"Brett McCracken offers a smart and timely peek inside our desperate quest to be cool. *Hipster Christianity* is an urgent but loving call to chase far more than the fashionable, to pursue enduring virtues rather than mere relevance."

—**Craig Detweiler**, Center for Entertainment, Media, and Culture, Pepperdine University

"Every pastor, youth pastor, college chaplain, and Christian college professor needs to sit down with *Hipster Christianity*, read it carefully, and take a good hard look at whether we are being faithful or being cool. The best example of generous orthodoxy I've seen yet."

—**Scot McKnight**, Karl A. Olsson Professor in Religious Studies, North Park University; author of *The Blue Parakeet*; blog.beliefnet.com/jesuscreed/

"Brett's book is a like a PhD course in Christian hipness. Part textbook, part cry for what matters more than being cool, Brett has accomplished something long needed in Christianity."

—**Jonathan Acuff**, author of *Stuff Christians Like*

"You're in for some surprises with this book. It's simultaneously more serious, more enjoyable, and more critical than you might think at first glance. Brett is able to put his finger on the pulse of hipster Christianity and yet point all of us back to the gloriously eternal and unchanging truth of the gospel."

—**Justin Taylor**, blogger at Between Two Worlds; managing editor of the ESV Study Bible

"What hath Kerouac to do with Christ? *Hipster Christianity* answers the question by taking a trip through the culture of cool, stopping along the way to explore its troubled marriage with the Christian faith. McCracken, the tour guide, provides the kind of loving critique only a reluctant insider could offer."

—**Drew Dyck**, editorial manager, Leader Training Team, Christianity Today International; author of *Generation Ex-Christian*

"Brett McCracken's critique of contemporary Christianity slices deep, but his love for the church heals the wound. As a new generation of Christians grow tired of manufactured relevance and long for a deeper understanding of what it means to be a 'new creation,' *Hipster Christianity* arrives at just the right time."

—**Jonathan Merritt**, author of *Green Like God: Unlocking the Divine Plan for Our Planet*

"*Hipster Christianity* is a thorough, accessible, and engaging ethnography of the often baffling landscape of 'cool' Christianity—from the wannabes to the effortlessly hip. . . . The truth is that the contemporary church could use a dose of hipster authenticity—and hipsters need the church to consistently point the way between love of their culture and wholehearted love of God."

—**Alissa Wilkinson**, associate editor,
Comment magazine

"McCracken writes with the cheekiness that only an insider of cool Christianity can have. . . . This is an invaluable contribution to the ongoing conversation about the shape Christianity should take in its relationship to the world."

—**Matthew Lee Anderson**, MereOrthodoxy.com;
author of *Body Matters: Overcoming the New Gnosticism of Young Evangelicals* (forthcoming)

"In this important work Brett McCracken notes that a church that was once out of touch with popular culture and the latest trends is now making the opposite mistake: trying way too hard to be cool and in the process losing its soul."

—**Mark Joseph**, The Huffington Post;
author, *Faith, God, & Rock 'n' Roll*

"Brett McCracken's well-researched and surprisingly insightful book is more than a passing fad. *Hipster Christianity* answers the question 'Who are we to be to the twenty-first-century world?' by skillfully defining what cool Christianity really is—centered on Christ, not consumption and image."

—**Stan Jantz**, cofounder, ConversantLife.com

"Weaving cultural trends, history, philosophy, and theology, *Hipster Christianity* accomplishes what previous books on this subject have failed to do. McCracken's writing is intelligent, winsome, sophisticated, self-critical, witty, and soundly biblical. . . . McCracken simply nails it!"

—**Anthony B. Bradley**, associate professor of theology and ethics, The King's College, New York; research fellow, The Acton Institute, Grand Rapids, Michigan

"Author Brett McCracken combines an insider's knowledge of the world inhabited by today's twentysomething hipsters with a remarkable aptitude for analyzing the intersections between the church and the larger culture (youth, pop, and otherwise). If you're a Christian hipster—and, maybe, especially if you're not—you need to read this book."

—**Larry Eskridge**, associate director of the Institute for the Study of American Evangelicals

hipster christianity

WHEN CHURCH AND *cool* COLLIDE

brett mccracken

BakerBooks

a division of Baker Publishing Group
Grand Rapids, Michigan

Published by Baker Books
a division of Baker Publishing Group
P.O. Box 6287, Grand Rapids, MI 49516-6287
www.bakerbooks.com

Printed in the United States of America

Library of Congress Cataloging-in-Publication Data
McCracken, Brett, 1982–
    Hipster Christianity : when church and cool collide / Brett McCracken.
        p.   cm.
    Includes bibliographical references (p.   ).
    ISBN 978-0-8010-7222-2 (pbk.)
    1. Non-institutional churches. 2. Popular culture—Religious aspects—Christianity. I. Title.
BV601.9.M33 2010
261′.109045—dc22   2010011027

Unless otherwise noted, Scripture is taken from The Holy Bible, English Standard Version, copyright © 2001 by Crossway Bibles, a division of Good News Publishers. Used by permission. All rights reserved.

Scripture marked NASB is taken from the New American Standard Bible®, Copyright © 1960, 1962, 1963, 1968, 1971, 1972, 1973, 1975, 1977, 1995 by The Lockman Foundation. Used by permission.

Scripture marked NIV is taken from the HOLY BIBLE, NEW INTERNATIONAL VERSION®. NIV®. Copyright © 1973, 1978, 1984 by Biblica, Inc.™ Used by permission of Zondervan. All rights reserved worldwide. www.zondervan.com

10   11   12   13   14   15   16   7   6   5   4   3   2

To J. Wilson McCracken and Sig Schielke
who cared little for anything hipster
but knew what it meant to live Christianly

contents

acknowledgments

*M*y family. Dad, Mom, Allison: thank you for all that you've taught me about God, love, truth, and hard work.

Robert Hosack, for believing in this idea and taking a risk with me; and everyone at Baker Books, for making the experience easy for a first-time author.

Dr. Stanley Mattison, Donna McDaniel, and all my friends at the C. S. Lewis Foundation, for involving me in such visionary work and allowing me to live a writer's dream at the Kilns!

Larry Eskridge, Laurel Dailey, Tracy Runyon, Albert Rios, Becky Pruitt, Tammy Uzzetta, Joanna Balda, Jim Kermath, and all those who either read through chapters, offered feedback, or contributed important thoughts and considerations to this project.

Others who played crucial roles in the endeavor of writing and marketing this book: Rebecca Ver Straten-McSparran, Kevin Sanner, Theresa Abueg, Adam Ferguson, Jessica Kemp, Jason Newell, Brian Bowman, Ryan Hamm, Tim Dikun, Lee Hough, Reid Boates, and all the pastors, church leaders, and churchgoers who spoke to me during my research. Thank you all!

introduction

I have some definite views about the de-Christianizing of the church. I believe that there are many accommodating preachers, and too many practitioners in the church who are not believers. Jesus Christ did not say "Go into all the world and tell the world that it is quite right." The Gospel is something completely different. In fact, it is directly opposed to the world.[1]

C. S. Lewis

*A*s I write this, I'm sitting at a table in the dining room of the Kilns—the home of C. S. Lewis in the outskirts of Oxford, England, where Lewis lived from 1930 until his death in 1963. I've written a few chapters of this book while staying here, and I offer my deepest gratitude to the C. S. Lewis Foundation for allowing me the opportunity to be a "writer in residence" here for a time.

C. S. Lewis is a man I've always admired for many reasons, but perhaps chiefly because he embodies for me the type of Christian writer I've always aspired to be—one that speaks to the culture of the day with both confidence and humility, logical clarity and literary flair, whimsy and gravitas. He was never afraid to tell it like it is, even when this ensured he'd have his fair share of critics and naysayers.

The quote I opened with—from a 1963 interview Lewis did in the final months of his life—reflects exactly the sort of firm, to-the-point rhetoric that makes Lewis so relevant and beloved even today.

And it's the sort of strong word the church needs more of today, at a time when the one thing most of us agree on is that Christianity is facing something of an identity crisis. Who are we to be to the twenty-first-century world? How should the church position itself in the postmodern culture? Through what cultural languages will the gospel be best communicated in this turbulent time? Is the gospel "directly opposed to the world" as Lewis declares, and what might this mean for hipster Christianity?

These big, background questions inform the work you have before you. But this book is about a more specific question—though a crucial, far-reaching question—that has come up time and time again for the church, especially in recent years. It is the question of cool; of whether or not Christianity can be, should be, or is, in fact, cool. This book is about an emerging category of Christians I've called "Christian hipsters" and an analysis of what they're about, why they exist, and what it all means for Christianity and the question of cool.

The title *Hipster Christianity* refers to the fact that this is a book about the culture and paradoxes of cool Christianity, but the title is also a slight nod to *Mere Christianity* by C. S. Lewis. Lewis's book was about what Christianity is at the core—the meat and potatoes of our faith. It attempted to make the case for Christianity based on rational arguments and substantive insights. By contrast, "hipster Christianity"—what I'm describing in this book—is a faith more concerned with its image and presentation and ancillary appeal. It assumes that mere Christianity isn't enough or isn't as important as how Christianity looks and is perceived by the outside world.

As I have blogged about the phenomenon of cool Christianity and Christian hipsters, the polarizing nature of this topic has become clear. Whether through the conversations I've had at the various churches I've visited throughout the country, on the blog boards that deal with my book topic, or just with my friends with whom I've talked through these issues, I have become more and more aware that the things I'm looking at are extremely complicated and deserve a fair, thoughtful, thorough treatment.

Yes, you heard that right. This is a serious exploration of hipster Christianity. It's not a joke, and though it is humorous at times and occasionally ironic, it is by no means an exercise in sarcasm (as in, say, Robert Lanham's *Hipster Handbook*).

And this book is not just about hipsters; it's not even just about *Christian* hipsters. Rather, the book explores the whole concept of "cool" as it pertains to Christianity. It looks at the way that—since the 1970s—contemporary Christianity has prioritized ideas like "cool," "relevant," and "countercultural," largely failing on an institutional level to achieve those things and yet succeeding in pockets and parts via individuals and otherwise organic incarnations of what you might call "hip Christianity."

The book is not an advertisement or rallying cry for hip Christianity, nor is it an outright chastisement. It's a critical analysis. It's about the contradictions inherent in the phenomenon of Christian cool and the questions Christians should be asking of themselves if they find themselves within this milieu. Are the purposes and/or effects of cool compatible with those of Christianity? If we assume that *cool* necessarily connotes the notion of being elite, privileged, and somehow better than the masses, how can we reconcile the idea with that of Christianity, which seems to beckon us away from self-aggrandizement or pride of any kind?

Whatever criticism I end up putting forward in the book, I hope that readers recognize that it is all for the ultimate refinement of the church and its mission in the world.

It has been very popular in recent years for Christians to bash on other Christians, to criticize the church and basically engage in a sort of "the church is totally f—d up and we know it" self-flagellation. A litany of books by Christian authors with titles like *Death by Church* and *They Like Jesus But Not the Church* have emphasized this point: it's *en vogue* for Christians to hate on Christianity in all of its mainstream forms.

But I love Christians, and I love the church. I even love hipsters, and I recognize why the label might offend some of them.

I'm writing this book not to position myself as some sort of expert on any of this or to make some audacious claim about anything, but because—like C. S. Lewis and countless others before and after him—I love Christianity and I love the church. She is the bride of Christ. I want to see her thrive, expand, and be all that she can be for the world. I want to see the cause of Christ advanced and not muddled up. And this topic—the relationship of the church to the notion of "cool"—strikes me as a vitally important issue that needs to be addressed with tenderness, nuance, and when appropriate, constructive rebuke.

The book is divided into three parts. Part One, "The History and Collision of Cool and Christianity," lays the foundation for what we're talking about—the history of the idea of "cool" (chapter 2), the meaning of the term *hipster* (chapter 3), the history of the development of hip Christianity (chapter 4), and the emergence of the Christian hipster (chapter 5). Part Two, "Hipster Christianity in Practice" looks at the specific qualities and attitudes of Christian hipsters, including what their churches are like (chapter 6), how they think about theology (chapter 7), where they line up politically (chapter 8), and how they approach art and culture (chapter 9). Finally, Part Three, "Problems and Solutions," gets into more critical and evaluative questions. What does it mean when churches bend over backward to be hip (chapter 10)? What are the conflicts and paradoxes between Christianity and cool (chapter 11)? Under what circumstances might hipster Christianity be a positive thing (chapter 12)? How can Christianity stop its skid to the periphery of culture (chapter 13)? And finally, what does it mean to be truly relevant in a culture so driven by evanescent trends (chapter 14)?

By the end of the book, my hope is not that readers will have learned how to be hip. Rather, I hope they will have been provoked into some necessary conversations, discourse, and soul-searching about the meaning of *cool* for their lives and their faith.

Am I a Christian Hipster?

One more thing. The question will inevitably arise (and has been asked of me countless times already), "Are you yourself a Christian hipster? Are you a part of the subject you're studying?"

The short answer is yes. I think by my own classifications (see chapters 3, 4, and 5) I would fit the category. But the last thing I want this book to be is some sort of how-to instructional or classification manual about whether someone is or isn't a hipster. Whatever categories and taxonomies of hipster that I might use in this book are not meant to be definitive introductions to some new type of people group; rather, they are meant to serve as examples of the larger questions at stake— the questions of what happens when Christianity becomes cool and whether or not a fashionable, edgy, countercultural Christianity is a good thing for the church.

part one

the history and collision
of cool and christianity

one

is christianity cool?

For most of my young life, I was afraid to let anyone know I was a Christian. It just wasn't cool to be a Bible-toting, churchgoing, penny-loafing goody-goody. I knew I was supposed to be proud of my faith in God and my devotion to Christianity, but in the midst of the "indie nineties"—when Kurt Cobain, computers, and Quentin Tarantino mainstreamed "alternative culture"—Christianity was (in my mind) about as far from countercultural coolness as Sandi Patty was from Madonna.

Still, I *was* a Christian; and not just a cultural, dragged-to-church type. I loved Jesus and prayed a lot, and not just because things like the rapture scared the hell (literally) out of me, though that was probably part of it. Thus, because I was devoted to Christianity, and cool was so evil (or so I was told), I had to resign myself to a life of less-than-nerd status. I wasn't a total nerd, mind you, but I wasn't the hippest kid in school either—because to be so was to take the broad path, the slippery slope, toward you-know-where. Being cool and Christian were not synonymous.

At times I struggled to keep secret my fascination with cool culture—a fascination I suspect everyone has to some extent or another. I remember watching MTV in the basement of my grandma's house because it was the only place I knew that had cable. I nervously kept one ear tuned to *The Real World* and the other to the possible sound

17

of parents on the stairs. The same thing happened while watching such "racy" fare as *Beverly Hills 90210* or *The Simpsons*. I felt so icky, so worldly, but I couldn't turn my eyes away.

The battle between fundamentalist guilt and worldly desire that played out in my developing soul was quite frequently sickening, because to a rural Baptist reared on apocalyptic boogeyman preaching, *any* hint that my salvation was in jeopardy was a punch to the gut. I understood that exposure to the temptations of the world was just too big a risk, so I gave up all pretense of being in on the cultural lexicon and just retreated to my fourth-pew cherub status.

I became a Bible-memory superstar in Sunday school, one of those idolized youth group leaders that the Awana kids looked up to; because if I wasn't getting respect in the oh-so-cool secular sphere, at least I had the Baptist crowd. It's funny—the overcompensation that happens when one denies an instinct in one way only to fulfill it in another. And looking back, this only proves to me just how instinctual and natural the drive for cool is in humanity. We want recognition and elite status; we want to occupy places of invidious distinction. Quite simply: we want to be the people everyone else wants to be.

Soon I was introduced to Christian rock music—specifically Audio Adrenaline, dc Talk, and later Jars of Clay—and I began to think that this thing called "cool" . . . by God, it could exist within the proper parameters of Christianity! I devoured Christian alternative music, went to concerts and festivals, and became a bona fide Jesus Freak. I became an authority on Christian music and rejoiced when, in the late nineties, some Christian bands (P.O.D., Switchfoot) began to cross over. Christianity was becoming so cool that MTV was paying attention—finally! Why didn't anyone see it before? Jesus is the bomb! Look at my awesome WWJD bracelet, my blue hair, and—gasp!—my fake earring! I'm so rad, and I don't even drink or smoke or cuss! Those were the golden days.

I'm not sure just when it happened, but in the midst of this Edenic phase in which I finally felt comfortable—almost legitimately cool—expressing myself as a Christian, I started to feel a little bit grossed out by it all. Christianity was definitely not the intimidating, "Gabriel's mouth is close to the horn," fundamentalist hideaway of my early childhood, which was good. But it had almost become *too* accepted. Christian clubs at my school drew hundreds of kids—even tons of the cool kids, the drinking jocks, the party girls, etc. What was up with this? Was Christianity really something so easy and mainstream and amenable to the popular crowd?

And in church itself, services were becoming completely different from the hymn-via-organ styles I grew up with. We started having guitars, drums, wireless mics, and bongos, and people began to dress like they were at a pool party. Church became *entertaining*, and people I once thought to be the world's worst sinners were increasingly welcomed with open arms. This was both a good and bad thing. People coming to church out of their own free will? Always a good thing. But what was it about church that was suddenly so appealing? This was what troubled me.

And it troubles me still, more than ever. Cool doesn't seem quite as cool to me as it once did, because I've borne witness to how distasteful it can be as a widespread economic philosophy—especially when fused with the sacred. The problem has not gone away, and in a culture that has increasingly co-opted cool and made rebellion and dissent the vernacular of any appealing movement, the body of Christ faces some difficult decisions. Will Christianity cower to the crown of cool, and at what cost? Is there really any other way to preach the gospel in the postmodern era—especially to young audiences—than to dress it up in chic?

As a longtime contributing writer for *Relevant* magazine, I've seen the tensions between cool and Christianity especially clearly. *Relevant*, after all, is the boundary-pushing, edgy-hip magazine that bends over backward to stylize Christianity and reframe it as "not your Grandma's Christianity." Their tagline is "God. Life. Progressive Culture." Keyword: *progressive* . . . hip, forward-thinking, trendy, current, *relevant*. The magazine traffics in the lingo and patterns of contemporary fashion to an extent that perhaps no Christian organization or product ever has before. But what are we to make of this new brand of "cool Christianity"?

Recognizing the extent to which the masses are entranced by the mystique of style and the temptation of trend, should Christian leaders resign themselves to the notion that "cool is necessary"? Or are there alternative means to reaching the culture for Christ than through the avenues of hip? And what does it mean to be a cool Christian anyway? Can or should such a category even exist?

The Question of Cool

Is Christianity cool? This question of whether Christianity can or should be comfortable with the image and labels that go along with cool culture lies at the heart of this book. And it seems to be the question of the moment for a large number of evangelicals desperately trying to keep their faith relevant in a changing culture.

But people rarely ask or discuss this question explicitly, because to ask if something is cool automatically negates its coolness. Everyone who is or has ever been hip knows that coolness is never analyzed or spoken of in any obvious way by those who possess it. Coolness is understood. It is *mystery*. It is *contagious, viral*. And this knowledge is the key for many—especially those looking to sell something or monetize hip potential. Bridled cool is an economic cash cow and can magically turn any idea, product, or personality into the next big thing. Pastors and twentysomethings-starved churches are increasingly the first in line to tap into a piece of that. Suddenly cool isn't a worldly indulgence from which Christians recoil; on the contrary, it is increasingly the chosen means of message delivery.

But as with all things cool, no one in Christianity is really talking about this in any sort of direct way. The talk is usually about "contextualization" or "postmodernity" or "meeting the culture where it's at." But it all really boils down to one simple desire: the desire to make Christianity cool. And this desire is bigger and stranger and more difficult than we'd like to admit. It comes with implications, baggage, and inherent problems that need to be discussed. The question of cool is loaded, and it's time we stopped dancing around it.

This book is about exploring, analyzing, and critiquing this desire for Christianity to be cool—but it also analyzes the already-existing cultures of Christian hip. The book addresses, in part, the phenomenon of Christian hipsters. I've observed this phenomenon firsthand for many years now, through writing for *Relevant* but also by being an evangelical youth group alumnus and a student and now employee at Christian colleges. I've observed the world of Christian hipsterdom at conferences and events from Michigan to Massachusetts, Oxford to Paris. I've seen it in the dozens of churches I've visited in preparation for this book—from a massive megachurch in Las Vegas to a tiny Anglican gathering in a centuries-old church in London. I've heard it from the mouths of pastors and in the ironic jargon and nomenclature of the specific hipster communities I've observed. It's fascinating to see these communities of Christian hip emerging, but it's also confusing and a tad bit troubling. What does it mean that Christians are suddenly becoming just as cool as the cool elites in secular culture? This is another question that drives the writing of this book.

This may be an odd book to write, I suppose, because as mentioned above, talking about cool in any sort of academic or serious manner is thoroughly uncool. There is a supreme dearth of meta-discussion of hip by those who *are* hip, though there are definitely a few caveats here: (1) Hip people, more so today than ever, do allow for hip self-reference in a postmodern sort of detached way. Talking about and making fun of hipsters is rather fashionable these days.[1] (2) Hipsters also allow for earnest self-referential discussion when in academic settings; say, a rhetoric class or a book discussion of *Nation of Rebels* or something.[2] But even this is partially involuntary, because when hipsters talk about hipsters, they are referencing entities they see as totally separate, totally bourgeois, totally manufactured phenomena—nothing like themselves. As *Adbusters* writer Douglas Haddow points out in his essay, "Hipster: The Dead End of Western Civilization," it is rare—if not impossible—to find a person who proudly labels himself or herself a hipster. "It's an odd dance of self-identity—adamantly denying your existence while wearing clearly defined symbols that proclaim it," he writes.[3] To label oneself a "hipster," then, is either a fun exercise in irony or just a misguided platitude that exacerbates our increasing inability to understand language, labels, and ourselves.

So on that note, why am I writing about the subject of cool? Obviously it must mean I am not in the inner circle of hip. I'm fine with that. But I know that I've *tried* to be cool, and that to an extent, everyone aims for this, struggles, fights the good fight of fashion. We seek cool because we understand it to be the capital of our culture—the holy grail, Gatsby's green light, the American dream—and that to ignore or write it off as "just how the kids are today" probably won't do anyone any good.

No, I'm writing about cool because I see its force, not only in the world at large, but in the church. To write a book examining the culture of cool and its tyrannous control of modern society from an economic or political standpoint would suffice, but there are already scads of books on this topic. What I want to know is, given the ubiquity of "cool is king" thinking, how are sacred realms—which seemingly teach and believe and survive on notions antithetical to coolness—coping? Specifically, how is Christianity dealing with a culture so driven by style? Is content taking a backseat?

The Essence of Cool

In examining this question of the coolness of Christianity, it behooves us to begin by examining coolness in general. In the next chapter I'll explore the historical roots of hip and the process by which this beast has morphed over the centuries.

But before that, I want to explore the basic meaning of cool—the *being* of it. I realize this is an inquiry that to many probably seems unnecessarily cerebral or even pedantic, but nevertheless, I think it is an important question: What does it mean to be cool? From where do we get this idea or notion of "cool"? First of all, the word itself

---

Definitions

Cool

My definition: An attractive attribute that embodies the existential strains to be independent, enviable, one-of-a-kind, and trailblazing.

Merriam-Webster: Fashionable, hip.

Urban Dictionary: The best way to say something is neat-o, awesome, or swell. The phrase *cool* is very relaxed, never goes out of style, and people will never laugh at you for using it; very convenient for people like me who don't care about what's "in."

Hip

My definition: Same as *cool*.

Merriam-Webster: Having or showing awareness of or involvement in the newest developments or styles; very fashionable.

Urban Dictionary: Cooler than cool, the pinnacle of what is "it." Beyond all trends and conventional coolness; the state of being in-the-know, including, but not limited to, being stylish or fashionable.

Hipster

My definition: Fashionable, young, independent-minded contrarian.

Merriam-Webster: A person who is unusually aware of and interested in new and unconventional patterns (as in jazz or fashion).

Urban Dictionary: People in their teens to twenties who generally listen to indie rock, hang out in coffee shops, shop at the thrift store, and talk about things like books, music, films, and art.

---

means nothing. In fact, in the language of hip, *cool* is probably way outdated as a descriptor of something fashionable, trendy, or hot (*hot* as in the way Paris Hilton uses it). But I don't want to get into a deconstructionist loop-de-loop here. The word *cool* indicates something that we can all—at this point in time—generally understand. So bear with me: *cool* and *hip*, whatever they may really mean, are the words I will be using (pretty much interchangeably) in this study.

And so, back to the topic at hand: defining *cool*. The word is often defined solely in terms of mere synonyms (trendy, fashionable, chic), which is unfortunate for a word that is infinitely more complex than people think. *Hip* is taken for granted in our culture—people presume its meaning with little deep thought as to why it exists. Why are certain things cooler or hipper than others? Who determines it? What is the appeal of it? What drives us to want to be the cool kid in class? These are questions we must ask if we seek to truly understand just where coolness comes from and why.

The following metaphors might help us in this pursuit of understanding the ontology of cool.

The Marathon Metaphor: Being Ahead of the Pack

Why do people race? Why is running in a marathon such an ancient rite of passage? What makes man compete? These questions, when taken to their logical end, allude to something within the human soul that spurs us toward winning, or at least to being ahead of others on the journey of life. We possess an existential drive to be in front, or at least not in the tail end. As anyone who has ever walked through a dark haunted house with a group of friends can testify, bringing up the rear is the place you *do not* want to be.

And this instinct—to be one step ahead, with an advantage and not at the mercy of anyone—speaks to the existence of cool. Any time you have a culture where everyone tries to be a leader rather than a follower, or a "head" rather than a "tail," you will naturally find that those who rise above and move ahead of the pack become the idolized. They are worshiped, esteemed, imitated. Everyone wants to be that, and thus the possessors of "that" become prized possessions themselves. People start to pay attention to these people: what they do, what they like, how they act, etc. In this process of esteeming the front-runners, however subliminally, a codification of cool begins to take shape.

The Divergent Path Metaphor: The Road Less Traveled

Robert Frost wasn't just anticipating inspirational office landscapes, Hallmark shelf life, or *Dead Poets' Society* cheesiness when he wrote "The Road Not Taken." He recognized an existential truth: we are drawn toward the unexplored, the unfound, the unexpected. The key line for me in Frost's famous poem is not "I took the one less traveled by," but rather, the line that follows: "And that has made all the difference."[4] What is "the difference"? How appropriate that we don't know, because Frost didn't know either when he took that lonely path. All he knew was that "the difference," whatever it might be, excited him and spurred him on.

Humanity, under the strain of mortality and danger on all sides, seeks comfort but also risk. To survive is one thing, but to really *thrive* on earth requires trailblazing ventures that might be fearful but are ultimately desirable. We sense that a glorious inheritance, an imminent difference that will put us ahead in the struggle, is waiting just beyond the borders of where we are. And with everyone looking for it, we have to be creative and sometimes stealthy in our pursuits. We have to forge new paths and circumvent the highways. While hordes of people are stuck on the thoroughfares—too afraid or else mired in traffic to get free—there are those who veer off and take a different route. Though everyone in life is in motion and keenly aware of the percussive rhythm of time passing and mortality coming, a select group of people chooses to march to a different drummer, hoping that in so doing they might control a bit more of the tempo.

The Darwin Metaphor: Survival of the Hippest

In any situation in which society is stratified (with cultural leaders, a conditioning elite), our instincts tell us that survival means playing by the rules of the ruling party. If we are not the marathon leaders in the cultural rat race, or the pavers of a less-traveled road, we can still hold some power if we simply pay close attention and follow the right people. We adhere to a rudimentary survival mechanism: if you can't beat 'em, join 'em.

As critical theorist Theodor Adorno writes in "The Schema of Mass Culture," we fear being outside of the cultural dialogue: "Today anyone who is incapable of talking in the prescribed fashion . . . of effortlessly reproducing the formulas, conventions and judgments of mass culture as if they were his own, is threatened in his very existence, suspected of being an idiot or an intellectual."[5]

We sense the power of the merchants of cool, and we overcome our impotence by identifying ourselves with the hot ticket items. When something like *Jersey Shore* seems all the rage, or when "Vote for Pedro" becomes a buzzword, we jump onboard. We feel powerful if we are a part of the winning cultural trend. How else do you explain our need to acquire extraordinarily unnecessary things like iPhones? They satiate nothing in our lives, but the drive to possess them is unbelievably strong. Why? Because trends—however short-lived—fuel a successful economy, and our cultural survival comes from keeping abreast of these things and not falling too far behind the fast-moving train.

Dave Hickey puts it nicely in his essay "Romancing the Looky-Loos," when he describes the differences between cultural spectators (those on the outside looking in) and cultural participants (basically, hipsters):

> Spectators invariably align themselves with authority. . . . They just love the winning side—the side with the chic building, the gaudy doctorates, and the star-studded cast. They seek out spectacles whose value is confirmed by the normative blessing of institutions and corporations. In these venues they derive sanctioned pleasure or virtue from an accredited source, and this makes them feel secure, more a part of things.

But this is where hipsters distinguish themselves from the pack, because they are not satisfied to just feel "secure" or "a part of things." They want to find things for themselves, discover the new frontier, and uncover unknown wonders on no one else's terms but their own. Hickey continues:

> Participants, on the other hand . . . lose interest at the moment of accreditation, always assuming there is something better out there, something brighter and more desirable, something more in tune with their own agendas. . . . Thus, while spectators must be lured, participants just appear, looking for that new thing—the thing they always wanted to see—or the old thing that might be seen anew—and having seen it, they seek to invest that thing with new value. They do this simply by *showing up.*[6]

So while it is true that hipsters, like anyone else, feel the pressure of keeping up and playing by the established rules, they are also the first group to break the rules and move on to the next, marginally accepted thing—thereby pushing the whole imitative circus forward. The hipsters are the mavens; they are the early adopters who—once they show up and adopt a thing as their own and pronounce it fashionable—set the course for the rest of us. But don't be fooled. Even hipsters are subject to following a prescribed and accredited course. For them, it's the self-imposed regimen of constant stylistic evolution. And it's crucial for their survival.

The Declaration of Independence Metaphor: Life, Liberty, and the Pursuit of Individuality

The idea of "hip" really came of age in the United States of America (much more on this in the next chapter). A multitude of factors birthed this concept, not the least of which are America's founding principles of independence, autonomy, and inalienable rights.

The beauty of the American experiment was that it tapped into such a basic human drive for independence and freedom from an oppressive tyrant (socialists would disagree, but that's neither here nor there). But the spirit of independence that took hold in the early years of the United States stemmed from a desire for freedom not only from England or otherwise oppressive political forces, but also from the tyranny of imposed *ideas* or *worldviews*. As John Stuart Mill wrote in *On Liberty*, protection against a tyrant is not enough for liberty to succeed: "There needs protection also against the prevailing opinion and feeling; against the tendency of society to impose, by other means than civil penalties, its own ideas and practices . . . and compel all characters to fashion themselves upon the model of its own."[7]

Mill is keen to recognize that people generally reject any sort of imposition—whether the force-fed, assembly-line fashion of the moment, the current trend in philosophy, or whatever the case may be. We much prefer the freedom of choice, however illusory, in matters of life, liberty, and happiness. And this idea—of rebelling against the prevailing opinions and practices solely for some semblance of existential autonomy and choice—is central to the understanding of the existence of hip.

Hipster historian John Leland addresses this in his book *Hip: The History*. He argues that the inherent desire of hip is not for wealth but for autonomy:

It is a common folk's grab at rich folks' freedom—the purest form of which is freedom from the demands of money. It is an equalizer, available to outsiders as to insiders. Anyone can be hip, even if *everyone* can't. In a nation that does not believe in delayed gratification, hip is an instant payoff.[8]

Indeed, for this and other reasons, Leland situates the concept of "hip" inextricably within the concept of America itself. We are a nation built on freedom and beholden to no one. He who risks the most gains the most, and so it goes also in the world of hip.

The "Class Clown" Metaphor: Affirmation through Attention

I realize that not everyone is extroverted or strives to be the center of attention, but even the shyest person cannot survive without some sort of external affirmation. It's a basic human need. On Abraham Maslow's famous hierarchy of needs, just above meeting basic survival and safety needs is the need to belong, to be loved and accepted. And once we find acceptance, our next pursuit is usually to be affirmed, respected, and regarded in a way that builds our self-esteem.

To put it simply, humans act in large part for the acceptance of their peers. This fits perfectly in the context of cool, where the ultimate pursuit—in being different, standing out, or leading the pack—is to be noticed. Humans are an image-conscious creation. Once our basic needs are met, we become increasingly concerned not just with ourselves, but ourselves through the eyes of others. It's quite pitiful, really, but it's just who we are. And don't think that the übercool folks who seem so ambivalent toward the affirmation of the larger culture are any different. They just hide it better and make their style seem completely *ex nihilo* and personal. In truth, all cool is basically a perception of others—it can't exist as anything intrinsic or detached from public perception.

I hope these metaphors help us a bit in creating at least a moderately operational definition of *cool*. As we have seen, the ideas behind the term predate the word, as we know it, by a long shot. *Hip* probably originated—in waves—starting at the dawn of the Renaissance in Italy (more on this in chapter 2), though certainly the concept of "fashion" in civilized culture goes back indefinitely. But as a word, *cool* is perhaps more common now—indeed, ubiquitous—than ever.

So then, if I had to succinctly define *cool*, it might, again, be something like this:

Cool: An attractive attribute that embodies the existential strains to be independent, enviable, one-of-a-kind, and trailblazing.

For now, that will do. As mentioned earlier, the essence and existence of cool—while important and vastly complex—is not my primary focus in writing this book. It is enormously interesting to me that we are so attracted to and desirous of this thing called "cool" (and I will explore this in later chapters), but what is more vital and intriguing to me is how exactly the search and adoption of coolness affects our lives. Is our desire to be fashionable, hip, stylish, and ahead of our peers benign? Or, if not, how does it affect our personhood for good or ill?

The relative goodness or badness in the nature of cool is of utmost importance. I think we can all agree that, essentially, our society is one that is driven by style and trend. It is the currency of our culture, no doubt, but the question is whether we can survive in this market without compromising our core. Or, is compromise even necessary? Can we sustain integrity and substance in a world so driven by packaging? Must every work, every person, every message that seeks mass acceptance be formfitted to the hieroglyphics of hip?

And thus we come back to the question of Christianity and cool. Are the purposes and/or effects of cool compatible with those of Christianity? Such a question only raises many more.

If it is true that our culture today is most effectively reached through the channels of cool, does this mean Christianity's message must be styled as such? What does this look like, and are any alternatives available? How does the Christian navigate in this climate of cool? How can followers of Christ be significant or relevant in this culture without reducing the faith to an easy-to-swallow, hip-friendly phenomenon? Is the church's future helped or hindered by assimilation to cultural whims and fads? Do non-Christians find Christianity more relevant or less relevant when it looks pretty much the same as the secular culture?

We can probably all agree that the ultimate task of the church on earth is, as C. S. Lewis writes in *Mere Christianity*, "nothing else but to draw men into Christ."[9] But the challenging question is this: to what extent are humans drawn to Christ by the way or style in which Christ is presented to them? And to what extent does our answer to that question fuel our various allocated energies with respect to spreading the gospel? In other words, as the messengers of Christ, are we to let the message speak for itself or must we adapt and package it for a specific context?

It is certainly appropriate that packaging is at the forefront of the minds of many church leaders today. In a world so obviously obsessed with style as a gateway to substance, we are right in viewing this as an important issue.

But as with any issue, hasty actions and unstudied assumptions are a dangerous threat. Before we jump on the wagon and harness the horses of hip, we must be careful to examine the wagon itself. How has it traveled in the past? How has it lasted two millennia? Will it look any different if driven by hip?

I should make clear that there are really two distinct categories of hip in today's world: (1) the naturally hip and (2) the marketed hip. What I am speaking of above—about Christianity harnessing the horses of hip to help spread the message—is definitely the latter. If Christianity is *naturally* hip, well, that's a horse of a different color (and something this book will consider in later chapters).

And that *is* the question we must wrestle with: *Is Christianity cool in today's culture?* And I mean *naturally* cool. As in—are people attracted to and desirous of it on its own accord? Or must it be cool in the marketed, presentational sense? Or perhaps there is a third option—a much more insidious, countercultural idea: perhaps Christianity is hopelessly unhip, maybe even the anticool. What if it turns out that Christianity's endurance comes from the fact that it is, has been, and continues to be the antithesis and antidote to the intoxicating and exhausting drive in our human nature for cool (for independence, for survival, for leadership, for hipness)? I'm not saying this is the right answer; just that this book is about weighing the options.

two

the history of hip

*W*e talk about hipsters, and we talk about the notion of "cool." But do we really know what the concept means, or what it has meant historically? Where does this idea come from—this notion of being hip, cool, stylish, fashionable, countercultural? What is its history? Before we begin to look at how these concepts relate to contemporary Christianity, we must set out to lay a historical and cultural foundation for understanding just what we mean when we talk about something being hip. That is the project of this chapter—to chart the history and development of the idea of "cool," from way back in the Renaissance all the way up to the present.

The origins of the word *hip* are unknown but widely speculated. Some people, like John Leland (author of *Hip: The History*), have made the case that the adjective is derived from the West African language Wolof and its verb *hepi* ("to see"), which morphed into "hip" in the early 1700s among West African slaves in the United States. In truth, according to scholars of slang, little evidence indicates that the word is of African descent or that it was widely used until around the turn of the twentieth century, when in America it became commonplace to describe someone who was "in the know" as "hep" or "hip."[1] This usage is thought to have developed during the late-1930s, early-'40s African-American "jive" era. Urban Dictionary postulates that the word *hip* fully replaced its close cousin *hep* in 1946 when Nat King Cole recorded the song "(Get Your Kicks on) Route 66," with the lyrics "get hip / To this kindly tip / And take that California trip . . ."

But we're getting ahead of ourselves. "Hip" is but one specific articulation of the idea of "cool" that I argue goes back at least three centuries and maybe farther. To find its origins, we will look as far back as Enlightenment Europe, where I contend the notion or desire to be hip had its formal entry onto the stage of Western civilization.

Setting the Stage for Hip: The Dark Ages Turn Light

Before we get to the Enlightenment, however, we should take brief note of what happened in Italy in the twelfth through the sixteenth centuries; namely, the death knell of medieval Europe. The tumultuous rise of Italian city-states (Milan, Venice, Naples) marked a shift in political and economic power from the feudal lords and landowning nobles to a developing urban middle class. In these highly populous city centers, rising commerce, industry, and trade helped the previously powerless labor classes gain some leverage against the existing powers-that-be. As city-states became more autonomous powers and a *nouveau riche* class emerged, things got pretty volatile in Italy. For the first time, wealth was distributed beyond the hands of landowners and hereditary aristocrats. The productive and commercial classes now held some sway, ushering in an intense era of class warfare and intellectual and cultural ferment which eventually gave rise to the Renaissance.

So, what is the significance of all this for the history of hip? In short, it was the first era in which feudal systems were questioned and overthrown (in some cases) in favor of a more self-made-success situation. That is, because of a variety of changes in the economic and political climate of pre-Renaissance Italy, the old systems of fixed, hereditary classes were thrown into flux and a new class mobility emerged, paving the way for Europe's future forays into republicanism and capitalism. A new light of freedom was dawning on the long-dark continent.

Rousseau's Novel Idea

Fast-forward to eighteenth-century Europe. The Renaissance had brought Europe fully out of the dark ages, but vestiges of privilege

32

and class distinction remained. The concept of fashion was developing, but "cool" or "hip" (as in, a position of invidious prestige that had nothing to do with class but everything to do with style and attitude) was yet to be crystallized as an idea. When it did emerge, the desire for cool came out of its close cousin, the desire to be free—to be a self-directed, natural, sovereign creature not beholden to institutions with systems of stifling rules and requisite norms. Jean-Jacques Rousseau first, or at least most famously, articulated this desire in eighteenth-century Europe.

As with most European thinkers and philosophers of his day, Rousseau's view of the world was massively altered with the discovery of the New World. Explorers and settlers in the Americas and also the Pacific Islands reported the existence of civilizations that were not based on rigidly defined class structures and absolutist hierarchies of power. From this, Rousseau concluded that the natural condition of man was egalitarian—that civilized Europe had twisted it around in trying to impose hierarchies of privilege and power. In his most important work, *The Social Contract*, Rousseau began with an audacious, history-changing statement: "Man is born free; and everywhere he is in chains. One thinks himself the master of others, and still remains a greater slave than they."[2]

Rousseau's ideas in *The Social Contract*, published in 1762, changed political philosophy forever but had violent and revolutionary impact in Europe in his lifetime. By discrediting the default right to power of the ruling, aristocratic classes and championing the sovereign will of the common people, Rousseau helped instigate the revolutionary fervor that swept across Europe in the late eighteenth century, most notably in the French Revolution, which resulted in an almost complete obliteration of the French aristocracy.

Though the aristocracy took a major hit during these so-called bourgeois revolutions, it didn't go away; indeed, it survives and thrives even today, in the sense that there are still wealthy elites and a decidedly demarcated upper crust. But in the eighteenth century, the aristocracy was put on the defensive, and that is the lasting legacy of Rousseau's revolutionary idea: that rich people could never again boast some absolute claim to power, just because they had more money and resources than others. In some ways, the bourgeois revolutions dealt the aristocracy a blow that was mostly psychological. The masses disrespected, despised, and looked down upon the aristocracy, essentially revoking their divine rights and diminishing their high-and-mighty authorities. They became uncool, though no less desirable (let's not kid ourselves: no one has ever stopped trying to be rich).

Meanwhile, for the first time, the bourgeoisie held the cards. The working class—the laboring masses that had more grit and authenticity than the out-of-touch aristocrats—held a newfound romanticism. This idea has defined the cool strain throughout history: the idealization of the working class. Of course, the "cool" aspect of the working class is mostly that it is the foil (in the Marxist, "we will overthrow you" sense) to the aristocracy. And here we begin to see one of the primary, paradoxical dialectics of hip: it is at once a negation of the aristocracy and an affirmation of it. Cool can't survive without the aristocrat, because it is only in relation to the aristocrat (as a critic, a clownish pest, or a style-setting ward) that the hipster creates his identity.

The history of hip is the history of an ever-changing, always symbiotic relationship between rich and poor, high and low, convention and rebellion. Whatever the well-bred aristocrat elevates as fashionable or desirable, the lowly hipster sets out to deny, deconstruct, and destroy. And—especially in the twentieth and twenty-first centuries—whatever the hipster elevates as fashionable or desirable, the upper class tends to co-opt and appropriate for themselves. This continues in an endless, twisted articulation of class warfare. As a result of the aristocracy's post-Enlightenment crisis of confidence, the notion of "privilege" became about more than just political power. It became a dance of fashion and aesthetics, uncomfortably and inextricably linked with the emerging bohemian castes that reveled in taunting the tastes of their benefactors.

Beau Brummel, Dandyism, and the First Hipsters

Emerging around the time of the late eighteenth-century bourgeois revolutions were two of the earliest strains of cool: the bohemian artist and the dandy, separate but similar collections of nonaristocrats who, in Paris and London, forged the very first expressions of hyperindividualistic, subversive style.

The bohemians—immortalized a century later in Puccini's *La Bohème*—were mostly poor writers and artists who congregated in various enclaves of Europe's most fashionable cities, often participants in underground literary and journalistic projects that commented on the heightened political tensions of the period. They tended to be more socially conscious and politically minded than their cohorts, the dandies, who were for the most part preoccupied with audacious, over-the-top fashion and general pretentiousness.

Born in London around the 1790s, the dandy might be seen as the first ironic hipster. Though mostly from the middle class, dandies dressed and acted as if they were the richest, most gentlemanly aristocrats in England. An outgrowth of the new power of the merchant and industrial classes, the dandies wore all the latest fashions, walked around with white gloves and canes, and devoted hours each day to personal grooming, cleanliness, and primping. They were mimicking the aristocracy, brazenly appropriating the haughty, aloof, superior mind-set of the upper classes that were simultaneously being ousted from power (and frequently beheaded) across the channel in France. Often blessed with inheritances, dandies typically spent their time idling around or squandering money on frivolous pleasures, frequently winding up bankrupt or in bad debt.

The poster boy and most famous dandy was Beau Brummel, a relatively lowborn Brit who nonetheless rose to national prominence at the turn of the nineteenth century, carousing with Prince (and future king) George and setting the trends for men's fashion in Europe. Brummel spent five hours a day getting dressed and is credited with first introducing the modern man's suit (with tie). In true dandy fashion, Brummel was obsessed with hygiene and cleanliness and had some influence in

Victor Hugo on Dandies

From *Les Misérables*

[They are] parasites, nobodies . . . [who] think themselves gentlemen in a bar-room, who talk about "my fields, my woods, my peasants," hiss the actresses at the theater to prove that they are persons of taste, quarrel with the officers of the garrison to show that they are gallant, hunt, smoke, gape, drink, take snuff, play billiards, stare at passengers getting out of the coach, live at the café, dine at the inn, have a dog who eats the bones under the table, and a mistress who sets the dishes upon it . . . overdo the fashions, admire tragedy, despise women, wear out their old boots, copy London as reflected from Paris . . . grow stupid as they grow old, do no work, do no good, and not much harm.[3]

popularizing the practice of daily bathing. The extent to which he and his dandy cohorts emphasized opulent fashion, personal beauty, and decadence as divorced from necessary class prerequisites would have influence in nineteenth-century art movements such as the Symbolist and Decadent movements. Some famous figures associated with or influenced by the dandy lifestyle include Charles-Pierre Baudelaire, Arthur Rimbaud, Paul Verlaine, and Oscar Wilde.

We should note a few things about the dandies and Beau Brummel before we move on in the history of hip. First of all, they represent the sort of unsteady relationship between the aristocracy and the fashion world that would come to define hip in every generation thereafter. It might be hard to argue that the dandy's dress was meant to be subversive, but certainly the dandy's obsession with fashionable image and style for its own sake was a revolutionary approach to one's personal appearance. As we will see with later generations of hipsters (and especially today), image and audacious style are a huge part of their expressed identity.

Secondly, the dandy (and bohemian, for that matter) established early on one of the most crucial characteristics of the hipster: situation in the city; or more specifically, movement within a city. The dandy had a tendency to just sort of saunter or loaf around his urban environs, breezily strolling down streets with little in mind but to observe and be observed. Baudelaire later described the dandy as the *flaneur*—the "gentleman stroller of city streets." The dandy announced his presence to the world in this highly self-conscious, sometimes flamboyant or theatrical act. Ever since then (peaking perhaps with Jack Kerouac's *On the Road*), hipsters have championed this sort of aimless pursuit and wayfaring movement—eschewing such bourgeois things as walking in a straight line to get somewhere.

Though the counterculture, including the dandies, tended to sympathize with the working class, they have historically (paradoxically) tended to view work with much disdain, preferring to laze around writing poetry, smoking, or gambling. They love the look and customs (particularly arts patronage) of being rich, but they hate the societal systems that require working to gain wealth. Particularly in America, where from day one the highest cultural value was a hard, up-from-your-bootstraps work ethic, hipsters have defined themselves in opposition to the industrious ethics of sweat-and-labor capitalism.

In appropriately ironic fashion, it is capitalism itself that has sustained hip for the past two hundred plus years.

America: The Country Born to Be Hip

If Rousseau can be blamed for the development of the concept of hip (and I'm not sure that he can; it's a bit of a stretch), he might also be blamed for the development of the American Revolution and subsequent founding of what would become history's most important democracy. And here we can see the lineage of hip from Enlightenment philosophies to the founding of America. If, as I argued earlier, the desire to be cool stems from the desire to be free, then America was ripe for a hip revolution. Nowhere has the desire for freedom—for unshackled, self-made sovereignty—been stronger. We are indeed the country that was born to be hip.

Some historians, such as John Leland, argue that hip's distinctly American quality has less to do with political philosophy, however, than the friction and syncretism of black and white. Hip arrived in America when the first African slave ships arrived, he argues, and developed as a sort of privileged, secretive language wherein slaves could exercise some sort of cultural autonomy in the face of their white oppressors. Hip then went on to thrive in America because it fit so well with our cultural values. For Leland, the history of hip is very much a history of America, a place of eternal newness, ever committed to shedding the past and pushing forward in technology and culture. The principal fantasy of America, Leland writes, has always been the notion of reinvention—the ability to fashion a new identity at any given moment.[4]

And though I disagree with Leland on the origins of hip (I place it farther back in time and in Europe), I agree with him that it was America—and her distinct independent-mindedness—that proved to be the fertile ground upon which hip could thrive. From the earliest days of the Republic, Americans had an edgy, countercultural disposition. They weren't going to be controlled, all men were to be equal, and no tyrant or aristocrat would tell them otherwise. The founding fathers were a belligerent bunch and set a precedent in America that would become the battle cry of cool: no one can tell us what to do or who to be. We are our own masters.

Of course, one can believe this wholeheartedly and not be a hipster. And the majority of Americans have historically not been hipsters. But, oh, some have. And even as early as the antebellum period, we can see how some of America's distinct ideals parlayed into some very influential hipster lifestyles.

In America of the nineteenth century, Romanticism was the dominating current of artistic and literary circles. The Romantic ideal elevated the artist as the person and perspective most suited to distill the grandeur, newness, and potential of the new Republic. Artists, of course, are naturally inclined toward the individual pursuit: art is *their* unique contribution to and perspective of the world. But in America, the Romantic ideal of hyperindividuation only heightened that impulse.

Out of this fusion emerged some of the first American visionaries of the countercultural movement. Writers like Ralph Waldo Emerson, Henry David Thoreau, and Walt Whitman wrote about and stood for a uniquely American syncretism of ideas that formed the basis for subsequent generations of hipsters: the nonconforming individual, civil disobedience, live-off-the-land naturalism, freewheeling fluidity, mind-altering substances, dropping out of mainstream society, embracing "authentic" living, et cetera. They adamantly asserted that the shiny, polished accoutrements of mainstream society did nothing to free us from the truth that, in the end, we are all living lives of quiet desperation.

Meanwhile, writers like Edgar Allan Poe, Nathaniel Hawthorne, and Emily Dickinson broached decidedly dark subjects—devils, demons, death—in their work; subjects that were not a little racy and challenging to the average and proper reader. We might say that Poe was the first "goth" hipster—the forebear to untold numbers of black-eye-shadow-wearing, angsty adolescents preoccupied with the dark side. These sorts of preoccupations (with darkness, taboos, and so on) have been hallmarks of hipsterdom ever since. It is totally uncool to be naive about our own darkness, after all. There are deep and dark places in the human soul, and Poe and friends were committed to venturing to these places in the name of authentic living. It was the first time the edgy, racy, artist/hipster sensibility began to seep into mainstream consciousness. Kids today are still reading the works of these authors in elementary school.

The Birth of Mass Culture

In the nineteenth century, the ideals of hip developed most often in the context of art or literary circles—part of a romanticized notion of the authentic, daring, eternally new, and self-directed American individual; in the twentieth century, hip became decidedly more politicized. It was and always has been about art and artists; they're the natural champions of all things subversive and confrontational. But by the turn of the century, as America began to see its influence in the world grow, the things against which hipsters positioned themselves began to change. They no longer just sought to rebel against a way of thinking (conformity) or to challenge the cultural status quo. Their fight grew broader and bigger against institutions of power, systems of control, governments and politicians and wielders of capital.

But what had changed? Two words: mass culture. If the first half of the twentieth century was defined by anything, it was the idea of mass culture, fueled by burgeoning capitalism. This era birthed the gilded age, large-scale manufacturing, and mass media via new technological forms (radio, cinema, and later, television). It was the Fordist era: assembly lines, homogeneous products, increased efficiency, consumerism, advertising, Campbell's soup, home appliances. At first it all seemed so wonderful—a bustling, busy, exciting new world of industry and frivolities and commodities. It bothered few people that everyone drove the same cars, saw the same silent serials at the local movie houses, ate the same confections, and listened to the same music over the radio. Mass culture was bringing the nation together in unprecedented ways.

But then the wars happened. World War I opened up the world's eyes to the devastating effects of modern technology and announced America's entrance as a major player on the international stage. But it had an even greater psychological impact. Many who fought in this "Great War" were never the same, and many artists and writers of the so-called Lost Generation came home desensitized, cynical, and confused about the idealism and progressivism of the American dream. Writers like Ernest Hemingway, F. Scott Fitzgerald, Ezra Pound, and T. S. Eliot reimagined America in light of these dashed dreams. Painters like Edward Hopper and Joseph Stella captured the existential emptiness and urban isolation of post–World War I America. Even as America's economy boomed, many were feeling that so much of it was all a ruse. More and more people were questioning establishment values and embracing freer, more amoral lives with increasingly open views of sex, profanity, and wild living. This was the Jazz Age, the Harlem Renaissance, the Prohibition era.

All the while, a thing called "modernity" was wreaking havoc on Christianity in America and throughout the world. The same sort of Lost Generation disillusionment from the war that was turning

Victorian values into flapper licentiousness was also eroding respect for and trust in the church. The result was a split between mainline denominations—who were embracing more liberal ecclesiology and theology—and more conservative fundamentalists who were committed to shoring up the battlements to protect against encroaching liberalism and amoral values. The famous 1925 Scopes trial demonstrated the thick tension between modernity and science on one hand and fundamentalism on the other. As we will see later, cool Christianity these days is fervently trying to reconcile this tension.

In spite of all these tensions and reevaluations of formerly held values, the countercultural current in America remained relegated to the margins of society—the cities, the artists, the activists—in the first part of the twentieth century. As America's party ended in 1929 and the Depression began, the counterculture became more and more associated with socialism and the imported ideas of Marx and Engels. Was capitalism really the best system? Many people asked this valid question during the Great Depression.

But capitalism was resilient, and in spite of the "red" ideas floating around in the air at the time, America's breed of capitalism and democracy made it through the hard times and by midcentury was thriving again, thanks in no small part to the second great war of the twentieth century.

The impact of World War II on the world cannot be understated. It affected all aspects of life and culture and had an indelible, galvanizing impact on the history of hip. Most importantly for the hipster, it awakened the world to the extreme dangers of mass culture. Hitler's Nazi regime was nothing if not a massive, memorable advertisement for the underbelly of mass societies. Look at the damage that could be done, the horrors perpetrated, with the help of mass media, propaganda, standardization, and efficiency! Look at the evils done in the name of nationalism!

But it cut both ways. America during World War II was just as nationalistic as Germany or Japan was, and even more so after the war ended. Could America's nationalistic fervor and patriotic unity ever lead to similar atrocities? The ensuing cold war exacerbated this question and pitted the world's two emerging powers against each other in a contest that everyone assumed would have to end with some sort of nuclear holocaust. America or Americans were not inherently evil, but the systems and subtle ideologies of a mass society often lent themselves to negative, unintended consequences.

In 1963, Hannah Arendt famously concluded, in her book *Eichmann in Jerusalem*, that some of the worst villains of the Nazi regime were not necessarily evil as much as they were terrifyingly *normal*—simply following directions and doing right by the authorities and nation which called them to her service. They were simply by-products of totalitarianism—pen-pushing bureaucrats acting not out of individual directive but out of a terrifying, unthinking acquiescence to the institutions and ideologies in power.

And ideology was central in the postwar world. Building on Marx, Antonio Gramsci popularized the word *ideology* and its negative connotation as the beliefs and values espoused by a dominant hegemony meant to control a population not by force but by subtler methods of psychological, system reinforcement. Gramsci argued that control was exerted not simply by a despot or fascist ruler but holistically throughout a culture—even the most free and democratic of cultures (like—gasp!—America). In our most apparently benign institutions—churches, elementary schools, pop music, films, Boy Scouts—the hegemony extended its reach and reinforced dominant values. Ideology was subtle propaganda, and it thrived in mass culture.

These theories worried the counterculture, which became increasingly suspicious not just of overt control or propaganda but of anything mass produced and mass consumed. A new generation of academics and Marxist philosophers reinforced these suspicions, led by Europeans like Max Horkheimer, Theodor Adorno, and Walter Benjamin, who formed the core of what came to be known as the Frankfurt School. These thinkers came up with the critical theory approach and terms like *culture industry*, which greatly informed the countercultural currents of the day.

In a way, these ideas were familiar iterations of that which had always fueled the counterculture, since way back in Rousseau's day: a suspicion of the wielding of power of one group over another for the purposes of control. Along the way came the idea of "hip" or "cool"—of being individually "in the know" and free from the stifling and boring systems of control and conformity. Now, in the mid-twentieth century, it was all coming together. The disparate threads of art and fashion and style were coalescing with politics and activism and rebellion against the mass culture behemoth, brewing a storm of resistance that would bubble up and over in the decade that would become hip's most significant yet: the 1960s.

Hip's Heyday

Since World War II, hip has enjoyed its heyday. The monumental impact of the clashing of superpowers, the bloodshed of "isms," and the scale of ideological aggression that was World War II gave a newfound legitimacy to the countercultural stance. Beyond just a loafing lifestyle of opium dens and meditative, off-the-grid living, the hipster cause was mobilized as a movement against "the man"—an important thorn in the side of the establishment, a checks-and-balances system for those who would otherwise lead the world irretrievably to the brink of destruction. After World War II, the logic of hip centered around the countercultural maxim that power and hegemony of any and all kinds could never be trusted again—that the majority must always be challenged, the authorities ceaselessly undermined, and the machine continually raged against. Cool became primarily about rebellion and protest, even if it was unclear what was being protested and why.

Douglas Haddow, writing in *Adbusters*, observes similar things about the postwar heritage of hip:

> Ever since the Allies bombed the Axis into submission, Western civilization has had a succession of counterculture movements that have energetically challenged the status quo. Each successive decade of the postwar era has seen it smash social standards, riot and fight to revolutionize every aspect of music, art, government and civil society.[5]

These waves of young countercultural hipsters have come and gone in their ardent protests and pot smoking for the entirety of history since World War II, all over the world. But the 1960s in particular saw the birth of the mainstreaming of hipster culture.

"The Sixties," however, actually started in the fifties. Before hippies, we had the beatniks: rebellious, urban artists and writers who refused to assimilate into the cookie-cutter postwar American dream so cluttered by consumerism and materialism. People like Jack Kerouac, Allen Ginsberg, and William S. Burroughs were the most famous of the so-called Beat Generation, articulating feelings of despair and hopelessness in the face of the oppressive standardization of modern life. They were self-described outcasts and exiles from the machinations of contemporary industrial America, which Ginsberg called "Moloch" in his iconic 1956 poem, "Howl":

42

> Moloch whose love is endless oil and stone! Moloch
> whose soul is electricity and banks! Moloch
> whose poverty is the specter of genius! Moloch
> whose fate is a cloud of sexless hydrogen!
> Moloch whose name is the Mind![6]

In contrast to the world of bureaucratic clones, Levittown suburbs, and white-picket-fence perfection, the Beats championed imperfect, carefree, *authentic* living. They romanticized the bum lifestyle—the aimless wanderer with no big plans or ambitions save an unbridled energy for freewheeling mobility and living life to the fullest, tapping into the very core of existence. Channeling the dandy-esque *flaneur* lifestyle, Kerouac wrote in *On the Road* of this truer, more authentic way of life:

The only people for me are the mad ones, the ones who are mad to live, mad to talk, mad to be saved, desirous of everything at the same time, the ones who never yawn or say a commonplace thing, but burn, burn, burn like fabulous yellow roman candles exploding like spiders across the stars. . . .[7]

The Beats eloquently laid out the vision that would light the fires of the next generation of insurgent youngsters, those who would come of age in the turbulent sixties. This younger generation of hippies and student radicals had been born after the war, growing up in the idyllic *Howdy Doody* era of optimism, consumerism, and capitalistic excess. And like their Beat forebears, they were convinced that there was more to life than this.

As Theodore Roszak describes in *The Making of a Counter Culture*, the driving force of the youth culture's rebellion in the sixties was a rejection of the "technocracy" that had come to define America in the postwar era—the massive bureaucracy that was ruled by experts who deified technology, rationalism, and science, and trusted in mechanization and specialization to solve the world's problems. This technocracy, argued Roszak, was a detached system that dismissed creativity, personality, and emotion, but was singularly focused on efficiency, expertise, and "objective consciousness." In contradistinction to this, the young, emerging counterculture in the sixties was increasingly characterized by an elevation of the personal, subjective, and experiential rather than the broad, objective, or ideological.

Channeling countercultural pioneers like Emerson and Thoreau, and feeding upon current European Marxist and existentialist thought, the sixties hipsters were convinced that the impersonal technocratic regime was waging war on human joy, on the preciousness of life and consciousness. True to the eternal hipster spirit, the emphasis was on the individual, on private and personal experience. It was less about class consciousness than it was about "*consciousness* consciousness."[8]

It was a generational rebellion, the mobilization of a youth culture that was larger and more prosperous and better educated than any American generation prior. And the world was spinning out of control in the sixties, which galvanized the restless youth in their revolt. People were getting assassinated right and left (John F. and Robert Kennedy, Martin Luther King Jr., Malcolm X), the Vietnam War was increasingly unpopular, the fight for civil rights was at a tipping point, there were riots and protests all over the world, rock music was being born, and so on and so forth.

Importantly, the sixties was also a time of heightened race consciousness. For many restless young white kids, whose eyes were opened for the first time to systemic injustices and race inequalities, the countercultural fights of their black counterparts proved to be a convenient model and ideal resource in their own countercultural development. Black hipsters were near-permanent outsiders, after all, and had been forced to develop their own language, style, and subculture in order to survive. Though their hipness largely came out of instinctual necessity rather than conscious ideological transgression, it nevertheless inspired the burgeoning white counterculture.

The sixties was also a time of pop cultural ferment; of Bob Dylan, the Beatles, the Stones, Woodstock, the Black Panthers, and Hell's Angels. It was the decade of *The Graduate* and *Easy Rider*—the mainstreaming of the art film, we might say. High and low art blurred, and the most self-conscious hipster provocateurs like Andy Warhol became household names. Cool had never been this high profile before.

And never had it been more global. America's cultural exports dominated the world following World War II, and before long the hipster styles of Berkeley and Greenwich Village sprouted up in Paris and Tokyo and every other major urban center in the world, sometimes with the accompanying take-to-the-streets activism (as in the Paris '68 riots). Whether it was Charlie Mingus, Elvis, or Hollywood gangster films, many of America's coolest exports took root throughout the world.

Likewise, in the increasingly globalized, mass-media world, the influences of a myriad of cultures and traditions cross-pollinated with Western fashions and notions of cool. American hippies appropriated Asian and Indian religions, the Beatles started playing music with sitars, the French filmmakers started making American gangster films, and so on. Cultures were mixing and melding, and hip was thriving. Hip always thrives where diverse cultures, ideas, and traditions intersect, which explains why America, with its melting-pot demographics (particularly in America's immigrant-heavy cities), has historically been the seat and source of hipster culture.

But even as the counterculture grew bigger and stronger than ever before, and the hipster movement more prevalent worldwide in the postwar era, the threat of cool "crossing over" or selling out loomed large. On top of everything else, the sixties was also the decade when the advertising industry took the driver's seat in the American econ-

Woodstock: The Hippie High-water Mark

Woodstock—the three-day festival of "peace and music" in the summer of 1969—was the climax of all things "sixties counterculture" and an unparalleled expression of generational solidarity. The hippies were there, along with the SDS activists, the bra burners, gay activists, yippies, performance artists, yoga gurus, shamans, Vietnam vets, suburban straights, and everyone in between. It was the culmination of decades of cultural change and political ferment, a final consequence or celebration of all that had been building and bubbling up as the relatively new youth culture came into its own and established itself in opposition to the dominant hegemonies and systems of accepted technocratic order. When Jimi Hendrix performed his iconic electric guitar rendition of "The Star-Spangled Banner" at the close of the festival to the remaining 40,000 muddied young Americans, it was the apotheosis of so much. In that moment was George Washington, Davy Crockett, manifest destiny, JFK, the GI Bill, Bob Dylan, "I have a dream," Montgomery, Berkeley, Nixon, Hiroshima, Hanoi, Chicago '68, Ozzie and Harriet, and Huckleberry Finn. It was the youth, adolescence, and future of an entire generation. But it was also the end of an era. Less than four months later, the violent, disastrous Altamont Free Music Festival in California ("Woodstock West") would strike the deathblow to '60s hippie idealism and close the book on the most illustrious chapter in hip's history.

omy—and Madison Avenue discovered that cool was the ultimate advertising cash cow.

Steal This Hipster: The Co-opting of Cool

No hipster wants to be a sellout. They strive to stay off the radar and out of the loop of mainstream, mass-market culture. But while they can always avoid selling themselves—their style, their attitude, their anger—they cannot help it when these things are *stolen* from them. This is precisely what happened in the sixties when hip became the romanticized, stylish, sought-after commodity that it was.

The irony, of course, lies in the fact that thievery has always been central in the story of cool. From the dandies stealing the "top hat and coattails" look from the Fleet Street aristocrats, to Elvis pilfering black gospel music, to Dylan appropriating Mississippi Delta blues, hip was always about taking for yourself whatever exotic thing you wanted. And it was also about encouraging theft or otherwise pesky acts of culture jamming, such as yippie superstar Abbie Hoffman's notorious *Steal This Book* stunt in 1971.

But in the sixties and ever since, the tables have turned. Now the corporations and advertising agencies are on the prowl—larcenous scavengers looking to co-opt and commoditize whatever is cool. Trends that were initially intended to be transgressive acts of rebellion in the sixties—like long hair on men, miniskirts, blue jeans, and bell-bottoms—quickly showed up in *Ladies' Home Journal* ads or on the racks at Macy's. Madison Avenue gladly assumed the role of intermediary between hipster fashion and the consuming marketplace. Styles and symbols originally meant to subvert the system began to reinforce it, even fuel it. The anger of rock music, the hyperindividualism of hippie styles, the antiestablishment vibe of student radicalism—it all fit so perfectly into the marketing goals of postwar American capitalists seeking to tap the exploding new youth market.

Hipsters were forced, then, to become even more evasive, more transgressive, more shocking, more innovative and elusive. They simply amped up their never-ending cat-and-mouse game with the suits and squares, becoming sneakier in articulating things like meaning, purpose, and rationale. If "the man" was committed to stealing their style, fine. He could come and get it. The hip train would be long gone by the time he got to the station.

The legacy of the sixties' mainstreaming of cool is that cool became infinitely more fleeting. What is cool today is lame tomorrow, all in the name of staying ahead of the pack. It's an extension of the age-old flirtation with power and riches and cultural authority that hipsters have always been defined by. On one hand, they love the fact that their style is so desirable; they love setting the cultural agenda. Hipsters take pleasure knowing that rich soccer moms in suburbia are shelling out big bucks at Nordstrom and Anthropologie to mimic what the hipsters are wearing at thrift-store prices. But on the other hand lies the unseemly aspect: once something edgy gets co-opted by soccer moms, it becomes considerably less edgy and must promptly be abandoned.

Joseph Heath and Andrew Potter talk a lot about this cycle in their book, *Nation of Rebels: Why Counterculture Became Consumer Culture*:

> Countercultural style begins as a very exclusive thing. It starts out "underground." Particular symbols—a love bead, a safety pin, a brand of shoes or cut of jeans, a Maori tattoo, a body piercing, an aftermarket muffler—will serve as points of communication among those who are "in the know." Yet as time passes, the circle of those who are "in the know" expands, and the symbol becomes increasingly common. . . . "The club" becomes less and less elite. As a result, the rebel has to move on to something new. Thus the counterculture must constantly reinvent itself.[9]

Since 1970, the counterculture has been nothing if not defined by constant reinvention. The seventies, eighties, and nineties were eclectic, ever-changing days in the history of hip. After Woodstock, music became a driving force, and the fact that music has been so hard to pin down for the last forty years serves as a testament to the chameleonic nature of hip. New styles of music have come and gone (for example, disco, funk, heavy metal, shoegazer, techno, grunge, ska), along with various lifestyle aesthetics (glam, punk, goth, and emo). Hip-hop emerged as perhaps the hippest of all styles, though as with everything else, it was quickly co-opted by MTV. All along the way, the antiestablishment theme has been strong. From Public Enemy ("Fight the Power") to Kurt Cobain, from The Cure to Rage Against the Machine, the currents of hip have retained the old spirit of challenging authorities and refusing the dictates of mass culture, even if it means biting the hand that feeds them.

These days, hipsters are running out of new things to do and be. After decades of constant evasive maneuvering and reinvention, the new cool emphasizes repackaging, repurposing, and remixing. It takes bits of this and bits of that from cultures and historical periods far away and long ago and combines them in unexpected and audacious new ways. It centers on nostalgia for the heyday of hip. So many bands today are intentionally trying to sound like sixties retro or trying to imitate the Bob Dylan-esque folk troubadour aesthetic. Hipster folk artists like Sufjan Stevens, Conor Oberst (aka Bright Eyes), Devendra Banhart, and others certainly seem to have a heavily retro quality to them. And kids these days (well, as I write this in early 2009) do seem quite taken with the skinny jeans and horn-rimmed sunglasses from the fifties and sixties (but we'll talk more about this in the next chapter).

In Summary

Of course, this short history of hip does not do the word complete justice. *Hip* is a complicated, contested word with many definitions and applications. But insofar as we can trace the origins of the notion of cool and how it has been formed and re-formed over the past few centuries, I think we can conclude a few things:

- The desire to be cool develops wherever the values of freedom, liberty, and democracy are introduced. To bestow the individual with the powers of autonomy and self-sovereignty invites self-styled rebellion, subversion, and countercultural behavior.
- Hip is always a rebellion against someone or something, a performance of an alternative, presumably superior way of thinking and living. At the core, it is an existential mechanism whereby humans can frame themselves as better or more privileged than everyone else (or at least more "enlightened").
- Hip is about image. It is informed by ideas—philosophies, politics, religions—but its dominant expression is always in the material realm: dress, hygiene, artwork, furniture, cars, *things*.
- The biggest enemy of hip is control—that is, being controlled, restricted, or imprisoned by some system of authority or power. Whether it is a titled aristocrat in eighteenth-century England, a government bureaucracy in 1968, or simply an oppressive system

of rules and cultural decorum, "the man" is always the spark that ignites hip rebellion.

- Ironically, hip has become a crucial sustainer of contemporary capitalism. The marketplace has embraced cool as the primary symbol of consumerism and material desire, and the result is that true and mass-marketed hip are increasingly hard to distinguish from one another.

In the next chapter, we will talk exclusively about the state and plight of hipsterdom today. Given that hip has become the new mainstream, what and who are the real hipsters anymore? Has the history of hip reached its apex? What does "counterculture" even mean anymore?

From there, we will examine the phenomenon of the Christian hipster and Christian cool. Which form of hip are Christians adopting? The mass-marketed kind? Or the authentic, truly countercultural kind? And where does the Christian hipster fit into the whole spectrum of hip?

But before we answer those questions of Christian hipsterdom, we have to define the twenty-first-century spectrum of hip and understand more precisely what we mean when we call someone a "hipster" today.

three

hipsters today

*C*ool is so ubiquitous today, it is almost a meaningless word. Corporations and soccer moms use it; so do nerdy youth pastors. The authentic *cool*, pseudo *cool*, and inauthentic *cool* are sometimes indistinguishable. The word *hipster* is not especially clear either these days, though it seems to have more definite connotations than *cool* has.

Hipsters absolutely loathe the word *hipster*. And yet, ironically, the word is almost exclusively uttered by hipsters themselves. The word shows up now and again in the *New York Times* or *Entertainment Weekly*, but in everyday conversation, hipsters use this insider term to express a weird blend of self-loathing, jealousy, and irony.

The term unfortunately communicates something very negative and derogatory; however, there are just no better terms out there. Hipsters are hipsters. They come in many shapes, sizes, and degrees of hipness, but you know them when you see them.

I am probably a hipster, though if you call yourself a hipster you immediately become a sort of Hester Prynne exile, a sellout to a label imposed by those oppressive hegemonies and corporate hacks who like labels. I'm okay with being a hipster exile. I might prefer it that way.

The word *hipster* contains within it the entire history of hip as outlined in the previous chapter. It's the culmination of all the counter-cultural, individualistic, artistic, competitive, apathetic, rage-filled rebellions that we've discussed thus far. The prodigious heritage that birthed *hipster*, however, threatens to undermine it; the word could implode at any moment and already suffers under the burden of over-use and disparate understanding.

For now, though, *hipster* still means something—enough that, for our purposes in this book, we can still use it. In ten years, it might be cutely outdated, like *beatnik*, *teenybopper*, or *slacker*. But if so, just remember that at its core, *hipster* means simply: "fashionable young people."[1]

This chapter will paint a picture of contemporary hipsters in the following manner: first, by describing what they look like and where you might find them; second, by summarizing their general philosophies; and third, by speculating as to the future of the hipster phenomenon. Hashing these things out might get a little more snarky than you or I would prefer, but it comes with the territory of writing about hipsters. Having a working definition (albeit my own, admittedly subjective definition) of contemporary hipsters will be useful later when we look at how the movement has been appropriated by Christianity.

Who They Are

Hipsters are a disparate bunch. You can be a hipster jock, a hipster nerd, a hipster Muslim, or a hipster Baptist. You can live in Brooklyn (the hipster Mecca) or in rural Ohio, employed as a salesman or an accountant. You can even be a hipster Republican (though these are rare). The only real requisite to being a hipster is a commitment to total freedom from labels, norms, and imposed constraints of any kind. And this attitude must be very public, which is why hipsters are fairly easy to spot. A person who is philosophically at odds with "the man" will possess a certain look, which can come in many different forms (and often ends up being inadvertently allied with the very "man" that is meant to be subverted).

Hipster logic (being totally unique and style-setting) almost precludes any sort of coherent, stable classification. Hipsters are aggressively elusive and indefinable, and yet certain hipster tropes seem relatively static. They are all very self-conscious about image, and—

hearkening back to Beau Brummel and the dandies—spend lots of time thinking about how to dress, accessorize, and fix their hair. The hardest part of the whole endeavor is also the most crucial: they must look like they don't care how they look.

Hipsters are also uniformly—and increasingly—defined by the media they consume, particularly music. As mavens of cool music, they cycle through bands with exhausting speed. The excruciatingly elitist music webzine, *Pitchfork*, exemplifies the tight-knit, vital relationship between the hipster and his or her music library. Hipsters also place importance on movies, though to a much lesser extent than music, and many hold dear their personalized cinematic preferences and DVD collections. Few hipsters admit to watching much television, but most secretly love a few horrible reality shows or CW teen dramas.

Any attempt to describe the superficialities of hipster culture inevitably comes across as grossly sardonic and almost mean-spirited. One need look no further than Robert Lanham's hilarious (but empathy-free) *Hipster Handbook*, which in 2002 was the first major book to describe in great detail the specs of modern hipsters. Today it feels remarkably dated, and what follows will doubtless be equally dated within a few short minutes after being penned.

The best way to describe the complex, vast, and chameleonic nature of hipsters is to break them down into specific archetypes, painful and demeaning though it may be. Such a project, of course, cannot be done with a completely straight face. So, take what follows for what it is: an all-in-good-fun attempt to describe contemporary hipsterdom by painting caricatures of twelve of its most common, stereotypical types. Keep in mind that no hipster falls 100 percent into any one of these categories; most of them have attributes of several or all of

Favorite Hipster TV Shows

If hipsters watch television, they gravitate toward HBO, FX, Showtime, AMC, or Comedy Central. Among their favorite shows (circa 2009):

Flight of the Conchords, Important Things with Demetri Martin, It's Always Sunny in Philadelphia, Dexter, Lost, 30 Rock, Mad Men, The Wire, The Daily Show with Jon Stewart, The Colbert Report, The Office, Big Love, Breaking Bad, Project Runway, True Blood, Sons of Anarchy, Jersey Shore

them. Many hipsters would look at this list and take issue with some of the types included ("How are yuppies hipsters?"), but the reality of hipsterdom is that its boundaries are very broadly defined, and it has room for widely disparate and even contradictory definitions. In any case, I think we can all visualize the "types" of people I'm outlining here.

Twelve Common Types of Hipster

The Natural

Seemingly without trying, The Natural attracts legions of horn-rimmed eyes at every soiree he or she walks into. This hipster typically comes from urbane parents or family who have long been attuned to or supportive of culture and the arts. Education is important, but so are social involvement and active participation in and appreciation of artistic endeavors. Good taste comes naturally for this person, who has every right to be elitist or snobbish. Naturals are well rounded, successful, and hard to denigrate. To be sure, they work very, very hard at maintaining their hipness, but for them it just comes easier and feels more authentic. If there is a downside to this kind of hipster, it is that observers tend toward jealousy or fear, and friends are usually in it for status or to learn pointers.

> **Fashion:** Impeccable and effortless, daring but not over-the-top. The consummate trendsetter.
>
> **Music:** Nothing too outré, hard to peg. Tends to have a nice balance of appreciation across genres and time periods, with lots of influence from parents and growing up amidst good music. Beatles, Dylan, Woody Guthrie, Simon and Garfunkel, Jeff Buckley, Dave Brubeck, Miles Davis, Chopin.

The Newbie

Intriguing and surprisingly common, The Newbie is fresh off of a former life of less-than status (that is, less than cool, less than stylish, more like the mainstream). The Newbie is found in large numbers in the sophomore classes of colleges, or sometimes the freshman (second semester) classes at more hip-friendly campuses. The Newbie often comes from a naive "everyone likes Dave Matthews and drives SUVs!" high school experience and then finds that in college, respectable uniqueness is the name of the game. Therefore, he or she scurries to find a hip niche, latching onto current fads and working hard to establish an individual style. Frequently Newbies will attend a concert or movie that will instantly change them into a lifelong devotee, which is very faddish, fickle, passionate, and irksome to many established hipsters.

> **Fashion:** Chameleon. Always trying new things, with many more misses than hits. Recycles current wardrobe in various new ways, vis-à-vis whatever prescribed trends are perceived (usually erroneously) as being "of the moment" and/or "easily pulled off." Tends toward over-the-top trendiness and chronic over-accessorizing (fedora, keffiyeh, necklace, etc.).
>
> **Music:** Very impressionable. Open to recommendations and attends lots of concerts for ideas. Scours old CD collection for salvageable records; usually only finds a few worthy of hipster repute. Johnny Cash, Death Cab for Cutie, Bright Eyes, Beach House, The Shins, whatever *Pitchfork* says is cool.

The Artist

The geographical origins of hipster—Montmartre, Greenwich Village, Haight-Ashbury—have one thing in common: they were all enclaves of artists, among other things. Thus, The Artist could be considered the original hipster. In modern times, The Artist is the hipster who lives and works in the bohemian art world. Whether painters, sculptors, musicians, poets, filmmakers, or whatever, these hipsters have talent and are committed to aesthetic triumph. They love art and have a deep appreciation for it, and they transcend most (but not all) trends and marketing whims. Artists thrive in urban settings, but can be found anywhere. They usually live with other Artists and rarely venture outside of the aesthetically minded bubble.

> **Fashion:** "Just rolled out of bed" by way of Berlin or New York City's Hotel Chelsea circa 1966. Very worn, lived-in, scuffed. Sometimes splashes of androgyny (guys in heels or skirts, girls in tank tops, worker shirts, or ties). Over all, messy and yet effortlessly on-fashion.

Music: Weird, eccentric, überartsy, or underground. Foreign music, ambient, and genre fusion . . . basically anything forward-thinking. Obscure sixties music is also big for them: Left Banke, Velvet Underground, Björk, Sigur Rós, Grizzly Bear, Danielson, Mum, Animal Collective, TV on the Radio, Nick Cave.

The Academic

Attraction to smarts is a broad trait of hipsters (all of them are more or less well educated), but a specific type of hipster finds identity in the bookish quality. The Academic guy comes late to philosophy class every day with tortured, tousled hair and a wild beard, but still blows everyone away in the discussion. The Academic girl has thick-rimmed glasses, drinks red tea, and reads Adorno for fun. These hipsters are really into intelligence and the image that accompanies it. They tend to be independent but thrive in academic circles and reading or writing groups. They like art and fun, insofar as they understand the sociocultural implications of it. You find these hipsters at colleges and in urban environments with a healthy culture and thought life.

Fashion: British intelligentsia couture. Glasses (trendy, horn-rimmed most likely), clean earth tones, lots of blazers. Has the look of Banana Republic or Burberry but often by way of a cheaper, more student-friendly alternative.

Music: Classical and jazz are cool to them, as are more mellow and intelligent singer-songwriters or anything that intelligently invokes post-colonialism. Rufus Wainwright, St. Vincent, Andrew Bird, Sufjan Stevens, Philip Glass, Nina Simone, Feist, Brian Eno, Arvo Pärt, Vampire Weekend, Yeasayer, Beck, Charlotte Gainsbourg.

The Dilettante

The Academic might use this term with negative undertones, but it fits. The word *dilettante* describes someone who has a superficial yet passionate admiration for the arts. In other words, this is the artsy-fartsy hipster who really doesn't know that much about art, but likes the image. The Dilettante took art in high school or college and fell in love with the sexiness of it. He or she loves art openings, gallery parties, and all things "fringe" in the world of cinema, music, theater, or whatever. When you quiz these hipsters on the difference between rococo and neoclassical, however, they brush you off as pedantic (because they do not know what you're talking about, but like using words like *pedantic*). Still, they have respectable taste because they associate enough with real artists who tend to have good taste. The Dilettante is a sometime-artist (mostly failed), but tends toward amateur art criticism and usually has a decidedly inartistic day job.

> **Fashion:** Cocktail party chic. The skinny jeans, T-shirt, and blazer look is popular for guys; heeled boots, slinky dress, and bohemian Anthropologie jewelry for girls. Lots of unnatural hair color.

> **Music:** Heavy on lo-fi, glo-fi, shoegaze, sh-tgaze, or whatever the indie music trend of the moment happens to be. Wavves, Neon Indian, Memory Tapes, Washed Out, Real Estate, Thievery Corporation, Air France, Lykke Li. Anything Swedish is also acceptable.

The Mountain Man

This oft-bearded hipster spends his day foraging roadkill for that night's supper (likely intending to swath himself in the unfortunate animal's pelt), illegally transporting raw milk across state lines, planting guerilla gardens, or just generally Pressing Onward Through Empire's Detritus. The Mountain Man (or woman) takes a special form of pride in carrying out the tasks most human beings were saddled with prior to the industrial revolution, but with a smug attitude of contrariness and a likely contempt for creature comforts unless they're found in the dumpster. Anarchist in attitude and painstakingly unkempt in disposition, this Paul Bunyan-esque agronomist is probably eschewing a bourgeois background; however, you may come across one who actually grew up in a rural environment or once had a tooth pulled without anesthesia. If so, God help you—*you will never hear the end of it.*

> **Fashion:** Anything found, plaid, or rugged, especially things that evoke mountain air or jagged cliffs, and shoes that appear to have traversed a great many miles of backcountry terrain. Though this hipster is not especially ethnic, and is in fact given to displays

that somehow both evoke and mock the American Frontier, he or
she may wear a necklace or vest found while learning taxidermy
from a friendly immigrant craftsman.

Music: Townes Van Zandt, Lightnin' Hopkins, Ramblin' Jack El-
liott, anything with banjo. May shun electrical devices but can
often be seen toting tattered instruments, hoping for an opportunity to play them in a self-satisfied and showy manner.

The Shaman Mystic

Usually named by a parent's guru, this unique hipster loves nature
and sequins in equal measure. When speaking, he or she gushes forth
canned psychedelic innuendo or strives (sometimes with almost farcical
awkwardness) to communicate ambiguity. He or she will do anything,
however unwieldy, to insert the word *energy* into a conversation as
many times as is humanly possible, along with any pertinent information about the return of Quetzalcoatl. In short, this hipster has
a tendency to take phoniness to heights undreamt by even the most
annoying of other hipster types, usually by plundering any and all
spiritual philosophies in the process of becoming more "in tune" with
nature, spirit, and self. Though hyper aware of irony and probably
theory-literate, The Shaman Mystic is one of the few hipsters who
unabashedly behaves with earnestness and is curiously comfortable
smiling, dancing ecstatically, and waving sunflowers around. These
hipsters are located in high concentration in Topanga Canyon, greater
Berkeley, Portland, and any Western state with large trees or aborigi-
nal topography.

Fashion: a sartorial jubilee. Often bedizened with feathers, stir-
ring displays of beads, and two-hundred-dollar haircuts, The
Shaman Mystic plumbs the depths of all spiritual/theatrical/
cultural traditions that are even remotely concerned with the
sacred, but will likely draw the line at stylized guardian angel
motifs or anything else embraced by middle-American women.
May sport a silk-screened unicorn T-shirt but will likely do so
with uncharacteristic irony.

Music: Devendra Banhart, Vashti Bunyan, Bat for Lashes, War-
paint, Espers, Ravi Shankar; anything obscure and evocative of
infinity, magick, or alchemy.

The Detached Ironic

Do you ever watch VH1? You know all those snarky, one-liner-spewing talking heads that make fun of pop culture all the time? Then you know The Detached Ironic. These media-savvy, tabloid-literate hipsters have a penchant for guilty-pleasure entertainment. Typically the "class clown" personality, this hipster holds an ever-ready arsenal of witty remarks about everything from O.J. to J-Lo. Extracurricular interests include watching trashy television with a bemused, self-satisfied irony (especially things like *The Tyra Banks Show*) and planning parties around cheesy movie marathons or televised awards shows. While popular in large groups and generally mood-lifting people, Detached Ironics can be annoyingly distant in close personal relationships due to their pervasive sarcasm and difficulty with serious situations. This genus of hipster contains a disproportionately large number of bloggers, Twitterers, and lifelong devotees to Captain EO.

> **Fashion:** Statement and vintage tees are where it's at—the most original, ironic, and retro, the better. Heavy on accessories like neon-framed sunglasses and trucker hats.
>
> **Music:** All about the eighties—the more outrageous and cheesy, the better. Hair metal, new wave, and drug music. When not wallowing in anachronistic pop, however, they turn to modern nerd-rock or punk. Animotion, Go Gos, Sex Pistols, Michael Jackson, Queen, Weezer, Morrissey, Surfer Blood.

The Yuppie

Webster defines this classic term as "a young, college-educated adult who is employed in a well-paying profession and who lives and works in or near a large city." In short: a young urban professional. These hipsters are city slickers extraordinaire, toting iPads in sleek suede book bags as they walk down the steps of their brownstone flat. They are heavily caffeinated, overworked gym rats who let loose only as part of a regimented schedule. For fun, Yuppies picnic at outdoor concerts, debate the merits of Bauhaus architecture, bar hop (monosyllabic bars only!), or attend *Mad Men*–themed parties. Groceries are exclusively bought at upscale retailers like Whole Foods or Trader Joe's, and table wine is served with most every meal. Though not as socially conscious as other hipsters, Yuppies do voice opinions loudly and forcefully. They tend toward blue-state ethics with red-state capitalistic verve.

Fashion: Lots of catalog and online shopping; no time for scouring store shelves. Dependable upscale department stores are the favorites. Generally lots of black attire, suits, and fashionable sunglasses. Even the gym clothes are designer. Overall very attentive to fashion "rules" and perfecting the right look for the right occasion.

Music: Very middle-of-the-road alternative. Nothing too risqué or indie, but certainly not straight-up pop. Music isn't hugely important to them, but Yuppies do fill their iPods with good stuff. Favorites include mellow brit-pop, sanitized hip-hop, and eclectic rock. Coldplay, Belle & Sebastian, Camera Obscura, Doves, Kanye West, John Legend, Mos Def, Arcade Fire.

The Flower Child

Born of progressive parents or former hippies, Flower Children are granola-eating, dreadlocked rich kids who stand in solidarity with the poor and, well, *everyone* except the white bourgeoisie. Aside from those stereotypes, they are actually quite diverse. Some are super socially conscious "no blood for oil!" activists, while others trade politics for pot. Additional concerns range from animal rights to fair trade to various third-world issues. Affection for all things natural and organic perhaps best defines The Flower Child. They love the outdoors (mountain climbing, biking, ultimate Frisbee), shun most television or "couch-potato" behavior, and are generally active in earth-saving politics, dumpster diving, and the aerobic/spiritual craze du jour (pilates, yoga, tai chi). They enjoy tofu, oats, soy, and kale, and frequent stores like Wild Oats, but are not always hardcore vegetarian. Flower Children are generally very mild in temperament and easy to befriend, if you can get past the "take a shower!" stigma.

Fashion: Dumpster chic or third-world imports. Cultural patterns and rebellion-driven fashions are key. Low-end thrift stores (such as Salvation Army and Goodwill) are the go-to, where plain plaid flannel shirts, Dickies, or old jeans that can be cut off or rolled up are great finds.

Music: Widely varied, but generally nonelectronic and mellow. Folk and old-school country are big, as are bluegrass, jam band, and progressive rap. Joni Mitchell, Ani Difranco, Iron and Wine, Patty Smith, Bill Mallonee, Joanna Newsom, Marisa Nadler, Vetiver.

The Expat

Otherwise known as the jet-setting international kids or the hostel-hopping backpackers, The Expats can't stay in one place for more than a year. They spend summers in Australia, winters in Chile, and spring breaks in Spain. Their passports are prized possessions and full of exotic stamps. These hipsters are typically multilingual and well versed in international relations. They work hard and spend almost all of their money on traveling, though often they combine work and travel by getting jobs or internships abroad. Expats frequently take interest in humanitarian causes and often do stints in Africa or other third-world countries. These wayfaring, *Lost in Translation*–type existentialists lack any sense of "home" and frequently utter such preposterous quips as "the road is my mistress" when they aren't busy quoting Hölderlin or Rilke elegies to the Dutch sitarist they befriended at a café in Caracas. Interestingly, this particular brand of hipster is disproportionately high in Christendom, what with the globetrotting missions sensibilities of YWAM and other similar organizations.

Fashion: Backpacker/safari/European. Jeans, hiking boots, all-weather outerwear. L.L. Bean for the preppies in the lot. Thrifty European cheapness (H&M) for the others.

Music: All about transition and changing moods and typically more international in scope than other hipsters. European roots, French ambient, folk troubadours. Air, Blur, Ray Lamontagne, Bob Dylan, Benjamin Oak Goodman, The Frames, The Jesus and Mary Chain, M83, Panda Bear.

The Activist

Hipsterdom has long been tied to that most expressive rite of democratic passage: protest. In the sixties the cause was clear: the Vietnam War. In the eighties and especially the nineties, the causes became much more diverse and decentralized amid the explosive information age. Today, hipster activism is usually antiwar or antiglobalization, or otherwise economic in nature (fair trade, third-world debt, etc.). Activist hipsters make their voices heard in many other social causes as well, such as urban poverty, education, civil rights, and immigration. They take pride in their solidarity with the trampled-on and disadvantaged in life, and often live in the midst of them. Though not nearly as violent or lawless as their Vietnam-era forebears, today's Activists are certainly passionate and feisty, especially during elections, summits, or large political gatherings. Favorite occupations among these hipsters include documentary filmmaker, immigration lawyer, or muckraking journalist.

> **Fashion:** Che Guevara chic (formerly turtleneck-and-beret mod chic). Sometimes militaristic, lots of army surplus and T-shirts with handwritten messages or pictures. Not huge on how they look.
>
> **Music:** Politically minded rock vis-à-vis Rage Against the Machine or some of the more retro, Vietnam-era protest acts. Any music remotely resembling subversive political messaging is welcome. Radiohead, Gorillaz, Nirvana.

Where to Find Them

In the past, hipsters predominantly inhabited major urban centers. Cities lend themselves to the development of hip culture for a number of reasons. As intellectual and artistic centers, cities invite the intermingling of perspectives, traditions, and cultures to the greatest degree. Prime examples are Montmartre in Paris, Haight-Ashbury in San Francisco, and Greenwich Village in New York City. Cities also provide the ever-important terrain for hipsters to saunter around like *flaneurs* and strut their shocking stuff.

To a large extent, hipsters are still most concentrated in cities. In almost every major city in the world, certain neighborhoods, streets, or enclaves tend to be the hippest. And in keeping with the cat-and-mouse impermanence of all things hip, these locations always change. In my home city, Los Angeles, for example, a new cool area of town emerges almost every couple years. When I first moved here a few years ago, the hipster areas of town seemed to be Echo Park or Little Tokyo, but in recent years I have heard more buzz about Los Feliz, Eagle Rock, and Silver Lake. Actually, Skid Row in downtown L.A.

Recent Hipster Strongholds Worldwide

In New York: Williamsburg (Brooklyn)

In Chicago: Wicker Park, Logan Square

In Seattle: Capital Hill, Fremont

In San Francisco: SoMa, Mission District, Potero Hill

In London: Soho, Hackney

In Paris: The 11th arrondissement

In Berlin: Friedrichshain

In Munich: Schwabing

In Madrid: Lavapiés

In Milan: Colonne di San Lorenzo

In Toronto: Kensington Market

In Vancouver: Kitsilano, Commercial Drive

In Tokyo: Roppongi, Harajuku

In Hong Kong: Sheung Wan

In Mexico City: Coyoacán, Condesa

In Rio de Janeiro: Ipanema, Leblon

is one of the new faves of gentrified hip. The point is, hip places to live are always necessarily shifting.

Within these neighborhoods, hipsters tend to hang out at certain key places. Bars are popular, of course, though not the bars where drunken frat guys hang out. Hipsters prefer really dumpy, roadside bars with names like Frank's or O'Fallon's, where cheap beers like Pabst and Old Style are on tap. Some hipsters prefer the chic one-word restaurant/bars with names like Aureole, Zen, Library, or Centimeter, and lately a trend has emerged toward vintage speakeasy bars where entrances are hidden in back alleys and bartenders with bolo ties measure ingredients with scientific precision. Hipsters also like to eat at greasy downtown diners and seedy dive restaurants off major highways. They like Vietnamese food, Viennese coffee, and farmer's markets, particularly if the farmer's market is not a touristy one. Other foods that hipsters tend to like include: arugula, cranberries, hummus, eggplant, pine nuts, French macaróns, kale, organic juice (organic anything), single malt whiskey, cask ales, high-end tequila, most obscure aged cheeses, and almonds. Or any food that Michael Pollan endorses.

Perhaps the surest bet for hipster-spotting is a music concert or music festival. Music is everything to hipsters, so of course they love going to concerts. This is where hipsters have their moments of truest community—when they are among "their people" and can experience a semblance of sincere, meaningful, shared joy. I've been there. I remember the transcendent joy in seeing the New York new-wave band Interpol play a concert in Chicago once during college. I was standing a few feet from the stage, surrounded by legions of sweaty, energetic hipsters dancing with abandon and sloshing beer to and fro. The guy next to me had enormous spiky hair and kept jumping up and down screaming "Happy birthday, Margaret! Happy birthday, Margaret!" while holding his plastic cup of Heineken triumphantly in the air. (Most of it ended up on me, unfortunately.) The experience was messy, nonsensical, kitschy, and primal. That's what hipsters want in a music concert.

In the summertime, hipsters all over the world flock to outdoor music festivals. In America, the big ones in recent years have been Lollapalooza and Pitchfork in Chicago, Sasquatch Music Festival in Washington State, South by Southwest in Austin, and Coachella in Southern California. These events have more hipsters per capita than just about anything anywhere.

Lest it sound from all of this that hipsters are a rare species of human that can only be spotted on rare occasions and only in certain ideal conditions, let me remind you that, in reality, hipsters are everywhere. You can find them at high schools in Oklahoma, behind the counter at Starbucks in Alabama, in trailer parks in Appalachia, and urban lofts in Denver. They are your teenage children, your youth group, your snarky nephews, and your angsty cousins. They're not all that difficult to find.

What Motivates Them

So, what makes hipsters tick these days? (I'm talking here about real hipsters, as I've defined above, and not the increasingly pervasive faux hipsters.) How do we get inside the mind of a hipster and understand what drives him or her? I'd like to suggest that it can be quite simple. A little bit of hipster resides in all of us. Hipsters are driven by most of the same instincts and preoccupations that drive anyone else.

Chief among them is the instinct to be better than everyone else. Let's face it: we all have this urge within us. We all manifest it in our lives in different ways; hipsters are just the most direct about it. They flaunt their elitism and arrogance where others take pains to hide it. In their aggressive trendiness, their daring fashion, and obscure music tastes, hipsters announce to the world that they have privileged knowledge about what is cool or valuable. But they don't actually try hard; their fashion-forwardness is simply an organic outgrowth of their closer connection to the truths of being, or so they would say. They dress outrageously because the idea of dress as a symbol of status and respectability is itself outrageous to them. They mock the system by refusing to play by its rules and instead changing the game itself and expecting everyone to play by the new rules.

Their very existence is meant to parody bourgeois consumerism, to slap in the face all the mall shoppers and country club wives who try so hard to look a certain part and adopt all the requisite accessories and accoutrements to advance in the social hierarchy. Hipsters view any sort of prescribed system or hierarchy as absurd, and they relish their ability to unnerve the rich folks and distress the soccer moms by being so flagrantly unconventional. The hipster loves nothing more than to confidently strut around in crazy clothes, covered in piercings and tattoos, frightening old people and Walmart shoppers by introducing illogical anarchy into their world. If a community has certain accepted notions about what styles and behaviors make sense and are proper, the hipsters purposefully embody styles and behaviors that are nonsense and improper. They gladly serve as the foils, the thorns, the impudent rascals and harbingers of unease in what might otherwise be a safe, boring, conventional world.

The highest virtue for hipsters is rebellion—from anything; it doesn't matter. More often than not, they rebel for rebellion's sake. Sometimes they have concrete things they are protesting against, but the core existential quality of the hipster is the drive to be *counter* or *against* things—to be different from, outside of, better than the tedious norm.

The hipster image centers on attitude. Performance. Exclusion. They project themselves as being totally independent of any controlling influence, and masters over their own life and meaning. As Paul Grant writes in his book *Blessed Are the Uncool*, "Cool glories in the spotlight, saying 'I am better than you. I am an individual; you are a clone. I know what's really going on here; you don't. I can get out of here; you can't.'"[2]

Hipsters recognize that they can only survive as a minority movement, and thus they exert tons of energy in trying to stay ahead of the pack, far off the radar of the cool-hunters and corporate mavens looking for the next thing to commoditize. When something they like becomes widely liked by the masses, hipsters begin to lose their privileged status, and they are forced to move on. Hipsters willingly accept this tiresome and endless cycle because their identity necessitates it. This is where the hipster wants to be: inside a circle that the majority is desperately trying to penetrate but never really can. The game must go on, but the hipster must always win. Here's a helpful description of this process from an article in *Salvo* magazine:

> Being a hipster means you buck convention by getting a job out of college that is unique, dress in non-conformist clothes, probably majored in some liberal arts degree at school, loathe the idea of ever living in the burbs, listen to NPR, go to bars that are off the beaten path, like quirky movies, and listen to bands that probably get very little major network radio time. And the minute a movie, band, restaurant, bar, or neighborhood, starts becoming mainstream, you no longer consider it "cool." Constantly looking for the new "it," hipsters religiously search for the latest trend—before it becomes too trendy. If everyone else is doing it, then it's not novel. And if it's not novel, it's not hip. Considering that being "hip" is about bucking the trend, hipsters ironically perform this ritual with clockwork.[3]

Being a hipster is hard work, but it's also hard play. Play and pleasure are a form of rebellion for hipsters. Work and discipline indicate succumbing to "the man." Ironically, hipsters have always had a romantic fascination with the working class, all things blue collar, and the proletariat. But when it comes to the values and vision of the capitalistic titans and moneyed class, hipsters have little sympathy. Hipsters (minus The Yuppie, perhaps) revile things like efficiency, synergy, corporate strategies, and the Protestant work ethic. Instead, they favor superfluity, fragmentation, inefficiency, and laziness. Remember the dandies' propensity to spend money frivolously and saunter aimlessly down city streets? Similarly, hipsters today spend their time lounging on blankets, playing music or loitering around someone's basement all day, drinking booze and watching crappy TV. It's their way of displaying conspicuous consumption. Superrich people buy boats and iPhones and summer in the Hamptons to show their importance and enviable position; hipsters shop at thrift stores, guzzle cheap wine, and download music for free. All the while, they smile and laugh and mock the suckers who sell their souls to climb the corporate ladder, buy a Mc-Mansion, and live boring suburban lives. Hipsters may not be laughing all the way to the bank, but they are constantly laughing.

Many hipsters today can perhaps be described as fashionable nihilists. A sort of gleeful glorification of meaninglessness directly inspires their extreme vanity and hedonism. Born in an era that has known nothing but prosperity and media saturation, when everything—including rebellion—is a commodity, and identity is as malleable and disposable as everything else, the young hipsters are desperately seeking something of substance but coming up empty-handed. Finding nothing profound to be particularly moved by, they instead opt to whimsically parade around in pleasure, experiment with style, upset any and all status quos, and announce themselves as pesky paradoxes totally at ease with a world gone mad (though, of course, they are not really).

The hipster commitment to meaninglessness, however, is both an organizing principle for the movement and a guarantee of its demise. That there are no causes or real philosophies undergirding hipsterdom ensures that, for all practical purposes, being a hipster is a style and nothing more. As a result, the hipster look becomes easily copied, easily mass-marketed. Everyone can be a "hipster," if it requires only a certain appearance and a mild enchantment with being countercultural. Thus, when you see people who look like hipsters, it's hard to tell whether or not they really are. Perhaps they are just rich kids from the suburbs who read fashion magazines and want to have the hipster look. Or perhaps their look was assembled from various thrift stores. Either way, the effect is minimal, and everyone is confused about what the word *hipster* even means.

As a result, hipsters today are facing a crisis of identity. Their identity has been utterly proliferated across the spectrum of late capitalism, and their indifference has made them an endangered species in a world where hip is largely just another thing to buy and sell, rather than a way of thinking or being. These days, we can almost more easily be "hip" than "not hip." We can just as easily shop at Whole Foods, Trader Joe's, or a farmer's market than at our neighborhood grocer. In nearly every store, from JCPenney to American Eagle, rebellious-looking clothes are now more common than preppy-looking clothes. With iTunes, Netflix, and other digital retailers, indie music and foreign films are just a mouse-click away. The Internet has made hip so achingly accessible.

Hip is losing its minority edge because it's becoming an empire. And, as Toronto blogger and self-described fringe hipster Sarah Nicole Prickett wrote in 2008, "In the hipster hegemony, so uselessly defined by antiestablishmentarianism, an empire falls merely by becoming one."[4]

The Poorgeoisie

A longtime popular aesthetic for rich hipsters involves looking poor and of the working class. But the recent widespread popularity of this style among hipsters prompted writer Steven Kandell to coin a term for it: The Poorgeoisie. In his 2009 *Details* magazine article, "How Looking Poor Became the New Status Symbol," Kandell writes:

> While Wall Street's hedge-funders have become whipping boys, those who have mastered the art of inconspicuous consumption are living as large as ever. But they're not easy to spot, resembling, as they do, Trotskyite grad students—a look that doesn't come cheap: $300 Acne jeans, $175 hand-stitched guayabera shirt, $150 mussed haircut with beard trim (not too short, please). This brand of consumerism escapes condemnation—it's okay to be a capitalist pig as long as you're the sort who roots around in your organic garden for truffles. . . .
>
> Just because the cultural moment is dominated by bloodlust for the heads of AIG executives doesn't mean public sentiment has turned against the accumulation of material possessions—it's just that the material in question is likely to be double-brushed flannel. And that's the advantage guys who look like Devendra Banhart have over guys who look like Patrick Bateman: The poorgeois are in cultural camouflage, blending in perfectly with a landscape full of genuine privation. The fact that their accoutrements may cost more than many suits is their secret pride.[5]

Later in the article, Kandell describes the philosophy that underpins the poorgeois lifestyle in Brooklyn, Silver Lake, and Portland as being "almost indistinguishable from the justifications of an I-banker who drives a Maserati and wears a bespoke suit: that quality, craftsmanship, and rareness are worth paying top dollar for."

Kandell is right in saying that the current hipster consumer sensibility privileges anything that is "a throwback to preindustrial times, when regular folks actually knew how to make things with their hands." Hipsters love things that are homemade or handmade, like hand-carved wooden jewelry, self-cured meats, and homegrown vegetables. They also love things that are old and vintage: antique tables, grandmother's dresses, sixties sunglasses. And Kandell also picks up on the current twenties-era speakeasy rage, which fits nicely into the new big-spending-and-yet-inconspicuous hipster trend: "Good-bye,

American Apparel stores now operate in every college town and many non-college towns. The days of hipsters having privileged access or secretive knowledge are over. Their esteemed place at the elusive margins, and their insider knowledge of the first instances of hip, are being threatened by an ever-more-clever consumerist mon-

$300 worth of bottle-service vodka in the back corner of a velvet-rope warehouse; hello, $300 worth of single-malt-and-Chartreuse Depression-era cocktails mixed by a mustachioed dude wearing an arm garter." I've seen this exact scenario in person, and it's exactly as Kandell describes—down to the arm garter.

Of course, on one level none of this is really new. Thorstein Veblen wrote all about this stuff back in 1899 in his book *The Theory of the Leisure Class*. Even back then in the Victorian era, Veblen picked up on the fact that the fashionable classes found authentic or handmade things desirable while mass-produced, machine-made products were deemed unsightly and pedestrian.

> The ground of the superiority of hand-wrought good, therefore, is a certain margin of crudeness. This margin must never be so wide as to show bungling workmanship, since that would be evidence of low cost, nor so narrow as to suggest the ideal precision attained only by the machine, for that would be evidence of low cost. . . . The objection to machine products is often formulated as an objection to the commonness of such goods. What is common is within the (pecuniary) reach of many people. Its consumption is therefore not honorific, since it does not serve the purpose of a favourable invidious comparison with other consumers. Hence the consumption, or even the sight of such goods, is inseparable from an odious suggestion of the lower levels of human life, and one comes away from their contemplation with a pervading sense of meanness that is extremely distasteful and depressing to a person of sensibility.[6]

How true Veblen's words are even today! Though the Victorian aristocrats he was writing about likely would faint at the prospect of dressing like a destitute vagrant, they share many other attributes with the contemporary poorgeoisie hipsters. Both seek things that are rare and hard to find (and thus inaccessible to the mainstream masses); both avoid the "common" things that are mass-produced and mass-consumed by people with negligible taste (today's examples would include McDonald's, Walmart, and pleated slacks). And though the Victorian aristocrat was a lot more conspicuous than the more socially conscious, "I can only spend $30 on a cocktail in the secret speakeasy darkness where no homeless person or starving child will see me" hipster, both are in the business of finding and accumulating (or imbibing) high-quality items.

ster that knows how to efficiently and aggressively turn what was meant by hipsters to be subversive into big business for the masses. The market has enlarged to the point that it allows for all the insane diversity and fragmentation and niche-orientation that had previously sustained the hipster cause. Now, every instance of interesting style or against-the-grain fashion is also an instance of moneymaking for "the man."

Hipsters are running out of ways to be unique.

The Death of Hip Has Been Greatly Exaggerated

For these and other reasons, spates of articles and pronouncements in recent years have declared the death of the hipster. One of the most prominent of these came in a 2008 article in *Adbusters*, which along with *Vice* magazine is probably the most hipster-friendly magazine anywhere. The article, entitled "Hipster: The Dead End of Western Civilization," was written by Douglas Haddow, who argues that hipsterdom is the culmination of all prior countercultures, but has been stripped of any sort of originality or authentic subversion. Instead, the current hipster generation is "pointlessly obsessing over fashion, faux individuality, cultural capital and the commodities of style." Their adoption of working-class decorum (white V-neck shirts, wife-beaters, Pabst Blue Ribbon beer, Parliament cigarettes), for example, amounts to nothing more than the "shameless clichés of a class of individuals that seek to escape their own wealth and privilege," notes Haddow. For him, the contemporary hipster represents the end of Western civilization—"a culture lost in the superficiality of its past and unable to create any new meaning. Not only is it unsustainable, it is suicidal."[7]

Other writers have offered different—albeit no less dire—takes on the future of hipsterdom. In an October 2008 article for *PopMatters*, Erik Hinton points to the hipster as a symbol of the broader culture's faltering sense of otherness and alterity—of being able to recognize something or someone as meaningfully different from oneself beyond superficial assessment of appearance. Hinton points out, quite correctly, that the hipster's tendency to collapse and collect bits and pieces of all culture and boil it up in one "totally unique" personal stew, ultimately creates a void of meaning wherein cultural distinction and difference is lost. As hipsters become more and more identified by the styles and tastes they accumulate, they lose their own sense of identity. "Who am I?" gets lost in the more pressing hipster question: "what bands, brands, and quirky styles do I like?"

Hinton writes:

Hipster Bashing/Backlash

At the close of the first decade of the twenty-first century, hipster bashing became one of the most popular recreational activities of hipsters and pseudohipsters alike. The unique brand of snarky self-flagellation known as hipster bashing was made manifest with the popular "Stuff White People Like" blog, which skewered white yuppie tastes; various viral videos like "The Hipster Olympics"; the "Unhappy Hipsters" blog, which put snarky captions to photos from *Dwell* magazine; and the granddaddy of all hipster-hating resources, "Look at This F***ing Hipster," a website launched in March 2009 wherein candid photos of outrageously attired hipsters are roasted with the most vitriolic and sassy captions imaginable.

As with any hipster trend, however, the hipster-bashing phenomenon has been met with a fierce backlash by hipster writers decrying the trend as "tired," "naive," and "more artificial than hipsters could ever hope to be," as *Hipster Handbook* author Robert Lanham writes in an op-ed in *The Dallas Morning News*. Among other things, Lanham cautions that in our fury to dismiss hipsterdom as empty and ridiculous, we forget that many hipsters are legitimate artists and thinkers whose place in the counterculture isn't artificial but rather an inspiration to their craft. We shouldn't get carried away with trashing hipsters, because in doing so we might throw out some truly talented people and important cultural contributions.

Lanham writes:

You get the sense that if Jimi Hendrix were to show up in Echo Park today, he'd be publicly mocked in a style section piece on blipsters for wearing a feathered fedora. Duchamp would have given up as soon as he appeared on dadaist-or-douchebag.com. And Warhol would be demonized as a hipster gentrifier for setting up his factory in a Brooklyn warehouse. Critics continue to complain that we live in an era where all art is derivative and devoid of substance. But if Hendrix, Duchamp, or Warhol were alive today, we'd be doing our damnedest to derail their self-expression, dismissing them as f—ing hipsters.[8]

Our lists of particulars become the whole of our personalities. This is why we see that kid at parties dressed like Hunter S. Thompson and break-dancing with gold chains around his neck, the girl reading Byron, wearing a Siouxsie T-shirt and hanging out at the bike shop. . . . The hipster is no more than a conscious manipulation of the freedom to live these piecemeal identities, comfortable in the awareness that identity can be constructed out of any bands, clothing, cheap, regionally esoteric beer, and inane micro-fiction that pleases. The hipster is a pastiche of old and new culture, free from the limits of meaning or the constraints of authentic identity.[9]

Within contemporary hipsterdom, unique identity is ironically lost in the all-consuming desire to fashion a unique, rebellious identity. Hipsters get lost in style and subversion and forget that skinny jeans and Parliament cigarettes can only go so far in setting them apart. Throwing all his eggs into the superficial basket of style, into the Facebook profile pictures and "bands I like" avatar identification, the hipster has rendered himself incapable of having the sort of significant identity that true countercultural revolution requires.

Obama and the End of Hipsterdom

When Obama won the presidency on November 4, 2008, hipsters everywhere were ecstatic. The vast majority of hipsters were Obama fans, and those that were not were mostly anarchists or otherwise apolitical or libertarian. But while Obama's election was a proud moment for hipsters, it was also a significant blow to their long-term viability. Hipsterdom blossomed during the George W. Bush presidency because he represented everything they were against. After 9/11, hipsters became more cynical than ever before, retreating into irony despite (probably because of) the government's calling us to be sincere, patriotic, and unified. Hipsters responded by becoming aggressively apathetic and cheerfully hedonistic. But during his campaign and ultimate victory, Obama unified the youth culture like it hadn't been unified in a long time, and hipsters were called out in droves from their cynicism.

In his postelection article "The End of the Hipster," Joshua Errett wrote in *Now* magazine that following 9/11, today's jaded counterculture "made a statement by making no statement, because no one was listening anyway." That is, until Barack Obama started making his way onto T-shirts, posters, and YouTube. "At some point during Obama's presidential campaign," wrote Errett, "an earnest, productive, engaged youth class was born out of a real desire for change. Hipsters essentially became hopesters."[10]

The same idea was expressed on the website Street Carnage (the thickly hipster site of *Vice* magazine founder Gavin McInness) following the election, in a blog post entitled "Obama Victory Renders Hipster 'Movement' Obsolete." In the post, Robert Dobbs Jr., a Brooklyn hipster who writes under the name blogn***er, declared that, a week after the election, hipsters must come to terms with the fact that their affection for irony and "neo-cynicism" now look less subversive than stupid and defeatist:

> Guess what—Obama has already changed the world by bringing hope and healing to B-B-BILLIONS of people around the globe. Neo-Cynisism [sic] can't f— with that—it's real.[11]

Elsewhere in the post, Dobbs discredits hipsters who allow themselves to believe, "for even a second, that there's any deeper 'meaning,' or 'movement' behind our chosen music-and-t-shirt collective." He's admitting what most of these gloom-and-doom hipster prognosticators have been pointing out for months: that hipsterdom is devoid of any substantial motivating logic. It emphasizes partying, being fashionable, being cool, and being cynical. The question is: are these things worth anything anymore? Some argue that, in a post-Obama world, hipsters who continue to proudly display the middle finger to all things establishment and all things idealistic are simply made to look the fool. Don't they know? Earnestness is the new irony.

Well, we shall see. I'm not convinced that irony will ever really go away. I'm not convinced that Obama's popularity among hipsters will lead them to throw in the towel on their supposedly countercultural existence. Hipsters will continue on, if for no other reason than because the human desire to be cool has not and will not go away. Hipsters will just have to redefine cool in an era when it is ever more meaningless. But rest assured: they will find a way to do it.

Hipster Becoming Uncool: Time for the Christian Version?

Christian cultural trends always seem to follow a few steps behind the secular culture. The relatively new definitive and unique subculture of Christian hipsters makes sense, then, since hipsterdom's heyday (at least in its current form) is on the wane. Christianity has a knack for getting in at the tail end of any movement—a problem that I will address in greater depth in later chapters of this book.

For now, we need to get a better grasp of the Christian hipster phenomenon. How is it the same or different than secular hipster culture? Where are the roots of Christian cool, and how have they shaped the state of Christianity today? How did it happen that something as square as Christianity became rebellious, countercultural, and—in some incarnations—truly hip? In the next chapter, we will address these questions.

four

the history of hip christianity

The history of hip Christianity is significantly shorter than that of "hip" at large. In fact, it's hard to locate any instance of hip Christianity prior to the mid-twentieth century. In the lifespan of cool, going back to the Enlightenment, Christianity is more commonly associated with all that is uncool. It represents the establishment, the ruling class, the aristocracy, the oppressive, violent imperialistic behemoth some call Christendom. It was everything that the counterculture—from the Parisian bohemians to the American transcendentalists—rebelled against.

And likewise, postenlightenment Christianity seemed to aggressively hide from all things cool or countercultural. Being cool was not something Christians were especially interested in. Rather, they were wary of, if not totally protected from, culture at large. Early evangelicalism especially seemed totally uninterested in being fashionable or attuned to progressive cultural trends. Particularly following the 1920s fundamentalist-modernist split in America, when fundamentalist Christians retreated into a sort of buttoned-down protectorate of conservatism, Christianity was much sooner labeled "sheltered," "prudish," or "square" than it was "hip" or "cool."

But obviously, something changed. The phenomenon of hipster Christianity at the beginning of the twenty-first century—coupled

75

with the crucial importance of things like "cultural relevance" to evangelical leaders today—did not just come out of nowhere. It has been building for decades. The history of hip Christianity is short but significant. Since around 1970, the idea of cool Christianity has in some ways reoriented the way evangelicals go about the business of being evangelical. They no longer focus on being safe and protected from culture, but being *in* culture—relevant to it, savvy about it, privy to what's "in," and totally comfortable with cool.

This chapter is about how we got from hopelessly square to effortlessly hip. It's a rocky story at times, so brace yourself. By the end we will arrive at the current batch of Christian hipster, but before that we must get through some important, pivotal history in the evolution of Christian cool.

The Seeds of Christian Cool: The 1960s and the New Youth Focus

As with the history of secular hip, the 1960s looms very large in the history of Christian hip. A lot of things changed in the 1960s, but one of the biggest things that happened was that "youth culture" exploded onto the scene and became the dominant force in American society and global capitalism. The teenagers and college students of the 1960s were the kids of the postwar baby boom, a massive block of youngsters who had grown up in peace and unprecedented prosperity. They had money to spend and time to waste. Things like "Beatlemania" proved the point of their consumer power. Everyone else took notice, especially entertainment and advertising industries. Movies started catering to the rebellious teenage crowd (think James Dean), television took aim at youth audiences (everything from *The Many Loves of Dobie Gillis* to *American Bandstand*), and rock music became the iconic voice of the new generation. No longer could kids be ignored or written off as insignificant proto-consumers that would one day grow up to have some measure of economic and cultural importance. From that point on, if something was to be successful, it had to take youth appeal seriously.

This shift was felt strongly in the Christian church, which by the mid-sixties realized that there was a need for churches to more specifically reach out to the youth. The idea of "youth ministry" as a function of the local church that went beyond Sunday school–type

Bible teaching was born. It had existed prior to the 1960s in the form of parachurch youth organizations such as Billy Graham's Youth for Christ organization, Young Life, Fellowship of Christian Athletes, Campus Crusade, and InterVarsity Christian Fellowship—all of which were started in the forties or fifties—but until the sixties, youth ministry wasn't the major force that it is today. In the sixties, more and more churches began hiring youth pastors and starting youth groups, aiming to provide fun and safe places for kids to hang out. Organizations began to spring up to resource the growing youth ministry needs of churches, such as Youth Specialties, founded in 1969 by some San Diego Youth for Christ staffers who realized that the future of youth outreach would be through the local church. These were the beginnings of the youth ministry industry, to which unlimited books, conferences, trade shows, and curricula are now committed on an annual basis.

The commoditization of youth culture within Christianity simply mirrored the larger commercial trends of the sixties—seeking to turn a quick dollar, "the man" was increasingly pursuing the explosive teen subculture. In the process, the youth culture was galvanized and unified with a new countercultural confidence. The power had shifted from the establishment to the fickle young consumer, which meant that, no matter what they did, the youth had their parents' generation in their pocket. This position was both an opportunity and burden for the youth. It offered them the unprecedented opportunity to set the agenda of the culture, but it also meant that any original idea or identity they might foster for themselves would quickly be co-opted and mainstreamed for the masses.

As Mark Oestreicher, former president of Youth Specialties, notes of this point in history:

> This is when and why the prioritization of the tasks of adolescence shifted. With a clearer sense of identity, a sense of confidence, and an undisputed place in culture, youth culture began a more earnest effort to define itself in opposition to the culture at large. This is in the very DNA of youth culture, really—it will always work to become "other" and unique, always mutate to stay counter-cultural and rebellious.[1]

For Christianity, as with establishment culture at large, this presented a unique and new challenge. The youth made up an increasingly desirable audience, but they were also increasingly elusive and belligerent, flaunting their autonomy and countercultural credibility. How, then, was the church to appeal to them? How could such a square institution as the church—perceived by many as an oppressive arm of the cultural hegemony—become desirable to these kids? This question has informed and shaped the development of hip Christianity for the last four decades.

The Jesus People and the Birth of Christian Hip

Looking back on the Jesus People movement of the late sixties and early seventies, it is hard to underscore just how unexpected and revolutionary the hippie Christian phenomenon really was. One of history's biggest ironies lies in the fact that so many of the sixties hippies—the most iconic of all countercultural youth movements— would seek out Jesus and convert to Christianity, perhaps the most iconic of all establishment forces.

One of the experts on the Jesus People movement is Wheaton College's Larry Eskridge, and even he is at a loss for an explanation as to just how this movement happened:

> Christianity represented pretty much everything [the hippies] were fighting against. . . . Evangelical Christianity in particular was viewed as the most oppressive, naive, ridiculous manifestation of religion you could possibly have. So the idea that any of them would ever fall into that trap is kind of amazing.[2]

When *Time* magazine first took notice of the movement in its June 1971 cover story, it also remarked on this unexpected marriage of seemingly opposing philosophies:

> It is a startling development for a generation that has been constantly accused of tripping out or copping out with sex, drugs and violence. Now, embracing the most persistent symbol of purity, selflessness and brotherly love in the history of Western man, they are afire with a Pentecostal passion for sharing their new vision with others. Fresh-faced, wide-eyed young girls and earnest young men badger businessmen and shoppers on Hollywood Boulevard, near the Lincoln Memorial, in Dallas, in Detroit and in Wichita, "witnessing" for Christ with breathless exhortations.[3]

So how *did* this happen? Though the movement seemed to start simultaneously all over the country, the story looms largest in California around 1967, when a few hippie converts and a handful of old-school evangelical pastors partnered to win the hippie world for Christ.

Appropriately, the story originates in San Francisco's Haight-Ashbury neighborhood, which in the sixties was the Mecca to which thousands of hippie runaways, dropouts, and ne'er-do-wells fled. There, in 1967, a hippie convert named Ted Wise and some Baptist pastors founded a Christian storefront coffeehouse called "The Living Room"—a friendly place for hippies and artists to just chill out, have free soup, talk about Jesus, and be cool (and a place where people like Robin Williams and Charles Manson sometimes hung out).

Ted Wise, whom Eskridge calls the "proto Jesus freak," was a drugged-out boho from Sausalito who one day opened a Bible and discovered Jesus to be totally different than he thought he was. From all that he'd ever heard, Wise imagined Jesus was sort of like a sergeant in the marine corps, "or at least a Republican."[4] But this Bible Jesus, to Wise, was actually cool.

Wise and his wife, Liz, started attending a Baptist church in Mill Valley, where Ted sang in the choir, sometimes while high on acid, and the couple started bringing their hippie friends. Eventually they convinced the church to start a hippie outreach in San Francisco, which led to the development of The Living Room.

Meanwhile, down in Southern California, similar things were happening. Recognizing the importance of music for the hippies, a youth pastor at Hollywood Presbyterian, Don Williams, created a place called "The Salt Company," a sort of Christian nightclub with a much bigger budget than The Living Room. Also in Hollywood was "His Place," a somewhat notorious coffeehouse founded by Arthur "traveled around the country carrying a twelve-foot cross" Blessitt. Soon it would spread across the country, however, with hippie Christian coffeehouses and communes showing up in the hip boroughs of all the major American cities—Greenwich Village in New York, Uptown in Chicago, the Ballard neighborhood in Seattle (interestingly, still a hotbed of hipster Christianity)—but also in such unlikely spots as Sioux Falls, South Dakota, and Ellwood City, Pennsylvania. The movement was truly widespread in a very short span of time.

Lonnie Frisbee, Chuck Smith, and Calvary Chapel

Lonnie Frisbee is probably the first and most important Christian hipster icon. A hippie in the strictest sense, Frisbee came of age in the sixties, ran away from home, and became an LSD-dropping, pot-smoking dropout. He explored meditation, hypnotism, and mysticism, but never found them satisfying. Like a true wayfaring hippie, he kept searching for enlightenment. Fortuitously, Frisbee started hanging out with Ted Wise and folks at The Living Room in San Francisco, where he converted to Christianity.

After his conversion, Frisbee returned to Southern California, where he had a chance meeting with a man named Chuck Smith, who pastored a church in Costa Mesa called Calvary Chapel. Smith—a suited-up "square" of the decidedly unhip variety—was dubious of reaching out to hippies, but he was so impressed by the barefoot, long-haired, bearded John the Baptist lookalike that he invited him to preach at the church. And that began a movement.

Frisbee's charismatic preaching and infectious zeal for God, all with a decidedly organic, hippie authenticity, attracted throngs of SoCal hippies to Calvary Chapel. The church grew from about two hundred to two thousand in a six-month time span and spawned multiple campuses, and soon pastor Chuck Smith was performing regular mass baptisms in the Pacific Ocean.

Having inspired the growth of the Calvary Chapel denomination, Frisbee—in true itinerant fashion—moved on to help found the more aggressively charismatic Vineyard movement, working with John Wimber. He didn't stay there long either, however, driven out because of lingering suspicions that Frisbee was a practicing homosexual. These accusations ultimately drove Frisbee from the churches and denominations he helped to start, and tragically left him shunned and written out of the official histories.

Frisbee is an early, symbolic case of what would become a fairly common dynamic in cool Christianity. He was an authentically hip novelty who brought in the crowds and understood the youth zeitgeist much more than the older church leaders ever could. Thus, they used him to grow the church, to reach the unreachable youth culture, and to spawn a revival. But he was ultimately disposable, because he—like whatever latest music style or film or fashion trend the church adopts for branding appeal—was never valued in and of himself. He was a utility; a gimmick that worked. And his shadow looms large over hipster Christianity today.

What Did the Hippies See in Jesus? (Answer: Themselves)

The famous "Wanted: Jesus Christ" posters serve as a lingering iconic image of the Jesus People movement. They could be seen on walls in the Haight and eventually as ads in underground newspapers like Berkeley's *Right On!* and the *Hollywood Free Paper.* The posters described Jesus as a subversive leader of "an underground liberation movement" who looks like a typical hippie (long hair, beard, robe, sandals) and is extremely dangerous, preaching an "insidiously inflammatory message" and often associating with "known criminals, radicals, subversives, prostitutes and street people."

"They liked him," said Eskridge, "because they were like him. He had long hair, a beard, wore sandals, wandered the land, was persecuted by 'the man.' They utterly related to him."

In that time, hippies in general, and not just the Jesus People converts, respected Jesus, who stood as a sort of icon for them. Hippies were sick and tired of establishment churches and organized religion, yes, but Jesus was different. He represented a more authentic, stripped-down, raw spirituality—a sort of "getting back to the real deal." And so while only a select group of hippies actually made the plunge to convert wholeheartedly to a life of following Jesus, most hippies found him to be a figure of countercultural inspiration and held him in high esteem.

But the hippie converts didn't just admire Jesus for being a figurehead of a countercultural movement. They truly believed him to be the Son of God, preaching a transcendent gospel of miraculous transformation to which they—having sought but not found answers in drugs, free love, and eastern religion—very much responded. Jesus also offered hippies the sort of direct, authentic, *real* experience of spirituality they so longed for. He was a man anointed by the Holy Spirit—that mystical, mind-blowing member of the Trinity that hippie Christians tended to play up. Not coincidentally, the Spirit-heavy, Pentecostal denominations were the ones that attracted hippies. To them, Jesus was not a stoic, stodgy, safe person. He was a wild, dangerous, rock star of a God whose existence and message could do nothing other than routinely turn the establishment upside down.

Counterculture, Subculture, and Christian Rock

Unfortunately, as tends to happen with countercultural movements, the energy and authenticity that made Jesus so attractive to so many young people was ultimately pursued, co-opted, and deflated by the mainstream forces seeking a piece of the pie. As soon as the Jesus People movement became so widespread that the media was taking note of it (in the early to mid-seventies), the end of its countercultural credibility was already on the horizon. Churches of all stripes were trying to get in on the act, pastors everywhere were affirming the new Christian youth movement, even Billy Graham—perhaps the last person you'd expect to reach out to hippies—was on board with it, a crucial aspect of the whole story, notes Eskridge.

"The fact that someone like Graham was sympathetic to these kids was huge. It showed America's parents that these kids were okay. If Billy Graham likes them, how bad can it be?"

Even the savvy media minds in the secular world were taking note of the Jesus People thing, turning it into mega profit with things like *Godspell* and *Jesus Christ Superstar*, the album version of the latter hitting number one on the Billboard charts. These pop culture touchpoints fused together the complex threads of the hippie Christian zeitgeist (hippies, young people, rock music, Jesus) and made it understandable and palatable for the masses.

Very early in the whole hippie Christian story, the countercultural impulse to portray Jesus as a dangerous subversive became victim of the inadvertent mollifying force of mainstream approval. Adults liked it because it got their kids interested in Jesus rather than drugs. Pastors liked it because it brought a new vitality and spirit to the church. Few people were offended by it, and those who were at least recognized the good that was happening on account of it. However countercultural the Jesus People were in their earliest days, by the end they were fostering a massive and mainstream subculture that was less about being risky, wild, and revolutionary *for* the world than it was about being safe, fun, and alternative *from* the world. It was a shift from "cool people becoming Christians" to "Christian cool as selling point."

The history of Christian rock music, which got its start alongside the Jesus People in the early seventies, nicely demonstrates this shift. Early on, Christian rock (or "Jesus music") was as genuine and bottom-up as you can get. Its pioneers were typically musicians and bands from the secular rock scene that became converts, were invited to play in churches like Calvary Chapel, and began writing songs about Jesus. They were people like Chuck Girard, a friend of Brian Wilson's whose band, Love Song, came out of the Laguna Beach dope scene; or Larry Norman, "the grandfather of Christian rock," whose epic 1969 masterpiece *Upon This Rock* is considered the first Christian rock album. Other secular rockers who converted to Christianity included Noel Paul Stookey of Peter, Paul and Mary; Jeremy Spencer of Fleetwood Mac; and Phil Keaggy of Glass Harp. You might also throw Johnny Cash, Pat Boone, and Bob Dylan into the mix—major figures in music who played notable roles in the 1970s Christian scene.

These secular rockers' conversions to Christianity, and subsequent Jesus music, lent the whole movement some important credibility with the kids. There was an authentic vibe to it all. It wasn't fake. It wasn't in-house. It wasn't safe. Well, not yet.

It also wasn't commercial. In its earliest days, the Jesus musicians were highly mobile, fly-by-the-seat-of-your-pants types who were making music simply for evangelistic and worship purposes. These bands traveled around a circuit of coffeehouses, cobbling together just enough money for food and gas. It was unorganized, inefficient, and very bottom-up.

Soon enough, the grassroots, amateur, rough-edged Jesus music morphed into the polished, efficient, niche-minded industry called Contemporary Christian Music. Chuck Smith founded Maranatha! Music in 1971 to publish and promote his church's stable of artists, including Love Song, Children of the Day, The Way, Mustard Seed Faith, and Daniel Amos. Originally nonprofit, by the eighties Maranatha! was a major player in the exploding Christian retail music industry, spawning, for example, such era-defining icons as Psalty the Songbook (a sort of Christian Spongebob).

So it went in the story of Jesus music. It started as a movement and quickly became an industry.

Christian Cool, Kitsch in the Eighties and Nineties

Though by the eighties most of the Jesus People had cut their hair, shaved their beards, and traded in their tunics and sandals for argyle sweaters and penny loafers, the legacy of the hippie Christian movement was alive and well. For one thing, the deeply personal, experi-

Key Dates in the Formation of Hipster Christianity

June 5, 1955: Francis Schaeffer opens L'Abri in Switzerland.

1967: The Living Room coffeehouse opens in San Francisco's Haight-Ashbury district; origins of Jesus People movement.

1969: Larry Norman's *Upon This Rock* (Capitol Records) is released; first major release of a Christian rock record.

June 21, 1971: The Jesus Movement is profiled in *Time* magazine article, "The New Rebel Cry: Jesus Is Coming!"

1971: First issue of the *Wittenburg Door* (or *The Door*) is published by San Diego youth worker Mike Yaconelli.

1971: First issue of *Sojourners* is published.

June 17, 1972: Christian Woodstock. During the Expo '72 evangelistic conference sponsored by Campus Crusade and held in Dallas, a day-long Christian music festival draws a crowd somewhere between 100,000 and 200,000 and features the music of Love Song, Larry Norman, Randy Matthews, The Archers, Children of the Day, Johnny Cash, and Kris Kristofferson.

1977: Ron Sider publishes *Rich Christians in an Age of Hunger*, which will become a classic among later generations of Christian hipsters.

June 18-20, 1984: JPUSA holds the first Cornerstone Music Festival in Grayslake, Illinois.

1984: Thomas Howard publishes *Evangelical Is Not Enough*, charting his pilgrimage from evangelicalism to liturgical Christianity.

July 21, 1984: Christian metal band Stryper releases its first EP, *The Yellow and Black Attack*, launching a successful career which included one Platinum and two Gold records.

1984: Degarmo & Key's video "Six Six Six" is the first Christian music video selected for rotation on MTV, and almost as quickly banned for excessive violence and disturbing images.

March 9, 1987: U2 releases *The Joshua Tree*, cementing their status as the world's most epic pseudo-Christian rock band.

1988: dc Talk, a trio of students from Liberty University, signs a recording contract with Forefront Records.

November 1993: Brandon Ebel founds Tooth & Nail Records.

October 1995: Mark Noll publishes *The Scandal of the Evangelical Mind*.

April 1997: Pedro the Lion releases its first EP, *Whole*.

January 2003: Christian satirical website *Lark News* is launched.

March 1, 2003: *Relevant* publishes its first issue.

2005: Sufjan Stevens's *Illinois* is named the best album of 2005 by *Pitchfork* and countless other secular music critics.

February 2006: Shane Claiborne publishes *Irresistible Revolution*.

February 18, 2006: Icelandic post-rock darlings Sigur Rós perform a sold-out concert at Calvin College.

ential, Spirit-filled emphasis of the Jesus movement held over into the eighties and nineties, as the charismatic movement took off and a sort of "just how you like it," seeker-sensitive approach became common practice among evangelical churches. The legacy also included an emphasis on the *new* and an elevation of trend and cool. Following the lead of Chuck Smith, whose outreach to hipsters reaped huge dividends, evangelical leaders in the 1980s no longer shied away from cool but rather actively sought it out. They began to reach out to the youth culture and form church to fit its needs—motivated by a renewed desire to be contemporary, current, and relevant.

Os Guinness describes what happened in eighties and nineties evangelicalism in this way:

> Suddenly the air in evangelical conferences and magazines was thick with assaults on the irrelevance of history, the outdatedness of traditional hymns and music, the uptightness of traditional moralism, the abstractness of theologizing, the impracticality of biblical exposition, the inadequacy of small churches, and the deadly, new unforgivable sin—irrelevance.[5]

Part of the new "rethink everything!" disposition of evangelicalism in the eighties and nineties was an aggressively commercialistic development of an evangelical subculture. A mind-set of "whatever the secular culture can do, we can do too—only Christianly!" arose. As a result, we saw the birth of Christian retail chains and everything from Christian sci-fi novels to Christian computer games, Christian animated cartoon series (including *McGee and Me* and *Veggie Tales*) and Christian T-shirts (that often mimicked current popular T-shirt brands, such as No Fear). If the secular market produced anything remotely cool, trendy, or popular, you'd be sure to find a Christian version in no time.

This was all very clearly seen in Christian music. Throughout the eighties and especially in the nineties, the CCM machine very quickly churned out Christian versions of whatever style of music was currently cool. Desperately trying to stay relevant and appealing to the fickle tastes of the youth culture, the industry adopted a comprehensive "if you like so-and-so, then you'll like . . ." methodology of artist development. If you liked the Beastie Boys, there was dc Talk (circa *Nu Thang*); if you liked Nirvana, there was Audio Adrenaline; if you liked Hootie & the Blowfish, there was Third Day; if you liked

*NSYNC, there was Plus One; if you liked Korn or Limp Bizkit, there was P.O.D., and so on. And of course arena concert tours accompanied the music, along with all the appropriate merchandising. It was big business. But as much as it was a boon to the evangelical industry, it didn't exactly make Christians all that cool—at least by the standards of the MTV secular observers.

On occasion in the eighties and nineties, something from the Christian subculture had crossover success and became a talking point in secular culture. Amy Grant's "Baby Baby" is probably the earliest and best example. Also on the list was Sixpence None the Richer with "Kiss Me," a song without a shred of Christian baggage that made its way into every teen movie or TV show in 1999. Other examples of milder crossover success include P.O.D. (the biggest Christian success of MTV's *TRL* era), Switchfoot (songs on the *Walk to Remember* soundtrack in 2002), Jars of Clay (whose "Flood" was something of a secular chart hit in the mid-nineties), and the once-popular and now ridiculed Creed (whose Christian cred—let's be honest—was always a little nebulous). But the thing about these crossover "successes" is that they weren't exactly winning over secular hipsters. They were crossing over into the mainstream Viacom/Billboard/MTV establishment, not crossing over into the trendy New York indie scene. And however cool these bands seemed to their Christian fans, most of the time they lost significant cool points for "selling out" to the mainstream market. So while many a youth pastor spent time playing up Creed or Sixpence in efforts to show that, "look, the world sees how cool we can be!" most Christian hipsters in the nineties didn't really buy it.

Hip Christian Youth Culture in the Nineties

Hip always thrives most in rebellion, so as the nineties progressed and the insanity of Christian kitsch, retail, and evangelical big business became increasingly hard to stomach for many idealistic young Christians, the Christian counterculture showed some signs of resurgence. These Gen Xers were less idealistic than their parents, more cynical, more into grunge, and slightly disillusioned by Ronald Reagan. They were also disillusioned by the horrors of evangelical scandals in the eighties, which were numerous and inestimably damaging to evangelical credibility—especially for the young people coming of age at the time. Defamed televangelists like Oral Roberts, Jim Bak-

CCM Albums of the Nineties That Make Christian Hipsters Nostalgic

A lot of Christian hipsters today were raised in the evangelical Christian subculture in the nineties. Thus, while most of them have completely abandoned CCM by now, they still look fondly and nostalgically (with a smidge of irony) upon the Christian music they were reared on. Here are twenty albums that Christian hipsters today love to listen to for a trip down memory lane.

Amy Grant, *Heart in Motion* (1991)

Michael W. Smith, *Change Your World* (1993)

dc Talk, *Free at Last* (1993)

dc Talk, *Jesus Freak* (1995)

Jars of Clay, *Jars of Clay* (1995)

Audio Adrenaline, *Bloom* (1996)

Newsboys, *Take Me to Your Leader* (1996)

Rebecca St. James, *God* (1996)

Third Day, *Conspiracy No. 5* (1997)

OC Supertones, *Adventures of the OC Supertones* (1997)

Reality Check, *Reality Check* (1997)

Plankeye, *The One and Only* (1997)

Project 86, *Project 86* (1998)

Mxpx, *Life in General* (1998)

Sixpence None the Richer, *Sixpence None the Richer* (1998)

Plumb, *candycoatedwaterdrops* (1999)

Insyderz, *Skalleluia* (1999)

All Star United, *International Anthems for the Human Race* (1999)

P.O.D., *Fundamental Elements of Southtown* (1999)

Switchfoot, *New Way to Be Human* (1999)

ker, Jimmy Swaggart, and Robert Tilton represented the worst of the conflation of Christianity and capitalism. Combined with the unseemly ubiquity of Jesus dolls, socks, oven mitts, and gold bracelets, the corruption of a corporate, increasingly supersized "Je$us" would prove to be a significant element in the development of the current Christian hipster phenomenon.

In the 1990s, then, cool Christianity took on a couple different forms. On one hand, it existed as an industry, as an establishment: churches, pastors, conventions, and festivals that clamored for the attention of youth by branding Christianity as just as cool as anything on MTV. These were the big-budget youth groups with high-tech lighting, frenzied lock-ins, laser tag, paintball, and worship leaders with dyed hair and tattoos who played Plankeye songs. These were the glossy megachurches with in-house climbing walls, coffeehouses, skate parks, gyms, ropes courses, and everything your average X-Games fan would find appealing. This was a top-down method that believed the flashier, more entertaining Christianity was, the more kids would come and think it was cool.

But on the other hand, cool Christianity in the nineties—and especially as it gave way to 2000—existed as a more organic, bottom-up entity: Christian college students embracing a more intellectual faith, cynical kids who found youth groups pretty lame, and indie/alternative/emo teenagers who embraced the Tooth & Nail brand of Christian underground music. These Christian kids embraced the lesser known but more artistically forward-thinking Christian artists like Over the Rhine, Vigilantes of Love, Danielson Famile, Pedro the Lion, and any band of the sort that wasn't afraid of playing bars or occasionally cursing in a song. These pared-down, back-to-basics young Christians participated in Passion conferences and 24/7 prayer gatherings, and helped ignite the contemporary worship movement, all the while shunning the indulgences of corporate Christianity and feeling a bit unsettled by the Purpose Driven, megachurch, seeker-sensitive zeitgeist.

This latter group of hip Christians, still relatively a small group in the late nineties, were the precursors to the current incarnation of Christian hipsters—a generation of Christian youth culture that has, since the turn of the millennium and especially in the post–9/11 era, come into its own in a more savvy, ironic, post-kitsch sort of way.

Relevant Magazine and the Birth of the Christian Hipster

So, when was the Christian hipster born? I think the term *hipster* in general came into common usage around 9/11, but I'm going to arbitrarily place the birth of the Christian hipster at 2003, when the first issue of *Relevant* magazine was released. Certainly Christian hipsters were alive and well before this—because *Relevant* was in part created for this growing demographic—but the arrival of *Relevant* on the scene heralded a new kind of hipster: a Christian kind.

Relevant magazine and its accompanying website—Relevant magazine.com—are part of the RELEVANT Media Group, founded by Cameron Strang, son of *Charisma Magazine* publisher and Strang Communications CEO Stephen Strang. Strang, a graduate of Oral Roberts University (which ironically banned the magazine's first issue from the college bookstore because of the irreverent "Consumer Guide to Jesus Action Figures" feature), is undoubtedly a Christian hipster himself, at least on the surface. His trendy style, multiple earrings, shaved head, and scruffy facial hair make him, in the words of the *New York Times*, "a model alt-evangelical."[6]

Relevant represents a number of things, but I think it primarily embodies the rebellion among younger evangelicals against the moral strictures and general lameness of old-school fundamentalist Christianity. The magazine appeals to those of us who grew up in eighties and nineties youth group culture, where dc Talk's *Jesus Freak* was pushing the envelope and kids were exorcised if they admitted to liking Nine Inch Nails. The magazine eschews the "burn your secular records!" mind-set of our modernist evangelical heritage and instead embraces secular culture and art with an aggressive open-mindedness. The magazine has always covered secular music in a higher proportion to Christian music, as if to say to the other Christian publications, "We're not afraid of venturing outside of the CCM subculture, because kids are listening to everything anyway!" Indeed, throughout its six-year history, *Relevant* has featured on its cover everyone from Ben Folds to Radiohead's Thom Yorke to rappers like Mase and Common. In addition to music, *Relevant* has featured regular columns from such cool Christian figures as Waterdeep's Don Chaffer and Jars of Clay's Dan Haseltine, pages and pages of pop culture trivia ("Slices"), and lots of features about social justice issues like AIDS in Africa, human trafficking, and genocide in Darfur.

For many young evangelicals at the dawn of the new millennium, *Relevant* was a breath of fresh air because it voiced their own perspective on culture: that it is okay to like secular music, fashion, and movies, and that it's okay to be slightly less beholden to white-bread, Bible-belt Republicanism. I remember when I received the first issue of *Relevant* magazine back in 2003. I worked as the arts and entertainment editor at the Wheaton College *Record* and was constantly receiving flak from conservative readers and alumni for reviewing more secular music than Christian music, or for (gasp!) giving R-rated movies positive reviews. When I saw *Relevant*, I thought, "Finally, a magazine for Christians who don't exclusively listen to Christian music—this has been a long time coming!"

Soon I was sending in movie reviews to *Relevant*, and they started publishing them on their website. It was so refreshing to be able to write thoughtfully about movies without the oppressive "but how is this a *Christian* movie review?" burden. A year or so later, I wrote my first print article for them—an interview with David Bazan of Pedro the Lion. Since then I've been a fairly regular contributor, writing mainly on pop culture trends, music, movies, technology, and politics. For a while in 2005 and 2006, I was actually a section editor of the "Progressive Culture" section of Relevantmagazine.com, writing monthly columns, editing and uploading user-generated stories, and overseeing the movies, music, and books sections. In the time that I've been associated with *Relevant*, I have seen it cycle through many staffers and writers, but the core principle—of being an alternative/cool/slightly snarky and ironic magazine for the emerging Christian hipster class—has remained the same.

The New Christian Hipster Irony

The irony that has proven to be *Relevant*'s bread and butter must not be underemphasized in this short history of Christian hip. If you are a Christian of a certain age (let's say 21–50) and you grew up in the Christian church (especially in the eighties or early nineties), you probably love making fun of the evangelical subculture. I know I do. I love nothing more than laughing about and ironically consuming vintage Christian kitsch items. Whether it's *McGee and Me*, Newsboys, *Left Behind*, or any number of other bits of Jesus junk, I always enjoy reminiscing about it. In the same way that the rest of our generation ironically talks about Zach Morris or *Labyrinth* or those years when it was cool to roll up your jean shorts (actually, that's cool again), Christian hipsters find great amusement in recalling the nonsensical oddities of the evangelical world.

I remember how in college—Wheaton College, that is—my friends and I bonded so often over our shared history of growing up in evangelical Christian culture. (Christian colleges, it should be noted, are often the most fertile places for Christian irony to spread.) We would reminisce about things like *Adventures in Odyssey*, Ray Boltz, and the various mayonnaise-heavy casseroles that church ladies would invariably bring to potlucks in the fellowship hall. We loved watching horrible Christian movies like *Left Behind 2* and making snarky comments throughout. Sometimes we would buy things like *Carmen: R.I.O.T.* or *Amy Grant: The Heart in Motion Video Collection* on VHS and give them to each other as presents. We would dream of writing fake Christian Amish historical romance novels or starting a museum of Christian kitsch and pop-apocalyptic memorabilia. We had great fun, because the evangelical subculture that reared us was just so ripe for parody and ridicule. Anyone who grew up in it and has not made fun of it in later years is truly a miraculous anomaly of well-preserved sincerity.

Christian hipsters especially love to satirize just how sickeningly derivative evangelical culture is—that we always have to copy what the secular world is doing, usually a few months or years later (for example: *Guitar Praise*, the new Christian version of *Guitar Hero*). Once we realize how capitalistic and commercialized it all was, it frees us up to make fun of it—to joyfully revel (ironically) in the maudlin kitsch that reared us. It is the ultimate irony, then, that Christians have co-opted the irony industry itself to make out of it an evangelical alternative.

For the secular world, satirical newspaper *The Onion* is the pinnacle of hipster irony. Christians have several very similar alternatives. For example, *Lark News*—a fake news rag with infrequent but hilarious updates—features headlines like "Denominations reach non-compete agreement" and "Missionaries maintain obesity against long odds." The site, founded by Joel Kilpatrick in 2002, sometimes has a fake news story picked up by mainstream media outlets who think it's true, such as a story about Zondervan releasing a gay-friendly Bible for homosexuals called the gNIV. Though it may confuse the less ironic among us, *Lark News* is a great source of laughs at the expense of our evangelical ridiculousness.

Then there is the *Stuff Christians Like* blog, the Christian version of *Stuff White People Like*—the runaway blog success that revels in smarmy self-loathing and the purging of white bourgeois guilt. The Christian version features the same numbered format as its mainstream predecessor, including such entries as "#31: Occasionally Swearing," "#393: Family Fish Bumper Stickers," "#382: Perfectly Timing Your Communion Walk," and "#93: Riding on the Cool Van in the Youth Group."

Other purveyors of Christian irony include *Purgatorio*, which touts itself as "a panoply of evangelical eccentricities, unorthodox oddities and Christian cultural curiosities"; *Ship of Fools* ("The magazine of Christian unrest"); and the granddaddy of them all, *The Wittenberg Door* (aka *The Door*), which is sort of the *Mad Magazine* of Christian culture and has been parodying institutional Christianity since

1971. Not coincidentally, *The Door* sprang up in California in the early seventies (a publication of Youth Specialties). This was the seat of almost all nascent forms of hip Christianity, after all.

One of the poster boys of the *Relevant* brand of what I'm calling "post-youth-group Christian irony" is Matthew Paul Turner, former editor of *CCM* magazine. In 2004, Relevant Books published Turner's book *The Christian Culture Survival Guide*, which epitomizes the sort of nostalgic sarcasm that so many of us who grew up in eighties-era evangelical Sunday school can relate to. Another *Relevant* author specializing in this brand of sarcasm is Jason Boyett, who wrote *Pocket Guide to the Apocalypse: The Official Field Manual for the End of the World* for Relevant Books in 2005. End-times satire humor is a whole genre, actually, with books like *Right Behind: A Parody of Last Days Goofiness* by Nathan D. Wilson, taking direct aim at the megahit *Left Behind* series by Tim LaHaye and Jerry Jenkins.

The Literature of Post-Youth-Group Christian Hip

Relevant magazine and the various satire publications are just the tip of the iceberg in terms of the burgeoning purveyors of Christian hipster literature and media. If you are a Christian who grew up in the eighties and nineties and likes cool music, movies, and fashion, *Relevant* is certainly not your only option. *Paste*, a vaguely spiritual magazine that covers "Signs of Life in Music, Film, and Culture," was founded by a churchgoing Christian from Georgia, Josh Jackson. *Paste* features reviews and news stories on all the hot new indie bands and movies, and can be considered a legitimate tastemaker on the hipster scene—described by the *Chicago Tribune* as "hip without sacrificing credibility on the altar of corporately deemed cool." When I interviewed Jackson in 2006, however, he was quick to say that *Paste* had no interest in being hipster. "It's not about what's cool," he said. "It's about what's good."

There is also the San Diego–based *Risen* magazine—delivering the "Spiritual Edge of Pop Culture" through design-heavy pages full of cool photography and interviews with stars of music, film, TV, and X-Games–type sports. And for the older, more NPR-oriented crowd of Christian hipsters, there is Seattle-based *Image*, a literary and arts journal with an avid fan base of culturally astute Christians. And of course many, many other webzines and blogs regularly pop up to cater to the Christian hipster class—sites like conversantlife.com, patrolmag.com, and lookingcloser.org, among countless others.

But when historians look back on this Christian hipster moment, they will look at more than just magazines and websites. A spate of books also represent this phenomenon—books that have reflected upon and helped develop the Christian hipster culture. The one that comes to mind first is Donald Miller's *Blue Like Jazz*. The title, the cover, the subtitle ("Nonreligious Thoughts on Christian Spirituality") are all so very hip—and it came out in 2003, the year Christian hipsterdom was born. Other significant books that have helped shape the Christian hipster culture include Lauren Winner's *Girl Meets God: A Memoir* (2003), Rob Bell's *Velvet Elvis: Repainting the Christian Faith* (2006), and Anne Lamott's *Traveling Mercies: Some Thoughts on Faith* (2000). Scores of other books make the list too, many of which I will reference and talk about throughout this book.

The emergence of the Christian hipster, then, is not something that happened in a vacuum. The path of history and the cultural currents of the last half century, at least, have shaped its formation, and it was and will be well documented in the literature and arts of its practitioners and observers. This book, for one, is seeking to document the moment.

five

christian hipsters today

*H*ow do you spot a Christian hipster? The easy answer is to pay attention to young people's appearance in church. Do they look achingly trendy? Do they have visible tattoos and eighty-dollar haircuts? Do they have a beard? If you are still unconvinced after surveying their appearance, you can also identify Christian hipsters by taking note of their post-church activities.

Over the years, I've come to see this as one of the clearest distinguishing features of Christian hipster subculture. They usually do something as a group after church, and it frequently involves alcohol.

For example, one time I visited Grace Brethren Church in Long Beach, California, with several fellow twentysomethings. After the service, we spent the afternoon at Disneyland riding rides with synchronized music on our iPods. Radiohead's "Paranoid Android" on Tower of Terror, Coldplay's "Clocks" on the Teacups, and so on. Later, we attended a beer-tasting seminar as part of Disneyland's California Food and Wine Festival.

A few times after attending The Bridge, a Presbyterian church in downtown Los Angeles, I found myself with several other churchgoers at Seven Grand, the newest speakeasy hot spot just down the street. For irony's sake, some of us ordered "The Presbyterian," a whiskey sour cocktail with lemon and nutmeg. We sat outside on the dimly lit retro alley patio, straight out of Chaplin-era Los Angeles, and talked about Calvinism and phenomenology.

If you find yourself doing this regularly after a church service, chances are good that you yourself are a Christian hipster.

Seriously, though, who *are* Christian hipsters? What are they interested in? What are we to make of them? This chapter, and several subsequent chapters in this book, is about answering these questions.

Christian hipsters are in many ways not all that different from any secular hipster. You will notice quite a bit of overlap here, and I don't want to make it sound like Christian hipsters are some homogeneous, easily identifiable, totally unique category of hipster. They're decidedly not. Especially on a superficial level: If I were asked to pick out the Christian in a lineup of twentysomething hipsters, it would be impossible (unless, of course, he or she had a visible Bible-verse tattoo or something). But just like the Christian hippies in the early seventies—who for all superficial purposes appeared to be just like any other hippie (minus LSD and free love, of course)—Christian hipsters today distinguish themselves in rather subtle, behavioral ways.

Christian hipsters may look and act like your average antiestablishmentarian, image-obsessed subversive, but for the most part they still try to live a Christlike life. They are significantly less hedonistic than their secular counterparts, for example. Sure, most Christian hipsters still tend to drink alcohol and maybe smoke, but they do it less frequently and with more guilt. They also tend to abstain from drugs (though it isn't uncommon for Christian hipsters to have at least tried marijuana) and premarital sex, though they talk about sex just as frankly and freely as most other hipsters. In most cases Christian hipsters have cleaner, less expletive-heavy speech than other hipsters, trying not to use the f-word too much in public, for example. If nothing else, Christian hipsters exude a softer, less cynical spirit than their more jaded counterparts, and a stronger sense of optimism. And of course there is the matter of their belief that Jesus Christ is the Son of God and that he alone motivates their hope for transformation.

Other things can distinguish Christian hipsters, as well. And though this is totally simplistic and way overgeneralized (like chapter 3's "Twelve Common Types of Hipster"), it might help fill out our picture of contemporary Christian hipsterdom if we look at some specific things they tend to like, and some things they are not all that fond of.

What They Like and Don't Like

Things They Don't Like

Christian hipsters cringe at megachurches, altar calls, and door-to-door evangelism. They don't really like John Eldredge's *Wild at Heart* or youth pastors who talk too much about *Braveheart*. In general, they tend not to like Mel Gibson and have come to really dislike *The Passion* for being overly bloody and maybe a little sadistic. They don't like people like Pat Robertson, who on *The 700 Club* famously said that America should "take Hugo Chavez out." And for that matter, they don't particularly like *The 700 Club* either, except to make fun of it. They don't like evangelical leaders who get too involved in politics, such as James Dobson or Jerry Falwell, who once said of terrorists that America should "blow them all away in the name of the Lord."[1] They don't like TBN, PAX, or Joel Osteen. They do have a wry fondness for Benny Hinn, however.

Christian hipsters tend not to like contemporary Christian music (CCM) or Christian films (except ironically), or any nonbook item sold at Family Christian Stores. They hate warehouse churches or churches with American flags on stage, or churches with any flag on stage, really. They prefer the term "Christ follower" to "Christian" and can't stand the phrases "soul winning" or "nondenominational." They could do without weird and awkward evangelistic methods including (but not limited to): sock puppets, ventriloquism, mimes, sign language, beach evangelism, and modern dance. Surprisingly, they don't really have that big of a problem with old-school evangelists like Billy Graham and Billy Sunday, and they kind of love the really wild ones like Aimee Semple McPherson.

Things They Like

Christian hipsters like music, movies, and books that are well respected by their respective artistic communities—Christian or not. They love books like *Resident Aliens* by Stanley Hauerwas and Will Willimon, *Rich Christians in an Age of Hunger* by Ron Sider, *God's Politics* by Jim Wallis, and *The Imitation of Christ* by Thomas à Kempis. They tend to be fans of any number of the following authors: Flannery O'Connor, Walker Percy, Wendell Berry, Thomas Merton, John Howard Yoder, Walter Brueggemann, N. T. Wright, Brennan Manning, Eugene Peterson, Anne Lamott, C. S. Lewis, G. K. Chesterton, Henri Nouwen, Søren Kierkegaard, Pierre Teilhard de Chardin, Paul Tillich, Annie Dillard, Marilynne Robinson, Chuck Klosterman, David Sedaris, or anything ancient or philosophically important.

Christian hipsters love thinking and acting Catholic, even if they are thoroughly Protestant. They love the Pope, liturgy, incense, lectio divina, Lent, and timeless liturgical phrases like "Thanks be to God" or "Peace of Christ be with you." They enjoy Eastern Orthodox churches and mysterious iconography, and they love the elaborate cathedrals of Europe (even if they are too museum-like for hipster tastes). Christian hipsters also love taking communion with real port, and they don't mind common cups. They love poetry readings, worshiping with candles, and smoking pipes while talking about God. Some of them like smoking a lot of different things.

Christian hipsters love breaking the taboos that used to be taboo for Christians, such as piercings, dressing a little goth, getting lots of tattoos (the Christian Tattoo Association now lists more than one hundred member shops), carrying flasks, and smoking cloves. A lot of them love skateboarding and surfing, many of them play in bands, and most prefer buying organic. They tend to get jobs working for churches, parachurch organizations, nonprofits, design companies, or the government. They are, on the whole, a little more sincere and idealistic than their secular hipster counterparts.

Hip Christian Figureheads

Though Christian hipsters do come in all shapes and sizes and can be any combination of the twelve types of hipster outlined in chapter 3, it might be helpful to look at some specific examples of people they tend to idolize. The following are a few Christian hipster icons—the figureheads of the hipster Christian movement.

Sufjan Stevens

If contemporary Christian hipster culture could have only one iconic face, Sufjan Stevens would fill that role. When the highly celebrated singer-songwriter started making waves in indie music circles in 2003 with the release of his album *Greetings from Michigan* (an ode to his home state), he inaugurated a new era—an era when a Christian musician from Hope College could move to New York and establish a legitimate name for himself in literary, artistic, and otherwise hipster circles, all without abandoning a deeply Christian artistic sensibility.

The arrival of Sufjan, whose 2004 album, *Seven Swans*, is brimful of biblical imagery and what might be called low-fi folk worship songs, signaled the birth of a class of young Christian artists who were making their way in the world of secular culture by committing to high-quality, forward-thinking work rather than participating in the CCM juggernaut or otherwise unseemly establishment channels of religious commercialism. The explosive success of Sufjan's 2005 album, *Illinois*—which was the best-reviewed album on metacritic.com that year[2]—catapulted him to princely status in the broader hipster world and gave hope to the emerging Christian hipster demographic that had for so long been deprived of an artistically relevant voice to call its own.

On the coattails of Sufjan's success, and that of his Asthmatic Kitty record label, several other Christian hipster musicians have debuted on the scene or enjoyed renewed significance. These include Half-handed Cloud, Rosie Thomas, St. Vincent, Denison Witmer, Danielson, My Brightest Diamond, and The Welcome Wagon—the latter of which is a duo made up of Brooklyn Presbyterian minister Reverend Vito Aiuto and his wife, Monique, whose church is profiled in the next chapter.

But Sufjan is a Christian hipster icon in more senses than just his music. He's a soft-spoken, heady poet with quirky, child-like style (he sometimes wears large butterfly wings or retro college tracksuits in concert performances) and a strong sense of nostalgia. Like many Christian hipsters, he is working through his own religious heritage—sometimes ironically, sometimes earnestly, but always with a pious and personal reverence that accepts and glories in a faith that is perceived as equal parts nerdy, mysterious, and transcendent.

Shane Claiborne

Perhaps one of the most important Christian hipsters around these days—more of a Christian hippie, actually—is Shane Claiborne, self-described "ordinary radical" and author of *The Irresistible Revolution* and *Jesus for President*. The thirty-four-year-old cites as his heroes Dorothy Day, a "prophetess of peace" who founded the Catholic Worker movement in the 1930s, Mother Teresa, Rich Mullins, Martin Luther King Jr., Francis of Assisi, Dietrich Bonhoeffer, Justin Martyr,

Oscar Romero, William Wilberforce, and other rebel Christians and activists throughout history.

Claiborne, like most Christian hipsters, was not always cool. He was a Tennessee-bred, self-described Jesus freak who organized See You at the Pole gatherings and was committed to bringing prayer back to public schools. He handed out tracts at malls, did evangelistic skits, and worked on the 1992 Bush-Quayle campaign. But when he went to Eastern College, met sociology professor Tony Campolo, and started sleeping on the streets with homeless people, he became a different sort of Christian. Soon he was working alongside Mother Teresa in Calcutta, joining Christian peacekeeping efforts in Baghdad as the American missiles fell on the city, and starting a sort of new monastic community in inner-city Philadelphia, called the Simple Way. In his book *The Irresistible Revolution*, Claiborne invokes a hipster forefather to explain his own countercultural efforts with the Simple Way:

> Poet Henry David Thoreau went to the woods because he wanted to live deliberately, to breathe deeply, and to suck out the marrow of life. We went to the ghetto. We narrowed our vision to this: love God, love people, and follow Jesus. And we began calling our little experiment the Simple Way.[3]

Claiborne is a super earnest, likable guy, and though his dread-locked, homemade-tunic appearance can be off-putting, he's one of the nicest and most respectable voices of his generation. His passion and commitment to living an unorthodox, countercultural life seems genuine, and he is the first to say that he is not cool. He writes in *The Irresistible Revolution* that his coolness was ruined by "a God who has everything backward," and that "you don't get crucified for being cool; you get crucified for living radically different from the norms of all that is cool in the world."[4]

But this statement is a little paradoxical, because the types of things Claiborne does—serving the poor, fighting capitalism, being green, and opposing the Iraq war, for instance—are in fact very cool these days. The "norms of all that is cool" from which he rebels are actually totally uncool commodities of the establishment. So though he is acting very earnestly in his desire to appear uncool, Claiborne is nevertheless inescapably hip. His insistence on actively shunning the label only makes him cooler.

Lauren Winner

Lauren Winner represents the erudite, academic Christian hipster. She's a bookish sort—a black-clad, scarf-wearing writer with sixties cat-eye glasses and a compelling "colonial Virginia via the Bronx" accent. If you've ever heard her speak, you know that she has an impressive command of words and rhetoric, and an appealing, down-to-earth presence that toes the line between ivory tower and girl next door.

Raised by a Reform Jewish father and Southern Baptist mother, thirty-three-year-old Winner has a diverse religious history. She converted to Orthodox Judaism while an undergrad at Columbia University, but then became a baptized Christian while a student at Clare College, Cambridge. Today she's a member of an Episcopal church and teaches classes on Christian spirituality at Duke Divinity School, where she received a master of divinity.

Winner (that's Dr. Winner) is a prolific writer, having received accolades for her three books: *Girl Meets God*, *Mudhouse Sabbath*, and *Real Sex: The Naked Truth about Chastity*. She has also written for the *New York Times Book Review*, the *Washington Post Book World*, *Publishers Weekly*, *Books & Culture*, and *Christianity Today*, and has appeared on PBS's *Religion & Ethics Newsweekly* and has served as a commentator on NPR's "All Things Considered."

Winner's thoughts on sex and chastity—as detailed in her rigorously honest and personal book, *Real Sex*—have proven revolutionary for young Christians everywhere who desperately seek a frank, productive dialogue about the subject. It might come as a surprise that Winner, a progressive Democrat with decidedly European tastes, comes down on the side of chastity before marriage, even if she reevaluates how we look and talk about the issues altogether.

But so go the paradoxes of Christian hipsters like Winner. They are torn between the very liberal, humanistic impulses of academia and progressive culture on one hand, and the somewhat archaic, inescapably old-school values of Christianity on the other. But increasing numbers of young Christians are gracefully embodying this paradox.

Jay Bakker

Like many hipsters, Jay Bakker had a rough childhood. His parents—Jim and Tammy Faye—were rich and famous televangelists until everything came crashing down in a 1980s money-and-sex scandal that sent his father to prison for five years. Bakker naturally turned away from establishment Christianity, became an alcoholic teenager, and blamed Jerry Falwell for much of his family's hardship. Eventually he came back to God, and today is pastor of Revolution Church in hipster hot spot Williamsburg, Brooklyn.

The church meets every Sunday at 4:00 p.m. at a bar (Pete's Candy Store) in Brooklyn, where Bakker gives a brief sermon (often with a title like "Nobody Likes a Selfish Bastard" or "Jesus: A Friend to Porn Stars") that is then broadcast on the church's website to create an "online church" for those too afraid to step foot back into a church building (even if it is just a Brooklyn bar). In addition to pastoring the church, Bakker makes the rounds on the speaking circuit and has appeared on *Larry King Live*, *20/20*, *Good Morning America*, and was featured in the Sundance Channel documentary, *One Punk Under God*.

It's easy to see why the media finds Bakker so interesting. He looks nothing like your typical Christian. He's a heavily tattooed, well-dressed hipster with a pierced lip, and in 2008 he was featured in an ad campaign for American designer Kenneth Cole. He's a far cry from his fundamentalist evangelical past, and he describes himself as a liberal Christian, making no apologies for being pro–gay rights and pro–gay marriage.

Bakker epitomizes the strain of Christian hipsterdom that is primarily a reaction against the excesses and corrupt nonsense of the evangelical world he grew up in. He has managed to retain his faith, but it's a faith that is aggressively counter to nearly everything he experienced as a child. Angry with the church and skeptical of Christian institutions and power structures, he favors "following Jesus" over "following Christians."

Donald Miller

Donald Miller must be considered one of the leading figures in hipster Christianity, if for no other reason than because he authored one of its most important early works—*Blue Like Jazz* (released in 2003 by Thomas Nelson). That book, with its tales of rediscovering faith with the help of Mark the Cussing Pastor (aka Mark Driscoll of Seattle's Mars Hill Church) and setting up reverse confessional booths on the campus of Reed College, became a *New York Times* bestseller and a favorite of Christian hipsters everywhere. Like Lauren Winner, Miller is first and foremost a good writer, and his books (*Jazz*, *Search-*

ing for God Knows What, and *Through Painted Deserts*) provide an appealingly stream-of-consciousness, contemporary memoir style reminiscent of Jack Kerouac or, more recently, Anne Lamott.

Blue Like Jazz was perceived in the media as a curious paradox: a Christian book that was actually pretty cool. Was this the beginning of a new "cool Christian" literary movement? The question is somewhat frustrating to Miller.

"I don't know that Christianity can be cool," said Miller in 2006. "And I suspect that people who think I have made it cool don't realize that . . . it exists outside of cool—it's the sort of thing you come into when you're done trying to redeem yourself with people."[5]

Despite his reluctance to label himself or his work as cool, Miller has nevertheless become highly sought after on the speaking circuit and has become a notable figure in the emerging church movement. He also campaigned heavily for Barack Obama in the 2008 election, organizing rallies on Christian college campuses and even providing the closing prayer one night at the Democratic National Convention in Denver. Supporting Obama, of course, is a major Christian hipster trademark.

Mark Driscoll

Some might balk at ascribing the word *hipster* to Mark Driscoll, but the fact is, he presides over one of the most important hipster churches in America—Seattle's Mars Hill—and is perhaps the only pastor ever to have been the thematic focus of an amateur porn festival.[6] Controversy follows Driscoll wherever he goes, and he attracts it in nearly everything he says.

A prime example of Driscoll's controversial rhetoric is this now-infamous quote from a *Relevant* magazine interview:

> Some emergent types [want] to recast Jesus as a limp-wrist hippie in a dress with a lot of product in His hair, who drank decaf and made pithy Zen statements about life while shopping for the perfect pair of shoes. In Revelation, Jesus is a prizefighter with a tattoo down His leg, a sword in His hand and the commitment to make someone bleed. That is a guy I can worship. I cannot worship the hippie, diaper, halo Christ, because I cannot worship a guy I can beat up.[7]

Driscoll is a hipster of the fratboy/testosterone-driven/"I'm gonna f— you up" variety (more like a "bro"). He is famous for using salty

Reasons Why Calvinism Is Hipster-Friendly

Calvinism is about certainty. In an era in which certainty is hard to come by and ambiguity is frequently championed, more and more young people long for something that is rock-solid certain. Calvinism requires no second-guessing about whether I've done enough or prayed the sinner's prayer earnestly enough to be saved, because it has nothing to do with my own powers.

Calvinism has an appealing picture of grace. It is irresistible and unconditional. When God sets his eyes on us, we can't escape his pursuit (and who would want a God who couldn't capture those he sought to save?). As Sufjan Stevens beautifully sings in "Seven Swans": *He will take you / If you run / He will chase you / Because he is the Lord.*

Calvinism emphasizes sin (total depravity). It underscores both our desperate need for redemption and righteousness and our utter inability to achieve it ourselves. This resonates with younger people today, who have grown up in a world that has told them they are good boys and girls who can do whatever they want to in life. They've been met with yesses at every turn, but are longing for noes. They recognize they are far from the angelic harbingers of goodness that their parents, teachers, and advertisers have deemed them. Calvinism tells it like it is.

Calvinism fears God. A healthy fear of God is totally lost on contemporary Christianity, which sees him as more of a "buddy/friend/therapist/guru" than the Creator and Sustainer of the universe. More and more young people are growing dubious of "God-lite" and prefer thinking of him as a commanding, dominating, dangerous God who deserves our deferential fear.

Calvinism is a little bit edgy, dark, and punk rock. It is less about hugs, Sunday school pink lemonade, and "God loves you" than it is about discipline, deference, and "God hates you in your sin; you are a wretch who needs God's grace." It is not for the faint of heart or the easily offended. Kids like this.

language in sermons and talking explicitly about sex, and manages to offend pretty much everyone at some point—though hordes of people still love him and follow his teachings. He can be soft-edged and almost poetic, but at the core, Driscoll is a hell-raising, scruffy brawler of a dude—sort of like Charles Bukowski meets John Rocker.

A hardcore Calvinist, Driscoll loves getting all riled up about sin, the depravity of man, the atonement, and the bloody violence of the cross. He adores people like Martin Luther, a man's man who drank a lot of beer, didn't mince words, and wasn't afraid to be a thorn in the side of the stodgy establishment. Driscoll espouses stridently conservative theology but liberally embraces the sorts of vices—drinking, dancing, R-rated movies, and UFC fights—that old-school Christians (and some of his Reformed pals like John Piper) ardently avoid.

Driscoll represents a curious anomaly of Christian hipsterdom, one that breaks all the traditional rules of being a hipster and yet manages to be strangely attractive to many, many hipsters.

Rob Bell

On the opposite end of the spectrum from Mark Driscoll is Rob Bell, who ironically also pastors a church called Mars Hill (in Grand Rapids, Michigan). While Driscoll rails against a chick-ified Jesus and calls his congregants to a highly fortified, macho-man mind-set, Rob Bell goes around saying things like, "Weak is the new strong."[8]

Bell has been a very high-profile figurehead of hip Christianity for some time now. Back in 2004, Andy Crouch wrote in *Christianity Today* that Bell "puts the hip in discipleship."[9] Subsequently, his surprising hipness has been analyzed by the leading scholars of cool, such as John Leland—who wrote in the *New York Times* that Bell speaks "with the awed enthusiasm of someone describing a U2 concert"[10]—or Robert Lanham, author of *The Hipster Handbook*, who labeled Bell "the Evangelical Steve Jobs" in his book *The Sinner's Guide to the Evangelical Right*.[11]

Bell, typically clad in all-black, Banana Republic–looking duds with Buddy Holly glasses and well-coifed hair (when he has hair), turned an abandoned mall into a megachurch and became a household name in Christian circles in the early 2000s on account of his strikingly contemporary, thoroughly relevant, "let's rethink everything" vision. In addition to authoring influential books like *Velvet Elvis* and *Sex God*, Bell produced an intriguing short film series entitled *Nooma*, embarked on a few unorthodox (and packed out) speaking tours, and gradually elicited the respect of nearly every wannabe hip pastor in the world.

Like most hipster pastors, he speaks in controversial language almost constantly—causing hubbub with statements such as "Christians can't speak about homosexuality unless they have at least one gay friend." He also speaks in a decidedly hipster, ironic parlance, constantly dropping pop culture and kitsch references with a wink and a nod, in a manner that *Time* magazine described as "Letterman crossed with NPR's Ira Glass."[12]

Where to Find Christian Hipsters

So, having outlined a little more clearly just who these Christian hipsters are, the question is now: Where do you find them? One easy answer is: anywhere that secular hipsters would congregate. Naturally, large numbers of Christian hipsters reside in places like Brooklyn and Wicker Park, in college towns, or in the artsy neighborhoods of any city. But some specific hot spots are uniquely concentrated pockets of Christian hipsters. The following is a rundown of some of the places and circumstances wherein you are likely to find the most vibrant communities of Christian hipsterdom.

Christian Colleges and Christian College Towns

Colleges and universities have always been hotbeds of hip, for obvious reasons. They are concentrated pockets of highly diverse perspectives, ideas, and cultures—places where people (largely young people) learn to ask questions of themselves, each other, and the world at large. Hip thrives in such environments because hip is all about the new, and institutions of higher education specialize in newness: new thinking, new talent, and new fashion.

It makes sense, then, that Christian colleges would play a similar incubator role in the world of Christian hip. Indeed, the Christian college has probably been the most important site of development for the hipster Christian culture over the past decade or so, particularly evangelical-minded Christian schools such as those within the Council of Christian Colleges and Universities (CCCU). Though there are dozens of Catholic universities and otherwise religious-affiliated institutions that doubtless have thriving pockets of Christian hipsters, by and large the CCCU schools have produced the lion's share. This list includes schools like George Fox University in Oregon, Greenville College in Illinois (home of Jars of Clay!), Messiah College in Pennsylvania, and about a hundred others.

A number of things happen at Christian colleges that make them hotbeds for the development of Christian hipster culture. For one thing, the schools are cloisters of young people who have frequently come out of very similar (and similarly harrowing) childhoods in the evangelical subculture. Students have a lot of things to make fun of and rebel against. These schools also provide some of the first opportunities for many Christian students to intellectualize their faith and maybe question their evangelical paradigms and assumptions. With no parents around, students feel free to discuss controversial ideas and toy with things like liberal politics and Calvinism, and to question the merits of capitalism. Many of them get involved in clubs that engage in social justice activism, whether for AIDS relief, environmental stewardship, or whatever cause there is passion for. Some of them become Democrats or even socialists; almost all of them develop more confident and inquisitive minds. They discover a freedom to transgress the formerly rigid boundaries and structures of establishment, modernist Christianity, against which Christian hipsters are in rebellion.

I've had experiences with Christian college hipsters at a number of schools, but none more so than Wheaton College in Illinois, where I attended from 2001 to 2005. At Wheaton, my experience with hipsters came mainly through friends who were art or English majors, or with people who went to the same concerts in Chicago as I did. It seemed to me that the hipsters at Wheaton during this time were largely of the granola/hacky sack/dreadlock variety. Especially when the Iraq war began, the plowshare hipsters really came out of the woodwork. But these same people could also quote Augustine or Bonhoeffer and engage thoughtfully in a conversation about just war. They may have been pot smokers who chained themselves to federal buildings downtown, but they were also very pious Christians who took Jesus seriously.

Calvin College in Grand Rapids, Michigan, is similar to Wheaton in many respects, though it is decidedly more hip. Calvin College is to Christian hipsterdom what Brooklyn is to hipsterdom at large. It's the leading edge, the place that received national media attention when George W. Bush spoke at commencement in 2005 and sparked widespread protests among students and faculty. But it goes beyond politics. Calvin is also the only Christian college to boast a yearly concert lineup that (in 2008–09, for example) has included artists like Broken Social Scene, Fleet Foxes, Mates of State, My Brightest Diamond, Anathallo, Rosie Thomas, Anberlin, The Hold Steady, Lupe Fiasco, and Over the Rhine. They even had Sigur Rós perform on campus, for goodness' sake! I saw Sufjan Stevens play a show at Calvin in 2006 (as part of the überhip Festival of Faith and

Music), and—combined with the fact that students smoke freely on campus—it was enough to convince me this was the apotheosis of Christian hip.

On the West Coast and particularly in California, a number of CCCU schools have high concentrations of Christian hipsters—schools like Azusa Pacific, Westmont College, Point Loma, and Biola, the latter of which is my current place of employment. The Christian hipsters at these schools have a decidedly SoCal aesthetic—surfer/skater/punk with more earrings, tattoos, and hair dye than their counterparts in the Midwest. More of them are making short films or playing in bands, spending more time practicing and experimenting with art rather than learning or debating theories about it.

The importance of Christian colleges in this whole Christian hipster movement goes beyond the confines of the campus, dorm, or classroom, however. The towns and cities near these colleges also play an important role. Chicago, for example, has emerged as a major site of ex-pat communities of Christian college hipsters—whether from Wheaton, Moody, North Park, Trinity, Olivet Nazarene, or any of about a dozen other CCCU colleges or seminaries nearby. I have loads of friends and acquaintances from Wheaton who now make their home in downtown Chicago, in hipster-friendly boroughs like Wicker Park and Logan Square. Some of them even live communally, with pooled funds, in more run-down areas of the city. They throw parties, smoke hookah and clove cigarettes, go to art galleries, and frequent trendy wine bars or neo speakeasies. Most of them are still very active in churches, and many of them work for Christian organizations. The situation is very similar in other cities—New York, Los Angeles, Seattle—where Christian colleges are near. If the colleges are where the hipster mentality is born, it is in the surrounding urban environments where it becomes a way of life.

We have not yet mentioned one aspect of the relationship between Christian colleges and the hipsters who attend them: the importance of class and education. Christian higher education is an influential shaper of Christian hipster culture, which means that Christian hipsterdom inevitably has a decidedly "white suburban educated" demographic hue. Not every Christian high school student can afford to go to a private Christian college—the ones who can give these schools a noticeably privileged student population. This is also the case with hipster culture at large—it tends toward middle- and upper-class white kids who have the money to go to college and learn the lingo of countercultural subversion, and who can afford to take material goods for granted and still buy all the fashionable bric-a-brac that the maintenance of a hipster lifestyle requires.

Study Abroad Programs or Third-World Missions

Another likely spot to find Christian hipsters is anywhere outside of their home country. Hipsters in general are aggressively wayfaring and mobile people, and Christian hipsters are perhaps the worst offenders. Chalk it up to Christianity's missions-mindedness, perhaps. These kids love taking advantage of study-abroad semesters, mission trips, or stints with NGOs or missions organizations in places like Jordan, Honduras, or Zambia. Most Christian colleges offer spring break or interterm trips or study semesters to pretty much any exotic site on the globe. Because Christian hipsters love nothing more than "getting outside of the bubble" and experiencing the danger, excitement, and unfamiliar wonders of new places, they jump at the chance to go overseas—whether for a week, a semester, or a multi-year missionary stint.

I'd be remiss to not note that, in my opinion, the most popular abroad destination for Christian hipsters is the United Kingdom. The UK is familiar and yet exotic, modern and yet ancient in all the ways that hipsters love. It has cathedrals of epic scope and beauty, and the iconic, ancient Christian tradition that American churches can only dream about. In particular, Christian hipsters adore the city of Oxford. The spires and ghosts of people like C. S. Lewis, J. R. R. Tolkien, and Dorothy Sayers remind Christian hipsters that a vibrant and jovial Christian intelligentsia is not historically impossible.

I have witnessed the Christian hipster love of all things Oxford on a few occasions, having attended the C. S. Lewis Foundation's Oxbridge conference (in Oxford and Cambridge) twice (in 2005 and 2008). Here, a diverse assortment of Christian thinkers, poets, artists, pastors, students, and not a few hipsters converge for two weeks of philosophizing, theologizing, drinking pints, smoking pipes, singing hymns in cathedrals, punting down ancient rivers, and conversing with likeminded dreamers and immortals in the shadows of thousand-year-old gothic towers. If there were a picture of heaven for the Christian hipster, this would be it.

Christian Hipster Fashion

So we know where Christian hipsters live, and what they like. But what about what they wear? Is there a particular Christian hipster fashion or aesthetic? The likely answer to that question is no, Christian hipsters mostly shop at the same hip clothing stores as any other hipster. They are into fashion and trend and adventurous looks.

This is not to say that a hip Christian fashion industry does not exist. One does, though it seems to have come entirely out of Southern California. That Christian-hipster-heavy region has produced a number of successful faith-inspired clothing lines, such as the San Diego–based Jedidiah, Irvine-based Ezekiel, and San Clemente–based Truth Soul Armor, all surfer/skater/action-sportswear in orientation, with very subtle if any Christian messages.

Vince Flumiani, founder of Jedidiah, has since moved from California to emerging Christian hipster metropolis Kansas City, where he opened The Standard Style Boutique along with fellow Christian entrepreneurs Matt and Emily Baldwin. The trio hopes that the boutique (www.standardstyle.com), which carries high-end hipster brands like True Religion, Rebel Yell, Marc Jacobs, and Diane Von Furstenberg, shows that Christian values can meld with fashion.[13] The Standard Style Boutique is an interesting example of Christian fashion because it carries nothing ostensibly Christian on its shelves and yet seeks to bridge the gap between an appreciation of secular high fashion and a pious life of Christian faith. It's not "Christian fashion" as much as it is "Christians who do fashion for a living."

Christianity is popping up in other surprising places in the fashion world these days. Buy anything at a Forever 21 store (H&M-esque chain of low-cost trendgear) and turn over the bag: what do you see? John 3:16. That's because the owners of the L.A.-based chain, Don and Jin Sook Chang, are devout evangelicals. Flip through the pages of fashion magazines and you might see ads that feature Christian hipster preachers wearing designer clothes—such as the Kenneth Cole ad campaign that Jay Bakker recently modeled for.

Christian hipster fashion has come a long way since the 1970s, when *Time* magazine described the "Christ couture" look of the Jesus People as "Mexican-peasant style" with white pants and tunics.[14] These days the look is more "skinny-jeans-and-stiletto" or "Jesus-is-my-homeboy skater punk." It has grown more urban and more ragged, and aside from a few crosses and a touch more modesty, it's not really any different than your average *Vice* magazine hipster.

Christian Hipsters' Ten Favorite American Cities

Finally, as an entirely unscientific but perhaps accurate summary of its geographic loci, here is my suggested list of the ten most important cities for Christian hipsterdom. These may not be the cities with the most or the highest concentrations of Christian hipsters; they are simply the most important—for a number of reasons.

1. **Chicago:** In addition to the aforementioned prevalence of Christian colleges in the city and suburbs, Chicago is just a super hip place to live. Hipsters of all kinds—Christians included—flock there. It's the home of *Pitchfork* magazine, for goodness' sake. Chicago also boasts a hip heritage: the Jesus People USA are located in Uptown; the iconic 1968 DNC riots took place in Grant Park; and Wilco is from there. It is also in the Midwest—a convenient urban enclave in the middle of the Bible Belt. For many Christian hipsters, Chicago is the best option for thousands of miles.
2. **New York:** As it is for any other hipster, New York is the dream destination for many Christian hipsters. Whether they go there to be actors, artists, designers, or factory workers, hipsters love living in New York. Many Christian hipster icons (such as Sufjan Stevens, Welcome Wagon, and Jay Bakker) currently reside there. New York is also the site of dozens of very hip, urbane, trendsetting churches like Redeemer Presbyterian, All Angels Episcopal, and Journey, as well as ministries such as the International Arts Movement.
3. **Washington, DC:** This city has a remarkably large number of young, just-out-of-college inhabitants who go there to make a difference in the world, interning in government and nonprofit jobs for little or no money. Christian hipsters—highly idealistic, activist-leaning people that they are—migrate to DC in large numbers. Hip churches are not hard to come by in DC either, including such congregations as Grace Presbyterian, Falls Church, Covenant Life Church (pastored by Joshua "I kissed

dating good-bye" Harris), and National Community Church, which features a totally hip coffeehouse, Ebenezers.

4. **Kansas City:** I might be biased because I'm from Kansas City, but having traveled all over I can honestly say that, against all odds, Kansas City is one of the most influential cities for Christian hip in America. It's the place where the 24/7 prayer movement originated, where bands like Waterdeep got their start playing at hip Christian coffeehouses like the New Earth. It's the home of hipster churches like Jacob's Well, Beggars Table, Vox Dei, Redeemer Fellowship, and The Gathering. And some of the most high-end and fashionable clothing stores in the city (The Standard Style Boutique, Habitat) are owned and operated by Christian hipsters.

5. **Atlanta:** This Southern mecca for evangelicals seems to be a city of choice for youth-oriented, hip Christian conferences, most prominently Catalyst—which is to Christian hipsters what Comic Con is to *Star Wars* nerds. Atlanta is also home to Louis Giglio, who started the Passion movement, founded sixsteprecords (the label of people such as David Crowder, Chris Tomlin, and Matt Redman), and recently started Passion City Church. But the biggest concentration of Christian hipsters in Atlanta is probably Andy Stanley's North Point Community Church, the multicampus megachurch which has as one of its pastors Carlos Whittaker—a self-described "experience architect" and "Web 2.0 junkie" who is something of a figurehead in the hip Christian Twitterverse.

6. **Los Angeles:** Southern California as a region is, and always has been, a hotbed of Christian hip. From Santa Barbara all the way down the coast to San Diego, the greater L.A. area (particularly beach cities, L.A. metro, and Orange County) is full of Christian hipsters. Countless Christian colleges, and industries such as film, music, and media, naturally attract Christian hipsters. L.A. is also home to oodles of hipster churches, including Mosaic, Rock Harbor, Bel Air Presbyterian, Sandals, Reality, and countless others.

7. **Seattle:** This überhip birthplace of Starbucks and grunge is also a bastion of Christian hip. The presence of Mark Driscoll's Mars Hill Church is a huge factor, but Seattle also has Seattle Pacific and Northwest Universities, *Image* journal, the headquarters of World Vision, Tooth and Nail Records, and a whole

lot of design and tech companies. Hip churches there include Church of the Apostles and Mosaic Community Church, which at one point met at a bar in Capitol Hill, Seattle's hipster gay neighborhood.

8. **Minneapolis–St. Paul:** The Twin Cities, like Chicago, are sufficiently Midwestern and yet urbane enough to attract Christian hipsters. The area is home to John Piper's church, Bethlehem Baptist, Doug Pagitt's Solomon's Porch, Greg Boyd's Woodland Hills Church, and several other hipster churches with names like Spirit Garage and Bluer. It's also a Christian college–heavy town, with Bethel University, North Central University, and Northwestern College all within the Twin Cities metro area.

9. **Denver–Boulder–Colorado Springs:** Let's just call this the greater Denver–Rocky Mountain region, which is teeming with Christian hipsters. Colorado Springs is sort of the epicenter for evangelical ridiculousness, which means a number of postfundamentalist, post–Focus on the Family hipsters run around there. Denver is home to Denver Seminary and Colorado Christian University, as well as hipster churches like Scum of the Earth Church and Pathways. Boulder—"Berkeley East"—is a whole other story.

10. **Orlando:** This seems like an unlikely spot for a high hipster population, and indeed it is. But Orlando is the home of *Relevant* magazine, which immediately puts it on the Christian hipster map. It is also home of the ridiculously unhip Holy Land Experience, and hip churches with names like H2O, Status, and Summit.

Honorable mention: Portland, Nashville, Philadelphia, Boston, Grand Rapids, San Diego, Dallas, Las Vegas, St. Louis, and Tulsa.

Having sketched more fully the phenomenon of Christian hipsters as a people group, it is now time to look more closely at how it all plays out in the church. What does this newfound hip Christianity look like in practice? How does it influence the conceptions and practices of Christianity today? What are the pastors, thinkers, leaders, and practitioners of Christianity doing to make the faith more cutting-edge, relevant, and appealing to the ever-widening hipster audience? These are the questions that will inform the next few chapters, which focus on hip Christianity in practice by examining such things as the "emerging" and "missional" conversations; the importance of social justice and politics; and new approaches to art, technology, and the environment. But first, in the next chapter, I want to lay the groundwork for what follows by giving an account of some specific churches in America that I have visited and observed in recent years. These are the leading churches in the hip Christian movement, representing the reality of what might otherwise seem too strange to be true.

part two

hipster christianity
in practice

six

christian hipster churches

*W*hat makes a church a "hipster church"? People have frequently asked me this question as I've embarked on my cross-country, transnational hipster church tour over the past few years. My usual response is, "It's a church that is disproportionately packed with hipsters," because this is often the most accurate distinguishing mark. But these churches are distinct in other ways as well.

Does the church have a one-word name that is either a Greek word, something evocative of nature, or something otherwise biblically obscure? Does the pastor frequently use words like *kingdom, authenticity, justice,* and *N. T. Wright* in sermons? Does the church advertise a gluten-free option for communion? Do at least two members of the worship band regularly sport V-neck T-shirts or skinny jeans? Has a Sufjan Stevens song ever been performed as worship? If you answered "yes" to all of those questions, chances are good that you're talking about a hipster church.

But that's a bit simplistic. Hipster churches come in all shapes and sizes and represent a diverse cross section of contemporary Christianity. As I've traveled around visiting these churches, talking to pastors and congregants, I have learned primarily that each church faces unique challenges. Each church has a unique context. They might be hipster churches, but they are also just *churches* like any other—

trying to preach God's Word and spread his gospel throughout their community.

The churches I have selected to profile in this chapter are by no means an exhaustive representation of hip Christianity, but a closer look at them will help launch us into a more detailed examination of hipster Christianity in practice—which is the larger task of the next four chapters.

The common feature of these churches, of course, is that they all attract large numbers of hipsters. Also, they all tend to be very media savvy, fashionably designed, and friendly to art and culture. They all emphasize social justice and serving—not just *saving*—the community outside their walls. But they are also all very different from one another, with different thoughts as to how best the church should position itself in relation to cool culture.

Thus, I offer the following seven communities as examples of Christian hipster churches. There are countless more than this, but the ones that follow exhibit some of the most notable and significant traits of the hipster church phenomenon—or at least provide an interesting sampling.

Mars Hill Church

Church Name: Mars Hill Church
Location: Seattle, Washington
Head Pastor: Mark Driscoll (officially "Preaching and Theology Pastor")
Summary: Mars Hill Church's popularity is largely due to head pastor Mark Driscoll's strong, controversial personality. Founded in 1996, Mars Hill now holds services at seven campuses across the Seattle area, ministering to many thousands of young attendees every week. I visited the church on a Sunday in November, attending both the original campus (where Driscoll preaches live) and a satellite campus in Lake City where Driscoll speaks via a televised feed.
Building: The main campus of Mars Hill is located in a massive warehouse-style building in Ballard. The huge, dimly-lit sanctuary has modern hanging light fixtures and an elaborate stage complete with a large backdrop of LCD panels. The Lake City campus is an actual renovated church—a smallish church complete with vaulted ceilings, stained glass, and pews.

Congregation: According to Lake City campus pastor James Harleman, the congregation of Mars Hill is 40 percent churched, 30 percent ex-churched, and 30 percent unchurched. And just from my cursory observations, I would venture that the congregation is 80 percent under the age of forty. They're young, and they're hip. I saw lots of tattoos, skinny jeans, V-necks, and Jesse James scarves in the crowd.

Music: There is no one "worship band," but rather a stable of stand-alone bands that alternate playing at the main Ballard campus, and "house bands" for the various satellite campuses. With names like Ex-Nihilo, Red Letter, and E-Pop, these bands tend to play indie rock versions of classic hymns like "Nothing but the Blood" and "Come, Thou Fount of Every Blessing" more often than the flavor-of-the-week contemporary worship songs. At the Lake City campus on the Sunday I visited, for example, a band called Sound and Vision performed math-rock arrangements of songs including "How Deep the Father's Love for Us" and "All Creatures of Our God and King," complete with Nintendo-sounding beeps.

Arts: A lot of artists and designers attend Mars Hill, and many of them "tithe their talents" to the church, designing logos and websites and printed materials for the church's branding. As a result, Mars Hill has a very cool, cutting-edge aesthetic that doesn't feel top-down (because it isn't; most of it is made by church volunteers). The church also expresses its love of art by hanging up local artists' work on the walls and by hosting film screenings (called "Cinemagogue") and film review blogs.

Technology: Mars Hill is a very technology-happy church. The sound and light systems in the buildings are high-tech, and the use of video is widespread and of professional quality. During the service I attended, texting was also incorporated—with the congregation encouraged to text in their sermon questions, which Pastor Mark might answer at the end. Mars Hill's website is predictably high-tech and stylish, and features its own social networking site, called "The City," meant to enhance and deepen the community life of the church. This is the type of church that is always on the cutting edge of technology and finds a way to incorporate all the latest doodads and media into the life of the church.

Neighborhood: The main campus of Mars Hill is located in Ballard, in Northwestern Seattle. This trendy area is full of artsy shops, restaurants, cafés, theaters, and yuppies. Mars Hill emphasizes missional dispersion, however, and has other locations across Seattle and Washington: Downtown Seattle, Bellevue, Lake City, Olympia, Shoreline, and West Seattle.

Preaching: Mark Driscoll heavily stands in the Calvinist/Reformed camp and likes to preach on things like sin, human depravity, Christ's atonement, justification, the cross, and how dumb religion and legalism are. He also likes to be controversial and doesn't shy away from taboo topics and language. On the Sunday I visited, Driscoll's message was on the Dance of Mahanaim in the Song of Solomon (an "ancient striptease," as he referred to it, and "one of the steamiest passages in the Bible"). During his sermon—part of "The Peasant Princess" series—Driscoll, looking like a metrosexual jock in an Ed Hardy-esque tight T-shirt, cross necklace, and faux hawk, talked about how wives should be "visually generous" with their husbands (e.g., they should keep the lights on when undressing and during sex).

Quote from pulpit: "God doesn't look down and see good people and bad people; he sees bad people and the Lord Jesus."

Quote from website: "The great reformer Martin Luther rightly said that, as sinners, we are prone to pursue a relationship with God in one of two ways. The first is religion/spirituality and the second is the gospel. The two are antithetical in every way."

Grace Church Hackney

Church Name: Grace Church Hackney
Location: London, England
Head Pastor: Andrew Jones
Summary: Grace Church Hackney began its worship services in the East London borough of Hackney in April 2004, under the umbrella of the Church of England and as a plant of St. Helen's Bishopsgate in central London as well as the Redeemer Church Planting Center. Though they are Anglican by denomination and their services are liturgical, the church is fairly casual and hip. The pastors don't wear traditional vestments ("strictly urban street wear up front! No suits, ties, no neat sweaters!"), the church holds seminars about environmentalism and "How I learned to stop worrying and love John Calvin," and on Tuesday nights a group called "tabletalk" meets at the nearby Owl & Pussycat pub where anyone can "join the conversation about Jesus and Christianity." The church has a very friendly atmosphere and seamlessly blends ancient traditions and liturgy with contemporary

concerns. I attended on Pentecost Sunday and was greeted warmly by numerous people who were happy to speak with me about my project, including vicar Andrew Jones himself.

Building: The church meets in St. Leonard's, a striking Palladian-style edifice dating back to 1740. The age and antique grandeur of the structure definitely give Grace some hipster style points. The building contains a 192-foot steeple, a giant four-columned Tuscan portico, an amazing blue ceiling with shabby chic peeling paint, and aging walls. The morning service is still occupied by the St. Leonard's congregation, while Grace meets in the evenings at 5:45 p.m.

Congregation: The congregation—like the Shoreditch neighborhood of Hackney—is largely young (twenties and thirties) and fashionable. There are some definite hipsters in the lot (a "very Shoreditch" crowd, as a young hipster named Polly assured me), but also a good number of young couples and parents with babies. The congregation of about 150 is also pretty ethnically diverse, certainly more so than your average hipster church.

Music: The music mixes ancient and modern styles, led by a music director who is a classical saxophonist and jazz pianist. No guitars or drums were included in the music on the Sunday I visited—just a group of about eight singers and two violinists. This little ensemble kicked the service off by walking up on either side of the building singing a Gregorian chant. The rest of the service they led the music from a little circle at the front of the building, leading us in a few seventeenth- and eighteenth-century hymns. During communion (and to my delight), the musicians performed *Solfeggio* by contemporary minimalist composer Arvo Pärt. Nothing like dissonant minimalist drone music during communion!

Arts: The church very strongly supports artists and the arts and encourages its congregation "to engage with the contemporary art scene, in order to give context to our presentation of the gospel to those around us." Arts activities include book and film clubs, screenings and discussions of films like *No Country for Old Men*, lectures, concerts, and trips to galleries.

Technology: Largely absent. The liturgy and song lyrics were in the printed bulletins, requiring no overhead projection whatsoever. Sermons are recorded and available on the church's website for download. That's about it for technology.

Neighborhood: Hackney—a London borough of about 200,000 people—has historically been one of the poorest neighborhoods of

London and typically a first stop for many of the city's waves of immigrants (from Turkey, Bangladesh, South Africa, and other countries). This diverse community, with both blue-collar and middle classes, has attracted artists and students and creative types who now populate the area, living in converted warehouses and gentrified lofts. Jones describes the local population as being "socially liberal, politically left wing, culturally sophisticated, interested in spirituality but not in the institutional church as they've experienced it." The borough of Hackney is also known as the center of hipster culture in London. The place swarms with hipsters, trendy cafés, bars, and restaurants. As I walked through the neighborhood before and after the church service, I was among perhaps the highest concentration of hipsters (outside of Williamsburg, Brooklyn) of any of my travels.

Preaching: Preaching is about twenty-five minutes long and expository and includes a post-service Q&A time for about fifteen minutes where people can discuss what was preached. Vicar Andrew Jones, with long gray hair, a goatee, and a joyful countenance (and sporting a T-shirt and jeans on the day I visited), dropped references to New York musician Doveman (in preparation for communion) and philosopher Nicholas Wolterstorff in the sermon I heard (about Romans 8 and the Holy Spirit).

Quote from pulpit: "You have the Holy Spirit. God Himself lives in your heart. You can't have any more of Him than you already have."

Quote from website: "Because this gospel is truth for all people, in all times, and in all places we believe it's not stuck in the past. It is always contemporary. We aim to present and enact this gospel in a way which resonates with the culture and concerns of present-day urban individuals, families and tribes."

Mosaic

Church Name: Mosaic
Location: Los Angeles, California
Head Pastor: Erwin McManus
Summary: The multisite Mosaic Church is one of the world's most prominent evangelical church bodies. Constantly churning out books, sponsoring conferences and seminars, McManus and company are lead figures in the various "movements du jour" (emerging, missional, etc.). Mosaic itself is a lively congregation with seven locations and

an average Sunday attendance of over three thousand. But what does the name Mosaic mean? When I spoke with executive pastor Eric Bryant, he defined *mosaic* as "a metaphor for describing the broken and fragmented lives that God brings together to form a beautiful picture," and the church's website beckons seekers "regardless of where they are in their spiritual journey" to come to Mosaic "and discover how all the pieces can fit together!" The church is committed to "re-branding" Christianity in fresh and innovative language to bring in the unchurched and burned-by-the-church folks who can't relate to old-school Christianity anymore. Mosaic's unique branding is evidenced by their "core values/metaphors/environments" which include Wind (commission), Water (community), Wood (connection), Fire (communion), and Earth (character). Though it may sound suspiciously New Agey or pantheistic, the theological core of Mosaic is actually solidly in line with the Southern Baptist denomination.

Building: Mosaic has campuses all over Southern California and even one in Berkeley, but the original location at The Mayan nightclub in downtown L.A. remains the most iconic. Originally built in 1927 as a theater for Gershwin-type musicals, The Mayan was remodeled in the early nineties and is now one of downtown L.A.'s most popular nightclubs. Its trademark pre-Columbian style features hand-carved walls, vibrant colors, and a richly decorous "old Los Angeles" vibe. Worshiping in a venue like this—sweaty, dark, with a faint smell of alcohol—can be jarring, but I think that's the point.

Congregation: The crowd of about eight hundred at the Mayan service is predictably young (the average age is about twenty-one). The typical assortment of hipsters, yuppies, surfers, and well-dressed Southern California young people populate the service, with all the stylish SoCal accoutrements you'd expect to see: trucker hats, big glasses, V-necks, Element shirts, beards, messenger bags, tank tops, and flip flops. In terms of ethnic diversity, it's above average (at least by evangelical Baptist standards).

Music: On the most recent Sunday I attended, the music at Mosaic consisted of a DJ who—appropriate to the nightclub setting—spun throbbing club music as the congregation filtered in, as well as a traditional five-piece band (all guys) who performed about four worship songs throughout the service. On all of my visits to Mosaic, I never recognized any of the songs played by the band, so I suspect they write their own music (as is trendy to do these days, if churches are able). In any case, the music style was pretty standard evangelical rock worship (i.e., U2 anthemic), with prodigious accompanying light effects and high-tech lyric projection.

Arts: The arts are huge at Mosaic. There is an arts ministry called Artisans that encompasses music, drama, dance, visual arts, poetry, spoken word, film, stage design, and live production, and each service incorporates one or more of these elements. At various points I've seen live painting, dancing, and dramas performed during a Mosaic service. As part of Artisan, Mosaic also sponsors an annual artists' retreat called Terra Nova, which is described on the website as "an explosion of art and creativity that will inspire your soul to create and dream the life that God has uniquely designed you to live."

Technology: Mosaic is a high-tech church. The service at The Mayan is slickly produced with all the latest in audiovisual technology, including three huge screens, rock concert lights, and smoke machines. The Mosaic website is remarkably stylish and well designed—a product, according to Eric Bryant, of the donated services of Mosaic's talented congregation of tech-savvy designers. The site contains podcasts, twitter updates, and pastor blogs. Interestingly, however, Mosaic does not employ the popular "video venue" method in its various satellite campuses, but opts instead for physically present preaching at each location.

Neighborhood: The Mayan campus is located in downtown Los Angeles, in a mostly abandoned part of town that makes it almost entirely a commuter church. Skid Row is a few blocks to the east, and Staples Center and the new L.A. Live development are a few blocks west, along with a smattering of trendy bars and loft areas. The church stresses connecting to the larger soul of L.A., playing up the ethnic diversity, culture making, and general idiosyncratic identity of the City of Angels.

Preaching: The preaching at Mosaic is dynamic and frequently incorporates interactive audience participation. Erwin McManus doesn't preach every Sunday, but when he does he is quite engaging. On the last Sunday I visited Mosaic, the sermon series was "Dear L.A." and the topic was "diversity," one of the four aspects of Los Angeles covered in the month-long series (the others being "creativity," "influence," and "uniqueness"). Marcus "Goodie" Goodlow, who pastors the West L.A. and South Bay gatherings, spoke at The Mayan on diversity day. Preaching out of Jonah 1, Goodlow's sermon argued that if Christians are to advance the conversation of racial diversity, we've got to redefine it as a verb, not an inert, immovable noun.

Quote from pulpit: "Courage is not the absence of fear. It's the absence of self."

Quote from website: "We cannot wait for change to happen—we must enact it. We cannot simply imagine a new world, we must also labor to see change happen 'on Earth as it is in Heaven.' We cannot simply attempt to enact change through our vote—we must enact it through our lives and talents, our generosity and sacrifices."

Life on the Vine

Church Name: Life on the Vine

Location: Long Grove, Illinois

Head Pastor: David Fitch (officially just the "founding pastor" rather than "head")

Summary: This unassuming little church in the Chicago suburb of Long Grove may not be as flashy as some of the other hipster churches (it's not really flashy at all), but it represents the type of congregation that more and more Christian hipsters resonate with. This church is deeply rooted in early church traditions and believes in the importance of community, liturgy, symbol, and sacrament—but not in a pretentious or overly stylized way. It's a church that is very mission-minded and committed to social justice. Part of the Christian and Missionary Alliance denomination, Life on the Vine was founded by David Fitch, who teaches theology classes at Northern Seminary and authored the book *The Great Giveaway*. I visited on a cold, snowy Sunday morning in January and had the pleasure of going out to lunch with several of the church leaders (including Fitch) after the service.

Building: The church occupies an old, nondescript Christian and Missionary Alliance building in a quiet, leafy suburban setting. It's a very small building with a sanctuary that can't hold more than a few hundred people. The chairs are set up in a round, so that worshipers are looking at each other during the service and no one is all that far from the preacher or Scripture readers—who read or pray from the four sides of the square space.

Congregation: The congregation at Life on the Vine is slightly more diverse than the average hipster church. A fair share of fashionable young people and suburban yuppies attend, as well as some older folks and a lot of families and children. While the church does have a children's catechesis-type class, it doesn't have a youth group. "Youth groups destroy children's lives," Fitch told me. The church strives to involve the congregation in service and equip the laity for leadership. There are no full-time pastors or staffers, and the alternating schedule of preachers includes a handful of seminary students from the nearby Trinity Evangelical Divinity School. It's a very user-driven church.

Music: Geoff Holsclaw leads the worship band, which is situated somewhat awkwardly (but totally deliberately) in the back corner of the building. This unassuming position is meant to remove any "performance" element—this fits with the church's larger focus on facilitating a more communal experience where individuals are not emphasized as much as the collective group.

Arts: The church walls and projector screens are full of visual art, described on the website "not as decoration but as windows into God's goodness or as mirrors confronting our sin. In a culture dominated by deformed images, we believe God uses these holy images to renew our imaginations." The church seems to be open to secular art and culture as well. In the sermon on the day I attended, the young preacher referenced Coldplay's "Death and All His Friends" and Sufjan Stevens's "John Wayne Gacy, Jr."

Technology: Minimal. There was a projector screen with song lyrics and some art images, but that was about it. It might as well have been the early nineties.

Neighborhood: Wealthy suburban. Long Grove is part of the middle- and upper-class stretch of Chicago's northwest suburbs. It's an odd setting for a progressive, hipster church like this—but the presence of Trinity in nearby Deerfield feeds a lot of Christian hipster traffic.

Preaching: This is where Life on the Vine is perhaps most unique. David Fitch is not a fan of expository preaching or three-point "life application" sermons that isolate a passage of Scripture from its larger context. Rather, he advocates a preaching that is grounded in the larger narrative of Scripture. Before the sermon at Life on the Vine, two passages from the Old Testament and two from the New Testament are read aloud, as context for the main sermon's text. The preaching at this church is more descriptive than prescriptive; less about handing out to-do lists than unfurling the reality of who God is and what the world means in light of the gospel of Christ. Rather than how-to or self-help instructions, sermons focus on honestly telling the story of Scripture and letting its reality speak for itself.

Quote from pulpit: "We cannot reach up to Heaven. Heaven reaches down to us."

Quote from website: "Sermons inspire, but Scripture is inspired. Preachers motivate, but the Spirit moves. We want to preach the Word with humility, being wary of the pitfalls of topical preaching, proof-texts, and legalistic application. We think the Bible can speak for itself."

Mars Hill Bible Church

Church Name: Mars Hill Bible Church
Location: Grandville, Michigan
Head Pastor: Rob Bell
Summary: Rob Bell's church is the lesser-known, yet equally hip, Mars Hill. Founded in 1999, the church now attracts upwards of ten thousand visitors on any given Sunday. I visited on Palm Sunday in April and immediately noticed the lack of signage indicating that this was indeed a church. As I drove around trying to find it, the thing that finally tipped me off was the large parking lot and parking attendants with neon batons. Only when I got to the door of the building did I see any indication that I had arrived at Mars Hill Bible Church. No signs on the road, no signs on the building. It felt like a secret, unassuming, slightly underground gathering, which I'm pretty sure is exactly what they were going for. It reminded me of the new speakeasy bar trend among hipsters: bars that have secret, unadvertised entrances in alleyways and unassuming wall facades. If you don't know where you're looking, you won't find it. Very hip.

Building: Interestingly, the church meets in an abandoned mall (Grand Village Mall). The main worship space, called "The Shed," is the former anchor store, and classrooms occupy the space of what used to be the food court or other stores. It all adds to the camouflaged, "no one would guess that a church meets here" vibe. The sanctuary hall is a vast square room with the stage in the middle and chairs surrounding in all directions. The lighting and color scheme is very plain, and there are very few adornments and no art or decoration to be found. It's all very Puritan.

Congregation: More diverse (age-wise) than I expected. At the 11:00 a.m. service I visited, the place was packed with a mix of J. Crew yuppies, North Face outdoorsy types, and a formidable smattering of Dan Deacon hipsters with Civil War beards. Overwhelmingly white. Lots of people had coffee in hand. Most everyone seemed really excited to be there, and the congregation was certainly lively, as evidenced by the occasional whooping and the impromptu standing ovation at the conclusion of the sermon.

Music: The music at Mars Hill, like most of the rest of the church, is refreshingly nondescript. The band—your typical seven-piece church rock band—plays David Crowder and Hillsong from the stage in the center of the room. Band members dress in appropriately gratuitous scarves. A few songs played at the beginning of the service, and that was that. Following the benediction, Explosions in the Sky played over the house speakers.

Arts: Not a lot of art. None on display from what I could see. But the fact that they play Explosions in the Sky probably means they aren't opposed to art.

Technology: Very minimal. A four-sided screen above the stage displays the lyrics to songs—white font on a black background. Other than that, there were no bells and whistles. The church's website, however, is very extensive and well designed.

Neighborhood: Grandville, Michigan, is a suburb of Grand Rapids, which is a hotbed of Christian hipsterdom, what with Calvin College and a bevy of Christian book publishers nearby.

Preaching: Rob Bell did not preach on the Sunday I attended, and apparently he's only contracted to preach for a certain number of Sundays a year. When he's not there, speakers like Brennan Manning, Phyllis Tickle, and John Ortberg are on stage delivering the message. On the Sunday I attended, Dr. Don Davis preached on Lamentations 5. The theology at Mars Hill is narrative-oriented and heavily influenced by people like N. T. Wright. Covenant language is used frequently (you can become a "Covenant Member" of the church if you adopt the church's shared set of values, called "The Directions"), with emphasis on social justice and "bringing heaven to earth."

Quote from pulpit: "He will establish a new heaven and a new earth where peace and justice will rule forever."

Quote from website: "What we believe about God is at the heart of what we believe also about each other, ourselves, and creation: that ultimately everything is part of the one great story."

Jacob's Well

Church Name: Jacob's Well
Location: Kansas City, Missouri

Head Pastor: Originally Tim Keel; he ended his role as senior pastor in 2009. The church is currently seeking a new senior pastor.

Summary: I have attended services at Jacob's Well on three occasions, which is more than most of the churches I've visited (simply because I'm in Kansas City a lot). Jacob's Well has been a fixture on the "emerging church" landscape since the early 2000s, largely because founding pastor Tim Keel was on the board of directors for Emergent Village. The church feels totally new and fresh but upholds tradition and history and all things vintage. It's a hipster church because it has a large, young hipster contingent in the audience, but also because it fits firmly within the hip tradition of usurping the establishment. As described by *Christian Century*, Jacob's Well is "a rebuke to those churches that, in imitation of cutting-edge 1970s evangelicalism, deliberately strip themselves of historical symbols, creeds and practices in an effort to grow. [Jacob's Well] is succeeding by moving in precisely the opposite direction."[1] For example, JW embraces things like read prayers, weekly communion (by intinction, and with the option of gluten-free bread!), and lectio divina. It's all very mystery-minded and aesthetically pleasing.

Building: A formidable old Presbyterian structure from the 1930s, the church has been renovated but retains many traditional and ancient elements like stained glass, pews, candles, and churchy vaulted ceilings. On one wall in the building you will see this quote from Stanley Hauerwas: "The work of Jesus was not a new set of ideals or principles for reforming or even revolutionizing society, but the establishment of a new community, a people that embodied forgiveness, sharing and self-sacrificing love in its rituals and discipline. In that sense, the visible church is not to be the bearer of Christ's message, but to be the message."

Congregation: Granted, I've only ever visited the evening (5:30 p.m.) service, which probably skews the count of the especially young, but the JW congregation is remarkably youthful. There are some older people scattered throughout, but for the most part the crowd seemed college or twentysomething. Lots of guys with beards, girls with tattoos, and skinny jeans everywhere. Mix of yuppie-type hipsters and more organic, indie types. Not particularly high on the friendly-to-strangers scale, but twentysomethings rarely are. We all did hold hands for the last song, however, which was a cheerfully sung benediction.

Music: Led by worship pastor Mike Crawford, the Jacob's Well band is youthful, loud, and worshipful. It seems less performance-oriented and more a facilitator of community singing, which is not to say that it isn't good. They play quality, largely original indie rock. Crawford writes many of the songs himself, such as "Words to Build a Life On," which features the lyric "Sing your freaking lungs out / Jesus Christ is King!" When they play the music of others, the JW band is more likely to do a Sufjan Stevens song during communion than any sort of "Jesus is my girlfriend" chorus. On one of the Sundays I visited, they played the Welcome Wagon version of the nineteenth-century hymn "Hail to the Lord's Anointed," mere weeks after the Welcome Wagon CD came out. Their style is a bit grungy, imperfect, and unpolished, in true hipster fashion. Slick, overproduced songs with crazy lighting and fog machines are nowhere to be found at Jacob's Well.

Arts: Arts are huge at Jacob's Well. They host frequent gallery shows displaying the art and photography of the congregation. Members of the congregation are encouraged to take one of the "community journals" to write doodles, art, prayers, thoughts, or poems as they sit through the service.

Technology: Like most hipster churches, technology is important at Jacob's Well, but not in an over-the-top way. They do encourage texting in questions or ideas, and the church has a large online presence (e.g., MySpace, Facebook, Twitter).

Neighborhood: The heavily hipster midtown Kansas City area, near Brookside and Westport, has artists, bohemians, and Democrats in abundance. Far from suburbia, which is important.

Preaching: One interesting thing about the preaching at Jacob's Well is that the speaker preaches on the floor, in conversational style, at eye level—not elevated on stage or behind a pulpit. The preacher invites comments and questions from the audience throughout the sermon, steering the sermon according to where the congregational conversation goes. On one of the Sundays I visited, the topic of the sermon was child sex abuse—a topic rarely discussed in church, which is a problem made all the worse because "we let dark places remain dark."

Quote from pulpit: "We at Jacob's Well are trying to move away from a belief-centered community to a practice-centered community."

Quote from website: "Jacob's Well doesn't have a mission; it is mission."

Resurrection Presbyterian

Church Name: Resurrection Presbyterian
Location: Brooklyn, New York

Head Pastor: Vito Aiuto

Summary: Resurrection Presbyterian is a noteworthy hipster church for a number of reasons. Launched in 2004 as a plant of the Redeemer planting network, Resurrection is situated smack-dab in the heart of worldwide hipster culture: Williamsburg, Brooklyn. Not only that, but the church is pastored by Vito Aiuto, a full-blooded Christian hipster who is a reverend but also an indie musician. He and his wife, Monique, make up the duo, The Welcome Wagon, and released their Sufjan Stevens–produced debut album on Asthmatic Kitty in late 2008. The church itself bears many of the typical marks of a vibrant hipster Christian community: liturgy, pews, communion out of a common cup (with real port), and a strongly infused mission-mindedness that includes local social justice work, HIV/AIDS ministry in Africa, and a leadership development/church-planting initiative known as the Brooklyn Church Project. I attended Resurrection on a steamy, stormy May evening in 2009.

Building: The congregation gathers at St. Paul's Lutheran Church in Williamsburg. St. Paul's meets in the morning, and Resurrection Presbyterian meets in the evenings. The beautiful old building—with stained glass, organ, and dark wood pews—is a creaky, humid structure that fits well with the liturgy, read prayers, and quirky renditions of ancient hymns that make up a typical Resurrection service.

Congregation: About one hundred people worshiped at Resurrection on the Sunday I attended (granted, it was Memorial Day weekend), and the crowd seemed to be mostly twentysomething singles and a few young families, with a smattering of older folks here and there. Naturally, there were a *lot* of hipsters in attendance, with tattoos, scruffy beards, and skinny jeans galore.

Music: The music reflects the style of The Welcome Wagon: pared down, acoustic, vintage, thoroughly hipster but totally reverent. On the day I attended, I saw only two musicians in the worship ensemble—a woman who sang and a man who alternated playing guitar, piano, and a number of other instruments. The worship songs were entirely old hymns, including "Immortal, Invisible, God Only Wise" and "Fairest Lord Jesus." They also played a number of purely instrumental songs—a tenor sax prelude, a jazzy ragtime-sounding piano solo during offertory and communion. The music was quiet and worshipful and fit the building well. It was about the farthest thing you could get from your typical megachurch rock band or praise team.

Arts: Many artists and aesthetically minded people attend the church, and the fact that the pastor is an acclaimed indie rock artist indicates that this is a congregation quite naturally and organically artsy.

Technology: Almost nill. There are no overhead projectors of any kind, and the music has no bells and whistles whatsoever. It's a slap in the face to technophile churches everywhere.

Neighborhood: Williamsburg: the epicenter of hip. Though increasingly gentrified, the neighborhood still has its rough edges, ethnic diversity, and pockets of poverty, which makes it even more appealing to hipsters. This area of Brooklyn—bordered by Greenpoint, Bedford-Stuyvesant, and Bushwick—is packed with trendy bars, concert venues, vegan restaurants, record stores, vintage clothiers, and used bookstores, especially along Bedford Avenue. The arts and indie music community in this area of New York is particularly strong, with new *Pitchfork*-heralded bands emerging seemingly weekly from the lofts and dingy flats of the Brooklyn scene.

Preaching: Vito Aiuto speaks most Sundays, though he was absent on the day I attended. The associate pastor, Chris Hildebrand, spoke on the topic of Christ's ascension (the last part of the "He Is Risen Indeed! Stories of Resurrection Life" series). Hildebrand's sermon, which incorporated quotes from N. T. Wright and references to Google Maps, focused on Christ's kingly authority and the implications of the ascension on our lives—that Jesus calls us to both humility and hope. In subsequent weeks, I also listened to sermons online that Vito preached on a farmer's market–inspired sermon series about the fruits of the Spirit: "Organic, Local and Beautiful: Bearing the Fruits of God's Spirit." It was a fascinating series of sermons because it seemed entirely appropriate and directed toward the hipster Christian audience, and yet thoroughly biblical as well.

Quote from pulpit: "We don't want to be the man. We want to be as far away from that as possible. We know what we don't want to be. But the question is: what *do* you want to give your life to? What *will* this church look like? We have a pretty good idea about what church we *don't* want to belong to, but what kind of church *are* we going to be?"

Quote from website: "A look at our liturgy—the pattern of our worship together—shows that worship begins with God's gracious movement towards us: God calls us to worship; he tells us of the forgiveness of our sins; he speaks his word of comfort, rebuke, and encouragement; he feeds us at Holy Communion."

seven

the emerging church

*B*ob Dylan, a folk troubadour and cultural provocateur, exudes an insistently chameleonic persona that defines the hipster tendency to ever and always be a thorn in the side of "the man." Like the hipster impulse he symbolizes, Bob Dylan brings to mind terms like *new*, *edgy*, *elusive*, *antiestablishment*, *out-of-the-box*, *ambiguous*, and *hard-to-define*. When you ask him a question, he asks you three more. If you try to label his sound or fit him into old paradigms, he ridicules and reinvents his sound just to spite you. But the music he makes is still beautiful in its own gratingly imprecise manner. And hordes of people—young people especially—totally dig it.

We might describe the "emerging church" in a similar way. Like Dylan, the emerging church (or "emergent" or "Emergent" . . . but we'll get to that) announces to the world, "the times, they are a-changin,'" and it proclaims with great gusto (and perhaps some condescension) that "something is happening here / But you don't know what it is / Do you, Mister Jones?"

For the emerging church, "Mister Jones" is the establishment church, old-school evangelicalism, fundamentalism . . . the old fogey who is slow, cumbersome, and not easily changed. And the emerging church has no patience with such an archaic irrelevance, deciding that it is best to just leave it in the dust.

In the 1967 documentary *Don't Look Back*, Dylan has a field day toying with and turning the tables on the stodgy, square reporters who ask him questions such as "Do you love people?" (to which Dylan responds, "It depends on how you define terms like *love* and *people*"). In the film's famous final encounter between Dylan and *Time* magazine's Judson Manning, Dylan exemplifies his hipster tendency to be an artful dodger by saying, "I know more about what you do—and you don't have to ask me how or why or anything—just by looking, than you'll ever know about me. Ever."

Now compare Dylan's elusive statement to this statement from Tony Jones, a leader in the emerging church movement: "The emergent church defies simple explanation and categorization. It is pluriform and multivocal. It is . . . like a conductorless choir singing medieval polyphonic chants."[1]

I mean, how hip is that?

What Do We Mean by *Emerging*, and Why Does It Matter?

The so-called emerging church has been an ongoing "conversation" (i.e., discussed, debated, and slapped on book and magazine covers) for more than a decade. It hit its peak sometime in the early- to mid-2000s, and is now arguably on the decline. You don't hear quite as much emerging talk these days as in recent years, and several of its early proponents like Andrew Jones, Dan Kimball, and Scot McKnight increasingly avoid using the term. Some early proponents, like Mark Driscoll, have disowned the movement altogether.

This fate was somewhat predictable. Because the emerging movement relies so much on labels (i.e., the need to call themselves something like "emerging"), and because hipsters run away from labels, it was bound to lose its categorical gusto and cool credibility before too long. "Movements," when they are so vigorously defined as such, never last very long.

Whatever the label, however, the emerging church idea will likely be around for a while in some incarnation. It undergirds much of what hipster Christianity is all about these days, and we must understand *emerging* if we want to understand the larger conversation.

Thus, even though these definitions are somewhat passé now, let me briefly note some of the distinctions in language that might be used in this chapter. I will mostly use the term *emerging*, which refers to the movement in the broadest sense and the ideas and characteristics that tend to define it. But I will also use *emergent*, which more or less means the same thing as *emerging*, though perhaps more often refers to "those specific adherents to emerging church ways of thinking about and practicing Christianity." Finally, you might see *Emergent* with a capital *E*. This refers to a specific organization known as Emergent Village, a cohort of like-minded emergent pastors and leaders through the United States and United Kingdom, led by people like Brian McLaren, Doug Pagitt, Tony Jones, and Mark Oestreicher.

This chapter is an important crash course in the emerging church movement, included here because I think it will help us start to understand hipster Christianity beyond the somewhat simplistic rubrics of some of the earlier chapters in this book. In this chapter and the following three, we will wrestle with some of the more theological, philosophical, and existential questions at play in this conversation. I hope the following offers a meaty summary of this significant shift in how we do church.

Toward an Understanding of *Emerging*: Seven Key Assertions

Though the emerging movement—now more than a dozen years old—has been largely defined by its uncanny ability to avoid concrete definition, I think it is possible to summarize its main thrusts in the following seven assertions. I am by no means an expert on this, but I've read dozens of the emerging church books over the years and from what I gather, these are some of emergent's most commonly articulated arguments:

1. Modernism Is Lame

In the first place, and above all, emerging is a response to modernism. It is postmodern (more or less). Emergents contend that modernity has set the church off track, which has, among other things, turned the Christian faith into little more than an "x + y = z" ticket to heaven. Christianity is bigger and more complex than the self-help, "this is how you can live your best life now," cosmic ATM that modern evangelicalism sometimes makes it out to be. It can't be understood in one prayer or in forty days of purpose, they say. Jesus simply cannot be domesticated.[2]

Dan Kimball expresses the emergent frustration with modernism in his book *The Emerging Church*: "The Enlightenment assumed that human thinking can solve everything. So when modernism then assumed we could figure out God and systematize our faith, we went astray."[3]

The emerging church disdains rigid, systematized ways of looking at things. It loathes most of the twentieth century's most significant "isms," including fundamentalism, foundationalism, ethnocentrism, totalitarianism, fascism, consumerism, and so on. In fact, the idea that life can be reduced to or understood through any "ism" is essentially what the emerging church (ironically, under the guidance of postmodernism) rebels against. Isms represent the hegemony, "the man." They represent unchecked power and dangerously reductive ideological influence. And for emergents, contemporary evangelical-*ism* is one of the worst offenders.

In *Stories of Emergence: Moving from Absolute to Authentic*, Spencer Burke, emergent leader and founder of THEOOZE.com, describes his discontent with contemporary Christianity in terms of three isms: "spiritual McCarthyism" (the fear, intimidation, and control that derive from too much power in the hands of too few pastors or CEOs), "spiritual isolationism" (the unnecessary walls placed between Christian and secular spheres), and "spiritual Darwinism" (the assumption that bigger is better).[4] These isms, like all other things that invite narrow-minded, boxed-in ways of viewing the world, are enemy number one for the emerging church.

Emergents suggest that modernism is too analytical, too trusting of science and rationality, too arrogant in the face of a world that seems to always end up being more mysterious and powerful than our intellects can comprehend. We are beyond that now, suggest emerging church leaders, and so are nearly all the young people whom we need to be reaching.

Thus, the base-level principle from which all emerging ideas have developed is this: modernism is flawed and should be (mostly) abandoned. However, this is not the same thing as saying that the emerging church is first and foremost a postmodern movement. It is antimodern first and postmodern second.

Still, there are many within emergent circles who wholeheartedly embrace postmodernity. They argue that we cannot know absolute truth or at least know it absolutely, that truth is largely defined locally and must be understood through specific sociocultural contexts.

If modernism is the whipping boy of the emerging movement, postmodernism tends to be the de facto, rubber-stamp-approved philosophy. Emergents typically have little criticism or suspicions of postmodernism, something D. A. Carson points out as a fault of the movement in his book-length critique, *Becoming Conversant with the Emerging Church*.[5] But again, the question of emphasis is important—the primary assertion of the emerging church is not that the church should be postmodern as much as that it should *not* be modern.

2. *Christianity Is Edgier and Less Safe Than People Think*

To understand the emerging church, we must remember that it all started when a bunch of youth pastors got together to figure out how best to reach eighteen- to twenty-five-year-olds at a 1997 gathering in Colorado Springs called "GenX 1.0." The emerging movement, thus, has from its start centered around this question: How do we get young, postmodern people to stay in or come back to church? How can the church stem the tide of mass exodus and mass disillusion among young people in the increasingly post-Christian era?

The consensus among early emergents was that a sea change was in order; the church needed a major image overhaul.

The church had grown stale, boring, safe, and mainstream. It had become too powerful, too greedy, too corrupt, and was in cahoots with the most unseemly elements of Washington and Wall Street. And as a result (seemingly), church became extremely distasteful to the younger generations. Like hipsters who are always rebelling against things that are safe, mainstream, and powerfully status quo, the emerging church leaders felt that the church needed to toss aside and move beyond the status quo in Christianity; to break out of the box and rebuild the whole structure. Something totally new had to emerge out of the problematic past.

Emerging church leaders felt strongly that Christianity—the things Jesus did and called Christians to do—is way more dangerous and edgy and countercultural than recent church history would suggest. As a result, the prevailing tone of most emerging rhetoric is decidedly provocative and prone to hyperbolic statements meant more to shock people out of their comfort zones than anything else. Every emergent leader has a cadre of one-liners that typically blast the establishment church in some strongly worded manner. For example, "Churches today are answering questions that no one is asking."

Every emerging church leader has said something similar to that at one point or another.

Emergents would say modernism was wrong to domesticate Jesus and systematize Christianity, because Jesus and Christianity were never meant to be anesthetized and easily digestible. On the contrary, as Mark Driscoll might say, Jesus is a rebel, and Christianity is punk rock.

3. The Church Gets in the Way of the Gospel

One of the hallmarks of the emerging church legacy—and indeed, something that seems to be more popular than ever these days—is the energy spent bashing Christianity, Christians, and the church. Only Jesus himself escapes the vehement denouncements of emergent rhetoric.

You might say that the most popular slogan among emergent types is some variation on "The church is getting in the way of the gospel," "Jesus wouldn't be caught dead as a Christian," or "The biggest enemy of the cause of Christ is Christians." Most emerging church figureheads have at some point written a chapter in a book, or an entire book, about this idea.

Tony Jones declared in *The New Christians* that "church is dead" and "a new church is emerging from the compost of Christendom."[6] Dan Kimball said it another way: "Emerging generations are actually very interested in Jesus, but many times Christians get in the way."[7] But Brian McLaren—the most controversial and polemical voice of the emerging movement—takes the cake for saying things like this with the most panache. Here's one example, from *A Generous Orthodoxy*: "Jesus might consider [Christianity] about as useful as many non-Christians consider it today."[8]

In recent years this sentiment has translated to a litany of books by Christian authors with titles like *Death by Church* by Mike Erre, *They Like Jesus But Not the Church* by Dan Kimball, *Jesus Wants to Save Christians* by Rob Bell, *unChristian* by David Kinnaman and Gabe Lyons, as well as movies like Dan Merchant's documentary, *Lord, Save Us from Your Followers*. This chorus of "we want Jesus but not the church" represents a trend in Christianity toward what one recent author called "decorpulation"—not the cutting off of the head (Jesus) but the cutting off of the body (the church).[9]

For emergents, the church today embarrasses them because it is irrelevant, out of touch, and busy answering questions that no one is really asking. It has a reputation for being hateful, bigoted, stodgy, legalistic, and lame. But above all, emergents argue, Christianity is getting the gospel wrong.

4. Dialogue and Conversation Are Better Than Argumentation and Apologetics

The emerging church emphasizes community and relationships. The church, emergents argue, should never have turned into such an individualistic pursuit wherein the most important thing is one's solitary decision to convert and follow Christ. On the contrary, the church is called into community and away from individualism. It should be about relationship and dialogue with one another rather than theologizing our ways into heaven by way of our own individual cognitive devices.

Donald Miller, a literary voice of the emerging movement, writes often about how we should privilege Christian relationship over solitary, modernist rationality:

> Maybe the gospel of Jesus, in other words, is all about our relationship with Jesus rather than about ideas. And perhaps our lists and formulas and bullet points are nice in the sense that they help us memorize different truths, but harmful in the sense that they blind us to the necessary relationship that must begin between ourselves and God for us to become His followers. . . . Biblically, you are hard-pressed to find theological ideas divorced from their relational context. . . . In fact, few places in Scripture speak to the Christian conversion experience through any method other than relationship metaphor.[10]

A key corollary to this elevation of relationship is the emergent love of all things "dialogue." As Tony Jones readily admits, emergents are "virtually obsessed with dialogue."[11] Importantly, this term does not refer to *debate* or *argumentation*, but rather a happily civil discussion wherein the objective is not necessarily to win someone over to an idea as it is to mutually come to a firmer grasp of an idea and to enjoy the company in the process. Emergents do not really like apologetics or otherwise modernist approaches to epistemology (the idea that someone could or should be argued their way to the truth), but they do love a good conversation. They resonate with Rob Bell when he says a Christian's duty is to master "the art of the long meal."[12]

The Emerging Church Bookshelf

Interested in learning more about the emerging church? Check out these books, which offer some of the best material out there on the subject:

The Shaping of Things to Come by Michael Frost and Alan Hirsch

The Emerging Church by Dan Kimball

Listening to the Beliefs of Emerging Churches: Five Perspectives, Robert Webber (ed.)

A New Kind of Christian by Brian McLaren

The Church in Emerging Culture, Leonard Sweet (ed.)

Velvet Elvis by Rob Bell

Becoming Conversant with the Emerging Church by D. A. Carson

Why We're Not Emergent (By Two Guys Who Should Be) by Kevin DeYoung and Ted Kluck

The New Christians: Dispatches from the Emergent Frontier by Tony Jones

Blue Like Jazz by Donald Miller

When emergents approach dialogue, they don't think in terms of winning and losing. They value the process above all, the community-based pursuit of a new understanding of God. Their broader view of theology reflects this: it is not fixed or static but rather localized and fluid. They love talking theologically, but their theology is malleable and context-specific. Everything they say invites debate and should be discussed, all for the benefit of learning together and sharing openly whatever convictions, uncertainties, or doubts one may have. They sometimes call this a "humble hermeneutic."

5. Story and Narrative Are Better Than Propositions and Systems

As part of its makeover of contemporary Christianity, the emerging church movement tends to argue that the "old way" of communicating the gospel (e.g., through propositional language and systematic theology) is inadequate for these times, and that a more story-based, narrative approach is the way to go. This follows closely from #4, and further shows how averse emergents are to all things enlightenment and modernist.

Emergents are highly suspicious of systematic theology. God did not reveal a systematic theology, they argue; he revealed a storied narrative. As Scot McKnight puts it, the emerging movement tends to believe that, rather than a systematic theology being the final word, theology is rather more like an ongoing conversation about "the Truth who is God in Christ through the Spirit, and about God's story of redemption at work in the church."[13]

As a result, emerging church pastors and teachers tend to favor story and narrative-based preaching over propositional or expository preaching. David Fitch wrote a chapter about this in his book *The Great Giveaway*. He suggested that the first task of preaching should be description, not exposition. Rather than "seeing Scripture as a collection of truth propositions that need to be scientifically dissected, inductively sliced, and distributed to Cartesian, rational selves sitting in the pews," the church should instead approach Scripture as the grand narrative of God in Jesus Christ. Rather than a three-point preaching full of to-do lists, a descriptive preaching should simply present us with the reality of the gospel and "unfold before the eyes of our hearts what is true of the world we are called to live in under the lordship of Christ."[14]

6. Binaries Are Too Simplistic

Emergents do not like binaries. The idea that something must be this *or* that, and cannot be both, troubles them. A great fault of modern Christianity, they argue, lies in its emphasis on certain binaries: in vs. out, sacred vs. secular, good vs. evil, and so on. Though in truth, binaries may sometimes exist, they are never as black-and-white as modernity makes them out to be. Thus, while many emergents acknowledge a distinction between Christian and non-Christian, they are very reticent to assume any sort of final judgment as to how or where we can draw such a distinction. Their emphasis is not on who is saved or unsaved, in or out, but rather on the transforming power of the gospel for *everyone*.

This quote from Rob Bell's *Velvet Elvis* captures the sentiment:

> If the gospel isn't good news for everybody, then it isn't good news for anybody. And this is because the most powerful things happen when the church surrenders its desire to convert people and convince them to join. It is when the church gives itself away in radical acts of service and compassion, expecting nothing in return, that the way of Jesus is most vividly put on display. To do this, the church must stop thinking of everybody primarily in categories of in or out, saved or not, believer or nonbeliever.[15]

It goes against the core emergent principles to view the world through simplistic lenses wherein *any* idea is broken down to only two competing sides, or where the church is positioned as an "in" versus the "out" of everybody else. Categories, labels, fixed boundaries, and all other reductive machinations of modernity are loathsome to most emergents. They prefer more inclusive, fluid, nuanced, less legalistic ways of doing things. As Kimball writes, "there's no one-size-fits-all way of doing things, because you can't box in the emerging church."[16]

This Dylan-esque idea is perhaps best represented in Brian McLaren's book *A Generous Orthodoxy*, which plays up cooperation and inclusivity rather than competition and exclusivity. McLaren aggressively denounces the notion that one perspective or theological point of view within Christianity has a corner on the market of truth, and he argues that true Christian orthodoxy is bigger and more all-encompassing than the way in which moderns conceived it. He argues for an appreciation of all denominations and traditions within Christianity, for example, rather than the typical "we're right and you're wrong" divisiveness within the church. McLaren hopes we can acknowledge that "Christians of each tradition bring their distinctive and wonderful gifts to the table, so we can all enjoy the feast of generous orthodoxy—and spread that same feast to the world."[17]

7. *What We Do Is More Important Than What We Think or Say*

One final assertion of the emerging church—and a very important one—is the idea that praxis (the living out, daily embodiment) of Christianity should be as or more important than the way that we think or even talk about it. How do we live out the gospel? What does the church look like in practice? These are important questions for emergents.

For the emerging church, the proclamation of the gospel must always be accompanied by the living of it. It's not enough to just *say*, "Christ is risen." We must live in such a way that demonstrates this life-altering fact. A major outgrowth of this idea is the missional movement, which will be covered in depth in the next chapter. But the idea also translates into how emerging churches do worship, which is typically much more conscious of form, aesthetics, space, and experience. Emergents are very mindful of how form and content must work together, and they strive to embody the truth of the gospel in how they live and worship as a community.

Emergents believe that it does not suffice to simply call something a church and be done with it. Rather, they believe that the meaning of *church* and *Christian* comes about in part from the way those words *look* and *act*. Though somewhat cliché now, a typical emerging church worship service often contains mood lighting, candles, incense, artwork on the walls, and other highly sensory throwbacks to ancient church tradition and mysticism. Emergents tend to look mostly to the past for guidance, adopting the forms, liturgies, and sacraments of the early church traditions that have largely been abandoned by contemporary evangelicals. Whether they meet at a house church, a bar, or an actual churchy church, emergents like to style their worship in very deliberate manners reminiscent of the early church—typically on the simple side, highly experiential and participatory, with Scripture readings, communion, sermon, and music. In this way, emergents are very conscious of form and how they communicate the faith beyond words.

Critique: Three Themes

Obviously, the emerging church has been controversial. Since day one, the movement has faced opposition—mostly from other Christians who claim that emergent ideas necessitate a presumptuous, reckless rush to change. Books like the aforementioned *Becoming Conversant with the Emerging Church* and the more recent *Why We're Not Emergent (By Two Guys Who Should Be)*, by Kevin DeYoung and Ted Kluck, have become go-to resources for the anti-emergent (largely Reformed) camps. The critiques from all sides have been many and multifarious and could fill the pages of a whole other book, but in this short space I will highlight what I think are three of the main themes that come up again and again.

1. Who Are We to Reinvent the Church?

One typical critique leveled at the emerging church is that their whole rhetoric assumes a sort of privileged insight into what the church should be—a kind of chronological snobbery wherein change and progress are elevated above tradition and orthodoxy. The most concise book-length critique that I have read from this perspective is *Prophetic Untimeliness* by Os Guinness, a book that chastises the contemporary church for its obsession with relevance, image, and up-to-dateness. In the book, Guinness articulates his criticism in this way:

> The air is abuzz with the future. The "coming church" and the "emerging church" are everything. The talk is all of new ways of "doing church" through reinventing, revising, innovating, borrowing, mixing, and experimenting. Everything now has to be "intentional" and "on-purpose." Ministers are no longer theological authorities but the "chief storytellers" and "facilitators of a joint spiritual journey." . . . But where in all this movement is the prayer to match the punditry? Is the church ours to reinvent, or is it God's?[18]

Many critics of the emerging church point to the dangers inherent in any sort of organized reinvention of Christianity that is not thoroughly bound up within a rigorously historical framework. Sure, the church should understand itself based in part on its given context, but it also must understand the greater historical narrative of God's working through his church in history. Before we pronounce ourselves as a generation that will reinvent the church, we must first humble ourselves to realize that we are but a blip on the radar of God's grand historical plan.

As Paul Grant writes in *Blessed Are the Uncool*,

> It is a good idea for Christians to continually take a new look at Jesus. It is furthermore important for each generation of young Christians to encounter Christ in the context of the changing world around them. But Christians have been doing that for two thousand years. Sometimes in our innovations we've cooked up very bad ideas. In the first century, the Corinthians twisted the concept of love to come up with a free-love theology. . . . And within living memory, American Christians have actively taught that racial segregation is God's desire for the church.[19]

That the emerging church takes itself so seriously as a real sea change in the history of Christianity comes across as groundless at best and arrogant at worst . . . even heretical by some critics' estimations. Who are these guys to throw out centuries of theology so that church can be reimagined in a postmodern context? What exactly are we emerging from and toward? Why now?

2. Rebellion for the Sake of Rebellion

Other critiques refer to the emerging church as a glamorization of rebellion—a movement of hip young pastors who desperately seek to rebel against the uncool establishment church because, well, because rebellion plays well with young people these days. Rebellion is much easier to sell than conservatism, and it's much easier to organize a new movement around a common enemy (such as old-school, modern evangelicalism) than to rally around a boring status quo.

Again, Grant puts it well in his book:

> Was Jesus really a rebel? Yes, but Jesus didn't rage against some abstract machine; he called people to an old way, the way revealed in the prophets. . . . Jesus rocked the boat, and defied the status quo, modeling courageous resistance of the prevailing winds. But in our contemporary culture, rebellion is considered a good in its own right—and a thrilling one at that. We're out to transgress. But we don't really have any agenda beyond rebellion itself.[20]

To many critics, the emerging church advocates change for change's sake. It looks like a group of overzealous young pastors who got carried away in their prognosis that the church needed major overhaul on account of some vague notion of postmodernism's revolutionary impact. It looks like a knee-jerk overcorrection for problems and trends (e.g., young people leaving the church) that might have been better met with a more measured response.

3. Takes Cues from Culture, not Scripture

A third major criticism of the emerging church focuses more on its scriptural merits and theological rigor (or lack thereof). This notion claims that the emerging church tends to take its cues too much from culture and context, and not enough from Scripture. Perhaps this plays out most significantly in the heated issue of homosexuality and the church. In the face of a culture that increasingly normalizes homosexuality, emerging churches frequently have a hard time speaking out against it. Critics say this shows that emerging churches are ultimately accountable first to culture and second to Scripture.

Os Guinness describes the historic shift of authority within evangelicalism from *sola scriptura* (by Scripture alone) to *sola cultura* (by culture alone):

Is the culture decisive and the audience sovereign for the Christian church? Not for one moment. God forbid. The client and the consumer may be king for free-market enterprise . . . but the church of Christ is not under the sway of market totalitarianism.[21]

Critics suggest that emergent leaders tend to start not with Scripture but with the situation—looking at the world and its various needs and fashioning the church around that. But the situation is ever changing and the culture fickle, critics respond. What good is it to focus so much energy on adapting to the culture rather than holding strong to a message—the gospel—that has resiliently transcended culture, time, and circumstance?

The Future

Because of the strong resistance and vocal criticisms that the emerging church has faced throughout its short life span, many people associated with the movement have gradually divested themselves of the term. For that reason, emerging as a movement is probably on the wane. But the ideas that drove it (as outlined in the seven themes above) will certainly carry on and continue to inform the theologies of hipster Christianity.

In the remnants and wake of the emerging church, new coalitions and organizations are forming, such as the Origins Project, founded in 2008 by the likes of Erwin McManus, Eric Bryant, Margaret Feinberg, Dan Kimball, and Scot McKnight. That group, like many other networks of formerly emergent types, is now more likely to use the term *missional* to articulate its unique new perspective on the church. But what in the world is *missional*? To that question we now turn.

eight

social justice, missional, and the new christian left

*L*ike most who grew up in evangelical youth groups in the eighties and nineties, I experienced my fair share of Christian outreach, service days, and mission trips. This included the typical projects like raking old people's yards and giving toys to needy kids at Christmas, as well as the occasional trip to the inner city to do something with a black church or serve food to homeless people. One summer my Southern Baptist youth group from Kansas City went on a one-week mission trip to the Uptown neighborhood of Chicago, which was an even bigger city with even more needy homeless people. Another summer my youth group went on a "mission trip" to Montreal, which ended up being mostly an excuse to visit Canada and try to talk to people about Jesus in French. In college I went on service trips to Appalachia and Paris (the former being more, ahem, "service oriented" than the latter) and visited with old people on a weekly basis at a nursing home. All of this stuff was wonderful, and I'm very grateful to have been raised in a Christian environment where service of this kind was constant.

As I've grown older and reflected on my evangelical upbringing, though, it has struck me that we tend to view "service" and "mission" as different categories. "Service" means helping poor people, giving things away, painting houses, cleaning yards. "Mission" means evangelism, passing out tracts, holding evangelistic crusades in poor villages in India. I remember how after an evangelistic mission trip, my youth group would get up in front of the church on a Sunday night and report about the souls we saved or the gospel seeds we planted. We never really emphasized how many houses we painted or how much trash we picked up off the streets. But even back then, it seemed to me that the mission of the church in the world necessarily encompasses both the soul saving and the "soup can and paint brush" service.

This more holistic vision of the gospel and the mission of the church is an idea that emergent thinkers tended to emphasize, and in the late nineties, some of them began talking about it in terms of the word *missional*. They felt strongly that the Christian church should broaden its view of "mission" to include both preaching the gospel and living it, thinking of Christianity not just in terms of creeds but also deeds. "Missional" is a call to action, a call for the church to get off its self-serving butt and get to work—because the hope of Christianity is not just for us, but for the world.

Missional has recently become a more popular buzzword than *emerging*: whereas *emerging* focused so much on criticizing the establishment church and declaring that something new was abreast, *missional* doesn't waste time dwelling on what's wrong with the church as much as *what the church can do now for the world*. The church is an action-oriented movement, with much work to do, and the younger generations of Christians—especially Christian hipsters—love this activist core.

As stated earlier in the book, activism has always been important in the history of hip. On one hand, the sort of countercultural activism that defines hipsters simply pushes against those in power—those oppressors who want to run the world their way and step on whoever they need to in the process. We see this in the angry anticapitalist, anticonsumerist crowd who read *Adbusters*, protest World Trade Organization summits, and deride capitalism in all its forms. But on the other hand, there is a side of activism that sincerely aims to help those in need—the oppressed, downtrodden, suffering have-nots of the world. Either way, activism fits perfectly into the hipster value system: of always being active and fighting some foe (whether it's "the man" or the scourge of world poverty).

Christian hipsters are no different. A defining characteristic of the new generation of cool young Christians is that they are aggressively on the side of activism, of social justice, of getting their hands dirty to serve others and help the world (though they sometimes speak more about it than actually do it). Maybe it's trendy, and maybe it's predictable. But this trend toward serving the world can really only be a good thing.

Rediscovering Christianity's Social Justice Fervor

Christianity is always and inescapably service-minded and justice-seeking. Christianity has from its very beginning emphasized serving others and helping those in need. In the book of Acts, Luke describes the early church as a community in which there was no needy person because the believers pooled their resources and provided for any need that arose. From the outset, the church appointed deacons to care for widows and the sick (Acts 6:1; James 5:14). And though things haven't always been pristine, the church has been serving the needs of others ever since.

Christianity has done more to make the world a better place than any other organized movement or guiding principle in history. Almost every major reform movement or social-justice campaign can be traced back to Christians, or at least Christian teachings. Christians, including Wesley and Wilberforce, led the way in the abolition of slavery and were the first to publicly deem it immoral and denounce it as sin. Christians have historically been the first and most active responders to international relief, hunger, and justice issues, and most major charities and humanitarian organizations (such as Red Cross, Salvation Army, Habitat for Humanity, Samaritan's Purse, Feed the Children, and World Vision) have decidedly Christian roots. Christians were the first to establish hospitals, schools, and universities (such as Oxford, Cambridge, Harvard, and Yale). They led the way in literacy movements, adult education, prison reform, substance-abuse programs, and many other progressive reforms.

And Christian young people who are just now discovering that Christianity has historically been more about helping others than winning PR battles have a long line of godly role models to whom they can look. Everyone from Francis of Assisi to Mother Teresa,

Dorothy Day to Dietrich Bonhoeffer, provides examples of how Christian compassion has been humbly lived out.

There are reasons why the concept suddenly seems new again and warrants a chapter in a book like this. Back in the 1920s, during the modernist-fundamentalist split, the "soul gospel" became divorced from the "social gospel," with the fundamentalists orienting themselves toward the former (soul winning, evangelism, preaching) while the more liberal, mainline denominations focused on the latter (social justice, activism, service). As a legacy of this split, contemporary evangelicalism has struggled to rejoin these two integral aspects of the gospel. "Serving the world" in the social justice sense has bad, liberal connotations among many conservative evangelical denominations, and vice versa for mainline denominations that are wary of counting conversions or ever using the term *soul winning*.

Naturally, the discovery that this is a false dichotomy and one that has only been a debate in the church for less than a century comes as refreshing and revelatory to many young Christians who seek to live out the activist faith of the early church and the Assisis of the world. Many of them are encouraged by the writings of people like Tony Campolo (*Red Letter Christians*), Jim Wallis (founder of *Sojourners* magazine), Ron Sider (*Rich Christians in an Age of Hunger*), Shane Claiborne (*The Irresistible Revolution*), and N. T. Wright (*Surprised by Hope*), the latter of which provides an eloquent theological framework for living a gospel that is "for the world."

As I was researching this book, I heard these sentiments expressed by many Christian hipsters. One reader of my blog, Olivia, who described herself as a grad student hipster who recently converted to Christianity, told me that what attracted her to Christianity had nothing to do with "the stylish accoutrements of particular Christians or particular churches and everything to do with the vision of the New Testament and the lifestyle of confession, repentance, and passionate, engaged community it calls people to." Christianity is cool, she told me, "because it is the opposite of apathy, because it demands sacrifice, because it forbids autonomy—all things that run against the grain of twenty-first-century American culture."

Young people like Olivia want to get behind a Christianity that is equally concerned with the present, material world as it is with whatever lies beyond. They are drawn to progressive, hopeful faith that is not about fear or prejudice or division or debate, but rather a "new creation" for which Christ came and is working through us to bring to pass.

A quote from Shane Claiborne's *Irresistible Revolution* sums it up well:

> There are those of us who, rather than simply reject pop evangelicalism, want to spread another kind of Christianity, a faith that has as much to say about this world as it does about the next. New prophets are rising up who try to change the future, not just predict it. There is a movement bubbling up that goes beyond cynicism and celebrates a new way of living, a generation that stops complaining about the church it sees and becomes the church it dreams of. And this little revolution is irresistible. It is a contagious revolution that dances, laughs, and loves.[1]

Missional: The Church Exists *for* the World

In recent years, as I've mentioned, *missional* has overtaken *emerging* as the defining buzzword of cool Christianity. And as we saw with *emerging* in chapter 7, *missional* means many different things to many different people. This ubiquitous word has been showing up in the vernacular of preachers, theologians, and seminary professors; gracing the covers of almost every major Christian publication; and spawning books, seminars, conferences, and endless blog debates. Everyone has an opinion. Most who discuss it agree that *missional* is some kind of important moment in contemporary church history. But beyond that, what does it mean?

Most definitions state that, at its core, *missional* is a mind-set that asserts the church is not primarily about us, but about God's mission in the world. Originating from the Latin phrase *missio dei* ("the sending of God"), *missional* conceives of the church as a primarily *movement*-oriented body that was not created for itself, but for the glorification of God through the spreading of his gospel to others. Our God is a God who sends. He sent Jesus to earth, and Jesus said in John 20:21 that "as the Father has sent Me, I also send you." As followers of Christ, we exist in this sending tradition. But what's new about that? Hasn't the church always been this way?

Proponents of the missional movement agree that the term isn't exactly new, but rather a return to the mission-mindedness of the early church, which has been gradually lost as churches have focused inwardly and "missions" has become a separate category altogether. *Missional* is about bringing the church and mission back together. Missions isn't just one of many programs or purposes of church. It is the core, overarching, motivating logic for all that we do. A church exists neither for itself nor its parishioners, but for the kingdom and mission of God.

At the core of the missional idea is a reaction against the big-budget, "we have Starbucks!" excesses of McMansion churches and the seeker-sensitive movement. The focus shifts from a "come in and be blessed!" view of church to a "go out and serve" perspective. Whereas seeker churches tend to have big budgets, large staffs, and an emphasis on growing "my church," missional-minded churches tend to have small budgets, few staff, and an emphasis on growing "*the* church." *Missional* means being less encumbered by big build-ings, large overhead, and too many programs that divert attention away from the core mission of the church. It defines church as not just buildings and denominations and institutions but as the body of Christ—his people—at work in the world. As Dan Kimball says, it's the difference between "I go to church" (consumer church) and "I am the church" (missional church).[2]

Missional asserts that the church is and always has been an apostolic action first and an institution second, serving its function by extending itself in motion between the kingdom and the world.

Is My Church Missional?

Missional churches are sometimes best understood in relation to "attractional" or "seeker-sensitive" churches. This comparison chart lays out the differences.

Missional	Attractional/Seeker
"Go out" mentality	"Come in" mentality
Typically smaller churches	Frequently large or mega-sized
Often in urban settings	Often in suburbs
Small budgets, few paid staff	Large budgets, many paid staff
Thinking holistically	Emphasis on disparate programs
Priesthood of all believers	Clear demarcation between pastors/laity
Emphasis on action/demonstration	Emphasis on words/proclamation
Everything is mission-oriented	"Missions" is one among many programs
Goal to grow "the" church	Goal to grow "my" church
Younger congregations	Older, baby-boomer congregations

The Holy Spirit's working through us as Christians—as the church—bridges the gap between the kingdom and the world. This is the mission of the church—*missional* at its most basic level: the present extension and embodiment of those "powers of the age to come" that Hebrews 6:5 speaks of. The kingdom is not a place for the pleasure of Christians alone: it is a force of transformation and renewal for the world.

People often read Jesus's words in John 18:36 as, "My kingdom is not of this world." But as N. T. Wright points out, what Jesus actually said is, "My kingdom is not *from* this world."

"That's *ek tou kosmoutoutou*. It's quite clear in the text that Jesus's kingdom doesn't start with this world. It isn't a worldly kingdom, but it is for this world. It's from somewhere else, but it's for this world."[3]

From this thinking we get "missional," a decidedly more social-action, serve-the-world Christianity than the previous seeker-sensitive or church-growth eras.

Younger Christians have tended to respond well to the missional idea (even if they don't use that word to describe it) for a number of reasons. For one, it represents a Christian faith that concerns itself with correcting global injustices and righting the wrongs of this life, rather than focusing wholly on soul conversions and the afterlife. Young people today simply do not relate to a religion that has little this-world significance, and they certainly do not understand why the soul gospel and social gospel have to be at odds. For them, the missional mind-set is a welcome reunification of both essential purposes of Christianity. Additionally, a more missional Christianity puts a more appealing foot forward, image-wise—something that is crucial in this whole "cool Christianity" discussion. As David Kinnaman and Gabe Lyons report in *unChristian*, the perception of young secular people is that Christianity these days is rather dour, hopeless, and irrelevant. Only 23 percent reported that they perceived Christianity as offering a "hope for the future."[4] Christianity is uncool, they say, because it just has so little tangible hope to offer the world.

But the missional approach offers tangible hope. Though still about preaching the gospel and saving people's souls, it is also about *living* the gospel and meeting people's needs—their material needs like health and shelter and food and money. The gospel should be good and transformative in this life as much as it is for us in the next, suggest the proponents of the missional church. And it should be something that the secular world welcomes and is thankful for rather than afraid of.

Of course, some worry that the missional movement might end up overcorrecting (as is so often the case with movements like this) and abandoning the soul gospel in favor of the social gospel. Writing in *Christianity Today*, missional advocate Scot McKnight invoked Walter Rauschenbusch—the architect of the social gospel in early-twentieth-century America—to warn of the potential unintended consequences of the missional push:

> Without trying to deny the spiritual gospel, [Rauschenbusch] led his followers into the social gospel. The results were devastating for mainline Christianity's ability to summon sinners to personal conversion. The results were also devastating for evangelical Christianity, which has itself struggled to maintain a proper balance.[5]

The Missional Bookshelf

Interested in learning more about the missional movement? Check out these books, which offer some of the best material out there on the subject:

The Open Secret: An Introduction to the Theology of Mission by Lesslie Newbigin

Missional Church: A Vision for the Sending of the Church in North America, Darrell Guder (ed.)

The Radical Reformission: Reaching Out without Selling Out by Mark Driscoll

The Great Giveaway: Reclaiming the Mission of the Church from Big Business, Parachurch Organizations, Psychotherapy, Consumer Capitalism, and Other Modern Maladies by David Fitch

Breaking the Missional Code by Ed Stetzer

The Forgotten Ways: Reactivating the Missional Church by Alan Hirsch

The Ministry of the Missional Church: A Community Led by the Spirit by Craig Van Gelder

Compelled by Love: The Most Excellent Way to Missional Living by Ed Stetzer and Philip Nation

Church Unique: How Missional Leaders Cast Vision, Capture Culture, and Create Movement by Will Mancini

ReJesus: A Wild Messiah for a Missional Church by Alan Hirsch and Michael Frost

Time will tell if the missional idea can maintain a proper balance between the soul and the social, or if it too will have devastating long-term effects for Christianity's evangelical efficacy. But in the meantime, the idea seems to be a helpful trend, influencing the next generation of Christians to care for creation and all of her struggling, needy occupants; to spread the love of Christ and the new-creation, kingdom message of the gospel through service, stewardship, and social concern.

Christian Environmentalism

Specifically, the idea of participating in the new creation holds that creation itself must be protected, restored, renewed, and respected. This important issue is big for Christian hipsters and most of the key figures within cool Christianity. Call it what you like: environmentalism, going green, or creation care. The point is, Christians are getting on board and are more and more involved in the push for a cleaner, sustainable environment.

Beginning in the early nineties, several Christian organizations formed to speak out about environmental issues from perspectives of faith. In 1994, the Evangelical Environmental Network released the "Evangelical Declaration on the Care of Creation," calling for Christians to recognize how they had degraded creation and proclaiming that biblical faith "is essential to the solution of our ecological problems."[6] Then, in February 2006, a coalition of eighty-six evangelical leaders spearheaded the Christians and Climate Initiative, producing a document that called on Christians "to come together with others of like mind to pray and to work to stop global warming."[7]

Even the large and influential Southern Baptist Convention has turned its attention to environmental concerns. In March 2008, a group of more than 250 prominent SBC members did an about-face on a resolution adopted the previous summer, which had urged Baptists to "proceed cautiously" in the global warming fight. In a new document, penned by twentysomething seminary student Jonathan Merritt, the leaders said, "Our cautious response to these issues in the face of mounting evidence may be seen by the world as uncaring, reckless and ill-informed. We can do better. . . . The time for timidity regarding God's creation is no more."[8]

Though creation care is by no means mainstream or widespread within evangelical Christianity (it's still such a hard "liberal" sell for many), more and more pastors, theologians, and everyday churchgoers are beginning to speak of "being eco-friendly" as if it wasn't a four-letter word. Conferences are springing up, such as "Flourish"—which began in 2009 as an opportunity for pastors and church leaders to come together and dialogue about "one of culture's most exciting conversations: creation care."

Many Christian colleges have vibrant environmentalism clubs and are adopting green standards for recycling, new construction, and facilities management. Some schools offer environmental studies majors or creation care study abroad programs in places like Belize or New Zealand. Scores of Christian magazines and books now present the message that "God is green."[9] And if you really want to, you can even purchase your own Green Bible, a linen-bound, "green-letter edition" featuring soy ink, recycled paper, and essays from the likes of Desmond Tutu, N. T. Wright, and Brian McLaren.

At the core of the new green impulse is the biblical notion of stewardship—that everything we have, including the earth, is entrusted to us by God and that we must be wise, responsible stewards of it. Using verses such as Genesis 1:28 and 2:15 as their justification, green advocates point out that nature belongs to God but was entrusted to man, and thus we are accountable to God for how we do or do not care for creation. This mind-set puts little stock in eschatological debate; whether Christ is coming back tomorrow or in a thousand years, the mandate to be wise stewards of creation is still a mandate.

Social Justice Is Cool (or, That One Time Bono Spoke at Wheaton College)

When I was a student at Wheaton College in the early '00s, a lot of famous people came and spoke in chapel. But nothing got the campus more excited—in a veritable uproar, actually—than the time Bono came to speak in December 2002. It was a ticketed event, and students were allocated one ticket each on a first-come-first-served basis (if I remember correctly). It ended up being such a hot ticket that some students scalped theirs and made a hefty profit. All to see Bono talk about AIDS in Africa and maybe play a song by himself on his guitar (which he did: "American Prayer").

Bono was joined onstage by Ashley Judd and Chris "Rush Hour" Tucker, which collectively was the strangest and most star-powered trio to have ever graced the stage of Edman Chapel (at least in the time I was at Wheaton). The significant event—part of a DATA "Heart of America" tour in which celebrities joined Bono to convince the Bible Belt to care more about Africa's struggle with AIDS, debt, and poverty—made quite the impression on Wheaton, which went on to develop one of the most active university chapters of the Student Global AIDS Campaign. The day after Bono spoke, the first meeting of the Wheaton College Student AIDS Action Network convened. Within three months, the group boasted the second-largest contingent at the national convention. Evangelicals, it seemed, had begun to wake up to the material (not just spiritual) plight of Africa.

In the six or seven years since then, more and more evangelicals have developed the same concerns, and not just with AIDS in Africa. The call of social justice now encompasses a wide range of issues and places—everything from genocide in Darfur to sex trafficking in Thailand to urban poverty within American borders—that are motivating younger generations of Christians to give the gospel some wheels and shovels. They are passionate about serving the world and participating in the righting of wrongs for the renewal of creation.

Involvement in action-oriented, social justice work is a hallmark of cool Christianity, to be sure. Whether building water wells in Africa (such as the Jars of Clay–founded Blood:Water Mission), raising awareness of northern Uganda's night commuters and child warriors (Invisible Children), or calling on lawyers to stop slavery and sex trafficking around the world (International Justice Mission), countless Christian organizations are doing significant rescue work, enlisting many hip young Christians along the way who want to do something significant for the world.

But for all the big Christian relief organizations out there (such as World Vision, Compassion International, and Habitat for Humanity), many other smaller organizations do important service to communities on more local levels. Some friends of mine in L.A., for example, run their own mini mission to Skid Row—the section of eastern downtown Los Angeles where some eight thousand homeless people live permanently. They get groups of ten or so young people together every Sunday morning before sunrise to trek down to Skid Row with backpacks full of clean socks and food to distribute to the people there. They call it "Sock the Homeless" and are completely unofficial—just a group of young Christians desiring to embody Christ's love to a world in need.

Living Christianly is still about evangelism and sending missionaries across cultures to preach the gospel, but for more and more younger Christians, this is just not enough. Christianity must be about serving the world, easing suffering, and making the world a better place for everyone. And if this means adopting politically liberal stances (including pro-environment, pro-regulation, pro-universal health care), then many younger Christians say, "so be it."

A New Christian Left?

So, what does this all add up to? Is Christianity moving into a politically liberal phase? Certainly the vast majority of Christians and especially evangelical Christians still identify more with conservative politics (largely because of social issues like abortion and gay marriage), but in terms of the types of Christians discussed in this book—the emergent, missional, hipster Christians—I don't think it would be too big of a stretch to postulate that a large percentage, if not a majority, of them would increasingly identify more with the Democratic party.

The 2008 presidential election showed a lot of signs that hinted in this direction. Across the board, Obama improved upon Kerry's 2004 share of the Christian electorate, making his greatest gains among the "frequent churchgoer" group, narrowing a 29-point Republican advantage (64 percent–35 percent) in 2004 to 12 points (55 percent–43 percent) in 2008. The more specific category, "evangelicals," voted overwhelmingly for McCain, but it was a lower share (75 percent) than for Bush in 2004 (79 percent). By all estimations, Obama went some way toward closing "the God gap" that has been noticeably untraversable by Democrats in recent elections (pre-2006, at least).

Part of the reason Obama made inroads among evangelicals is certainly the fact that he actively, earnestly (it seems) courted their vote. His campaign worked with political action committees like the Matthew 25 Network to reach out to Christian voters, visited more than ten Christian college campuses in swing states, attended forums at Saddleback Church and Messiah College, and elicited the stump support of people like Donald Miller, who could probably serve as our archetype of the Christian hipster Democrat.

Ten Signs a Christian College Senior Has Officially Become a Democrat

It's a common story at evangelical colleges and universities: Students come in as freshmen, ardently conservative Republicans, and leave as seniors, more liberal and perhaps even Democrats. This "senior switch" has probably occurred if the student does the following:

Purchases *Myth of a Christian Nation* by Greg Boyd and gives it to Republican parents as Christmas gift.

Suddenly removes all Facebook pictures from Bush 2004 rallies.

Reads new favorite authors like Jim Wallis, John Howard Yoder, and Ron Sider.

Lobbies to have Tony Campolo speak at graduation.

Makes plans to live communally in an urban area postgraduation.

Spends a semester living in Zambia or Honduras.

Encourages friends and family to only take showers every other day.

Wears a bandana and cutoff jeans while playing ultimate Frisbee on the quad.

Exclusively listens to NPR for news and refuses to watch Fox News anymore.

Quietly removes NOTW and pro-life bumper stickers from car windows.

Obama was wildly popular among young people in general (the 18–29 demographic went 66 percent–29 percent for Obama) and younger evangelicals supported him more than they'd ever gone for a Democrat before. Obama doubled his support among young white evangelicals (those ages 18 to 29) compared with John Kerry in 2004.[10]

More younger evangelicals voted Democrat in 2008 than ever before for a number of reasons. A lot of it has to do with the things we've already discussed in this chapter. But some measure of rebellion factors in too; these young Christians desperately want to break out of Christian Coalition–type boxes and disown the Moral Majority–Pat Robertson–Jerry Falwell heritage many of them grew up in. Their world is far more complicated, globalized, and postmodern for all that. And to many of them, thinking of the world or themselves solely in Democrat-Republican categories just doesn't make sense anymore.

In a postelection analysis, Jim Wallis's *Sojourners* magazine put it this way: "A new generation of young Christians cast a 'Post Religious Right Ballot' this election. . . . Young religious voters refuse to get caught up in the culture wars of the previous generation."[11]

Later, notable Christian Democrat Tony Campolo told *Relevant* magazine that the Obama election was a "mortal blow" to the Moral Majority in part because of an increasingly obvious disconnect between older evangelicals focused almost exclusively on abortion and gay marriage, and younger evangelicals who care about a broader range of issues, including the environment and poverty.[12]

Clearly, the political winds are changing when it comes to young evangelical Christians in America. The generational disconnect is significant, and the theological shifts along emergent and missional lines tend to fall strongly to the left side of the political spectrum. There may not be a "Christian Left" in the same iconic, powerful sense as the "Christian Right" has come to be known, but at least in terms of hipster Christianity as explored in this book, the dawn of a new political era for evangelicals may come sooner than you think.

nine

reframing christian "art"

On a recent late-summer evening, I found myself lounging against a white picket fence in the front yard of a quaint house in Long Beach, California. College-aged Christian hipsters filled the yard, most of them alumni or students from a nearby prominent evangelical university. I saw blankets spread out on the grass, beer cans and plates of hummus strewn about, and various incarnations of tobacco floating in the air (hookah, pipes, cigarettes, cloves, Dokha). But there were no drugs. These were *Christian* hipsters, gathered together for an evening of aesthetic give-and-take they affectionately called "Beatnik."

It was my first time at a Beatnik event, but it was the sixteenth such gathering for these particular SoCal hipsters. The event consisted of roughly two hours of free-form sharing time, where anyone could walk up to the throne-like chair and perform or share something they'd either created or found inspiring. People played songs, recited Bukowski poems, and read excerpts from *Walden*, and after each sharing time, everyone in the audience snapped their fingers. You know, fifties beatnik style. One kid wearing facepaint and a red bandana played a Bright Eyes-esque song about the horrors of stem cell research. Another simply talked about his beautiful encounter with atheist pot-smoking hippies while he worked on an organic farm in Canada. One girl passed around her homemade moccasins and solicited the group's collective wisdom as to how she might improve as an amateur cobbler.

The night was a celebration of creativity, expression, and performance, but also community. Art and innovation were the ties that bound these Christian hipsters together, the things they all agreed upon. For them, art—the sharing and appreciating of it—seemed to be a sort of spiritual catharsis. But there was nothing particularly *Christian* about the art they shared that night. They performed no evangelistic dramas or worship songs. Aside from a mention of Augustine and C. S. Lewis, few Christian thinkers or artists were invoked; they didn't need to be. The spiritual relevance of art and aesthetic activity was evident apart from any heavy-handed religiosity. For Christian hipsters, art—whether sacred or secular in origin—should be made, engaged, and experienced as a *good* on par with any other of the spiritual disciplines.

But how is this approach to art different than that of traditional (i.e., "uncool") Christianity?

Two words: Thomas Kinkade.

For Christian hipsters, Kinkade represents much of what is wrong with Christian art. Why? Because his paintings are just so saccharine and idyllic, they say. The cottages and waterfalls and lush flower lawns as rendered by the so-called painter of light do not advance any sort of truthful or artistically credible vision of the world. His paintings are just so happy and naive and fake. Much more truth can be found, they argue, in works like Picasso's *Guernica*, or Munch's *The Scream*, or even Duchamp's *Fountain*. Anything but Kinkade. He's the Christian hipster's worst nightmare. I could almost end this chapter right here.

What They *Are* Saying

Actually, it would be a shame to boil it all down to something that Christian art is *not*. While it's true that the hipster Christianity we've surveyed thus far has frequently been defined in terms of what it is rebelling against and striving *not* to be, here we can actually talk fairly concretely about the Christian hipster's vision for what art *should* be. They talk about it all the time—at festivals, symposia, workshops, retreats, conferences, lectures—so there ought to be something we can say about it here, right?

I should say right off the bat that I can't be especially objective on this topic. I've been immersed in the contemporary dialogue about art and faith for a while now, through experiences like serving as the arts and entertainment editor of the Wheaton *Record*, editor for the "progressive culture" online section for *Relevant*, and—most recently—film critic for *Christianity Today*. I've read the books, written the articles, attended the lectures, and led the seminars. But this chapter will not be just a manifesto for my own thoughts. Rather, I will attempt to summarize what I see as the key assertions about art that the "cool Christian" community would be prone to make. Hopefully with this summary we can better understand why Thomas Kinkade is so gauche to many Christian artists and hipster Christians, and why a new framing of "Christian art" is so integral to the purposes of cool Christianity.

In any case, here are some of the things that Christian hipsters are saying about art:

1. Art Is Messy and Morally Complicated

Christian hipsters love to hammer this home—that art is not easy, simplistic, formulaic, or black-and-white. It's messy and challenging, and not always easy to swallow. This is reason number one why they loathe Thomas Kinkade. His work represents the idea that art should be some sort of utopian comfort food meant to look pretty above the mantel and soothe our souls by making us forget the harsh realities of existence.

In his thoughtful analysis of Kinkade for *First Things*, Joe Carter described Kinkade's "Cottage by the Sea" in this way:

> What is so dispiriting about this painting is that rather than being created in order to be challenging or even inspiring, it's intended only to be comforting. It invites the viewer to enter a world of un-natural nature, a world where the "light" comes from within, and the warmth comes not from the receding sun but from inside the walls of the perfect Anglo shelter. The cottage is a self-contained safe place where the viewer can shut himself in and get away from the harsh realities of creation, particularly away from other people. The Cottage by the Sea offers a place where the viewer can enter the perfect world of Kinkade's creation—and escape the messy world of Kinkade's Creator.[1]

But rather than an escape from the messy world of our Creator, the art that Christian hipsters advocate opens us up to reality and uncovers truths about existence, which are alternately comforting, harrowing, beautiful, and frightening. Art is about truth, they say, and truth is often a messy proposition. Sometimes art is the best way to convey such a huge, unmanageable, and mysterious thing as truth.

Hipsters will likely invoke Jesus for these sorts of arguments about art. When Jesus spoke in parables, many people were taken aback and annoyed. His stories were so confounding! So cryptic and hard to understand! But perhaps that is how truth must be told. Perhaps truth is bigger than the mathematical concepts and scientific boxes we'd prefer to have it in. Perhaps truth is most easily comprehended through aesthetic articulation. So goes the argument of many Christian hipsters who long for a renewed Christian appreciation for the arts.

The recent history of Christian engagement with the arts embarrasses many young progressives. Since the Reformation, the Protestant church in particular has been dubious about art and its seductive, idolatrous potential. They partly feared its uncontrollable nature. Art had uncommon power to make people feel passionately, to open their minds to new possibilities. It had the power to wake people up and make them see things they'd otherwise not see. But those in positions of authority or with vested interests in a tightly controlled regime would just as soon keep people half asleep or unknowing. Among other things, art is a dangerous force of insubordination. (Many hipsters elevate this insubordination aspect of art to the utmost place, valuing art chiefly for what it does to undermine established norms and status quos. Some Christian hipsters think this way as well, but for the most part they are more concerned with art being truthful—whether or not that means it is subversive.)

Over the years, the Christian fear of art has frequently manifested itself in a regulatory form. We see this overt institutional censorship in the church-organized production code of early Hollywood films, as well as more localized boycotting of offensive or antireligious artistic content (think picketing outside theaters, banning books, and burning CDs en masse).

The popular Christian approach to art and entertainment in recent years has largely been marked by a concern with content. An abundance of websites, magazines, and newsletters advise parents about how many cuss words or sex scenes are in newly released movies. Christian watchdog groups aggressively attack films like *Million Dollar Baby* for containing dangerous themes like euthanasia; others, like *Facing the Giants* or *The Chronicles of Narnia*, are promoted as safe, family-friendly diversions.

The idea that art must be safe or family-friendly is exactly what Christian hipsters are trying to move away from. Certainly we must be cautious about the potential ill effects of an artwork's moral content, they say, but we must have a broader view and more discerning eye when it comes to how we evaluate the merits of art.

In his book *The Culturally Savvy Christian*, cultural critic and arts advocate Dick Staub makes the point that discernment should mean "evaluating the nuances of art, not just evaluating it based on a superficial checklist of unacceptable elements."[2]

Indeed, the point that many artistic Christians are trying to make is that art has so much more to offer us when we engage with it beyond our simplistic moral rubrics. Think about the Bible, they say. It's full of offensive content: sex, beheadings, prostitutes, torture, infidelity, you name it. The Bible is R-rated; it's dangerous. But that's only because *life* is that way, and every story has to have conflict and resolution, darkness *and* light.

A favorite quote of many Christian artists—almost a cliché now—comes from C. S. Lewis's *The Lion, the Witch, and the Wardrobe*, when the Beavers are describing Aslan to the Pevensie children. Lucy asks about whether Aslan is safe, to which Mr. Beaver responds: "Safe? . . . Course he isn't safe. But he's good."

Something doesn't have to be safe in order to be good. Christian hipsters are desperately trying to communicate this about art. It should not be constricted by a prudish commitment to "safe," but rather it should be allowed to do what it is meant to do: unveil reality and expose truth in all of its messy, mysterious glory.

2. Non-Christians Can Make Christian Art

Following from the logic of assertion number one, this assertion suggests that Christians should not only appreciate secular art but recognize that sometimes secular art can be just as sacred and truth filled as Christian art. Indeed, "Christian art"—if it should be a category at all—should be broadened to include any and all art that truly unveils the holy or embodies transcendence. It's perhaps the most rebellious, in-your-face, contested claim Christian hipsters make about art: sometimes the art that leads us most readily to God

Secular Albums Christian Hipsters Might Consider Worship

In addition to their insistence that aesthetic transcendence can be found outside traditional categories like "religious," "sacred," or "Christian," Christian hipsters believe that secular music can be just as spiritually enriching as any overtly Christian music might be. Here are ten albums Christian listeners most likely consider worshipful and sacred, regardless of whether or not that was not the artist's intended purpose.

Jeff Buckley, *Grace*

Coldplay, *A Rush of Blood to the Head*

U2, *The Joshua Tree*

Radiohead, *OK Computer*

The Arcade Fire, *Neon Bible*

Sigur Rós, *()*

Explosions in the Sky, *The Earth Is Not a Cold Dead Place*

Wilco, *Yankee Hotel Foxtrot*

Animal Collective, *Merriweather Post Pavilion*

Bob Dylan, *Slow Train Coming*

is crafted by the hands of someone who doesn't even believe God exists.

This is an important belief for many Christian hipsters who have been profoundly moved toward God in and through the books, music, paintings, and films of decidedly irreligious artists. Maybe they've felt transcendence at a Radiohead concert; maybe they've seen God in the harrowing darkness of a Darren Aronofsky film; maybe they've experienced the enveloping emptiness of a Rothko painting. Perhaps they've felt saved by films like *The Thin Red Line, Lost in Translation*, or *American Beauty*. I know I have.

It's the idea of common grace—that Christians are not the only arbiters of truth and beauty; that God's general revelation is visible to and can be accessed by all. Even the most secular, irreligious, or un-Christian artworks can communicate profound truths, even of a religious nature. And it's not necessarily a new idea.

The Protestant Christian theologian Paul Tillich spoke a lot about aesthetics and common grace, saying things like "God is present in secular existence as much as he is present in sacred existence," and describing secular paintings like Picasso's *Guernica* as "the best present-day Protestant religious picture." Needless to say, artistic-minded Christian hipsters love Tillich.

Tillich was adamant that God—or "the ultimate concern," as secular people might prefer—was too big to be revealed only on the canvases of religious artists. For example, upon seeing Jan Steen's painting *The Dancing Couple* at the National Gallery in Washington, DC, Tillich remarked, "The Steen painting is thoroughly secular, and has no relationship to religion in the narrower sense of the word. But it expresses the power of being and everything which expresses the power of being is indirectly religious."[3]

Of course all of this problematizes any sort of categorical talk of Christian art. If we agree with Tillich that art is sacred or religious whenever it "expresses the power of being," doesn't this open the door to a whole lot of confusion as to the line between sacred and secular art? Certainly. But more and more, Christian artists welcome this ambiguity. Do (or can) such things as Christian art or Christian artists exist? The question has become increasingly complicated and is ultimately not as important as the question, is the work we produce *good*?

The consensus seems to be this: we should be deeply Christian artists. But that doesn't mean we should be something called Christian artists or that whatever we produce should be called Christian art. We should simply focus on our craft, on making the best art we can. We should understand that people will and should resonate with our work not because it is Christian but because it is good. Above all, Christians should make good art, true art; art unafraid of exploring mystery, portraying evil, and looking for truth wherever it appears. Which is exactly what the best secular artists are doing.

3. We Should Let Art Work on Us, not the Other Way Around

In a lot of hip-leaning churches these days, art is everywhere—paintings up on walls, artsy film clips in the service, secular music blared over loudspeakers. I have seen art at almost all the hip churches I've visited. But one wonders: Is all of it for some utilitarian purpose? Is it just to get the hipsters to come? To appear art-friendly and thus more cool?

If so, it will not work. Hipsters can smell artistic utilitarianism a mile away. And to them, it's an abomination.

When it comes to the purpose of art, Christian hipsters are not all that concerned to find an answer. "Purpose," "result," and "usefulness," as we have already seen, are concepts antithetical to the logic of most hipsters. Art, many Christian hipsters maintain, should just *be* what it is: beautiful, expressive, embodied truth. We should never approach it with some ulterior motive, trying to leverage it for some didactic purpose or impose some artificial justification for its existence. This point separates many true Christian hipsters from the poseurs. It's easy to adopt an aesthetic posture to fit in or look cool. It's easy to make art serve our needs. It's harder to cede ourselves to art and let it work on us, oblivious to what we want or hope to get out of it.

Here again, the Christian hipster turns to C. S. Lewis, who argued in *An Experiment in Criticism* that art should be an end in itself, something we *receive* rather than *use*. "We are so busy doing things with the work," wrote Lewis, "that we give it too little chance to work on us."[4]

Hipsters today—including Christian hipsters—prefer to let art work on them and confront them with some embodied reality; art need not have a point or message beyond this. It is enough for an artwork to just *be*; and indeed, that should be its point. The medium is the message, if you will.

Thus more and more Christian hipsters argue for the art of the banal, the everyday as being expressive of the transcendent—of "the ultimate concern," to use Tillich's phrase. A photograph of a candy wrapper might be just as holy as a sculpted crucifix. A painting of pure color or abstract line might evoke truth just as much as Caravaggio's rendering of David and Goliath. Rather than an overly cognized, analytical approach to aesthetic evaluation ("I don't get what this painting is saying!"), many Christian artists now argue for the *direct experience* of art. It's about what art does to you in the moment; it's about the experience.

Some argue this along phenomenological lines: where it's not so much about *meaning* as about *being*. Art isn't just a secondhand representation of reality we leisurely appropriate at our convenience. No, art presents its own reality, its own *being*, which is as real, or more real, than the reality we walk around in every day. Art has the power to isolate objects so that we can truly see them and experience their being. We need not know anything else about an object apart from the experience of its reality. But that, Christian hipsters might argue, is enough for us to experience the holy.

They resonate with George Steiner when he says:

> *Only art lets-be.* Only in and through the painting does the pair of shoes achieve a total, autonomous being *per se*. . . . Far beyond any

168

pair of shoes we encounter in "real life," it is van Gogh's work that communicates to us the essential "shoeness," the "truth of being" of these two leather shapes—shapes at once infinitely familiar and, when we step back from facticity and "open ourselves to Being," infinitely new and uncanny.[5]

All this to say that, when it comes to art, the Christian hipster cares less about what a piece of art says than about what it *is*. They're less interested in how they can use an artwork (to spread a message, for example) than in how they can experience it. Bottom line: they hold art in a higher place than mere utility.

4. Art Should Never Be Didactic

Building on the notion that art should work on us rather than us using it for our purposes, Christian hipsters adamantly argue that art is not art if it chiefly means to teach us a lesson. This is not to say that art cannot tell a story or be representational, just that its worth need not be derived from one's ability to locate any take-home value.

Make art that is superfluous or without utility, they say. Make art that is opulent, expensive, and beautiful for its own sake. Baptist preachers might cringe at the thought of commissioning a top-tier artist to paint a massive abstract work with no overt evangelistic content on a wall of their sanctuary; but Christian hipsters would relish it.

At the 2007 Festival of Faith and Music at Calvin College, Lauren Winner (*Real Sex, Girl Meets God*) presented what I thought was a compelling case for superfluous art—art that exists for itself, for beauty. "God cares about senseless beauty," Winner said, citing the Exodus passages of building the opulent-for-its-own-sake tabernacle. While our culture promotes the logic of scarcity, Winner argued, we know that "God is a God of abundance." Winner's ultimate message was that, contrary to what most evangelicals would probably argue about art, "useless is high praise." Needless to say, this went over extremely well among the large crowds of Christian hipsters in attendance. When it comes to Christian art, useless is the new useful.

On this point, many Christian hipsters look to theologian Karl Barth, who in spite of being totally old school, had a progressive, nonutilitarian view of art. Barth was over the moon for the music of Mozart. It was pure, holy transcendence for him—and not because Mozart had anything to express or a point to necessarily make but because he was a master of the craft and a conduit of the beautiful, mysterious, elemental form we call music.

Mozart was "remarkably free from the mania for self-expression," wrote Barth. "He simply offered himself as the agent by which little bits of horn, metal, and catgut could serve as the voices of creation."[6]

Even without a Christian message, art like Mozart's can still be a harbinger of the holy, Barth would suggest. And this is a rallying cry for many Christian hipsters, who believe art isn't about the message as much as it is about being well-crafted and truthful.

At the 2008 Oxbridge conference put on by the C. S. Lewis Foundation in Oxford, I heard a lecture from Dana Gioia, the chairman of the National Endowment for the Arts. He spoke about evanescence as the core purpose of art. Like life, art is simply a momentary glimpse into reality and is always ephemeral. "Every work of art at some level has the skull in the garden," said Gioia. It speaks to us subtly about our own mortality while simultaneously helping us live fuller lives enriched by the aesthetic imagination. Whatever "use" the arts might have has less to do with a didactic message and more to do with what they lead us toward in our enjoyment and experience of them.

Some in the Oxford audience were perhaps surprised that Gioia—a Catholic—went so far as to say this: "Art provides the most immediate and useful way in which God's voice is heard in the world. Dante, Mozart, Michelangelo, Gaudi, have brought more souls to God than any minister. Because they speak to us in a way that is fundamentally human and memorable."[7]

For Christian hipsters, art validates its purpose when it connects with us on a human level—when it captures the beauty and mystery of our existence. It need not make any obvious point about anything; indeed, it should avoid this. Rather, it should just be beautiful, extravagant, and exceptional. This is when art is at its best. This is when it brings us closer to God.

5. We Are Created to Be Artists

Here is the crux of the matter—the practical point to which all of the theoretical assertions bow in deference: art only exists insofar as there are artists, and Christians need to get in on the act. Art must be made, not just appreciated. And if anyone has a motivation to create, it is Christians. We believe in the one Creator, after all, who created us in his image. We are creators, in cooperation with the God who took on human form and redeems all creation, making all things new.

170

Dorothy Sayers articulated this idea well in her book *The Mind of the Maker*, where she writes:

> Looking at man, [the author of Genesis] sees in him something essentially divine, but when we turn back to see what he says about the original upon which the "image" of God was modeled, we find only the single assertion, "God created." The characteristic common to God and man is apparently that: the desire and the ability to make things.[8]

So there it is: creation, the ability and the drive to create, is something we share with God. It's a crucial part of the image we inherit from the divine; it's part of what makes us human. We are sub-creators, as J. R. R. Tolkien would say, and to express the divine mark within us through our own creative activity is an act of worship.[9]

Because this creative capacity is in our DNA, we should be creators. We should make art, write poems, create culture—and not just consume it. The Christian artistic community emphasizes this point. Books like Andy Crouch's *Culture Making* have made big splashes by simply pointing out that we are called not only to be culture consumers or culture critics, but also culture makers. But we should not settle for mediocre cultural production. The church has far too often settled for kitsch and ephemera with little lasting value for the church or the world. No, we should commit to making high-quality cultural artifacts that "have a chance of furnishing the new Jerusalem," writes Crouch.[10]

This sort of future-minded, new-creation language is common in Christian hipster discussions about what kinds of art we should be making. If the kingdom of heaven is still to come on earth—and more and more young Christians think this way—then the earth's wonder and materiality and object-ness take on a new sacred importance. If the earth is destined for renewal and not just fiery extinction, perhaps the cultures and creations we derive from it are more important than we used to think.

Makoto Fujimura, a Christian visual artist who founded the New York City–based International Arts Movement, represents a lot of the things I've mentioned in this chapter. Fujimura spoke at the 2009 Calvin College Festival of Faith and Music on the topic "Creating and Transgressing in Love," in which he suggested "every act of creativity is directly, or indirectly, an intuitive response to offer back to God what has been given to us." Since God has gifted us with extravagant grace,

171

said Fujimura, we respond extravagantly back to him through art. Furthermore, faith is the answer to the questions art poses. Art reflects both God's abundance and our need for him. Artists should "engage the culture that is and create the world that ought to be."[11] Art exists in the "now and not yet" place between the hopeless despair of death and impermanence (the "Friday") and the hope-filled renewal of the resurrection (the "Sunday"). Art is our guide through the long day's journey of Saturday, to borrow an idea from George Steiner.[12]

Christian hipsters are convinced that people of faith should be artists not to convert people or have "alternatives" to secular art, but because our deepest beliefs and convictions—that we exist between a risen Savior and a renewed world—beckon us to make art and create culture reflective of a broken world that will one day be healed. It is our heritage as people created in God's image, and we worship God when we fulfill this purpose.

What This Looks Like in Movies

The two most obvious areas of aesthetics in which the Christian hipster perspective can be seen today are movies and music. As someone who has edited and written both film and music reviews for nearly eight years, I have seen the development of the Christian hipster aesthetic sensibilities firsthand.

When it comes to movies, the Christian hipster approach is largely defined by what it is *not* concerned with: "morally objectionable" content. Rejecting the "curse counter" philosophy of aesthetic evaluation as represented in websites like *Plugged In* or *Movieguide*, Christian hipsters believe that a film's worth—even for a Christian—goes way beyond how much sex, violence, nudity, and language it contains. This isn't to say they don't consider these elements at all; just that they will praise a scandalous film—like *Requiem for a Dream* or *Breaking the Waves*—even if it has a decidedly unsettling grittiness to it.

As a critic for *Christianity Today* over the past few years, I've seen how this sort of progressive, thoughtful, Christian engagement with cinema can happen. Over the years, our diverse cohort of critics has included Protestant, Catholic, and Orthodox voices such as Jeffrey Overstreet, Steven D. Greydanus, and Frederica Mathewes-Green. Unlike some Christian film sites, *CT Movies* offers longer, more in-depth reviews that look at films holistically. We cover R-rated films just as often as G-rated films, and we assess a film on more criteria than just how family-friendly it is.

But we are just one of a number of intellectually nuanced Christian film outlets. Others include *Hollywood Jesus, Paste, Relevant, Patrol*, and a multitude of blogs and critics' collective websites that constantly come and go. The beauty of the Internet is that Christians who like thinking deeply about film can find like-minded critics pretty easily. I know I have been encouraged to find so many talented, thoughtful writers about film lurking around obscure corners of the Web.

When it comes to Christian hipster thoughts on movies, the perspectives and tastes are diverse. But perhaps it will be helpful to list some of their typical favorite movies, to get a better sense of what they generally like: *The Mission, Ordet, The Passion of Joan of Arc* (or anything by Dreyer), *Diary of a Country Priest* (or anything by Bresson), *Babette's Feast, Blue, Decalogue, Tokyo Story* (or anything by Ozu), *Chariots of Fire, Breaking the Waves, The Son* (or anything by the Dardenne brothers), *The New World, Silent Night, Night of the Hunter, Andrei Rublev* (or anything by Tarkofsky), *Magnolia, Wings of Desire* (or anything by Wenders), *Becket, Crimes and Misdemeanors, Into Great Silence*, and pretty much all the films Paul Schrader mentions in *The Transcendental Style in Film*.

What This Looks Like in Music

In the summer of 2005, in Oxford, England, I heard pastor Rick Warren make a statement that represents the opposite of what many Christian hipsters would argue about music.

"There is no such thing as 'Christian' music," said Warren. "There are only Christian lyrics."[13]

The statement, though a popular one for Warren (it appears verbatim in *The Purpose Driven Life*), offends many Christian artists who insist that in any art—especially music—truth and meaning (the content) are inseparable from the forms (melodies, brushstrokes, etc.) themselves. The music of composers like Handel, Bach, Vivaldi, and Vaughan Williams, often without lyrics, was nothing if not Christian. Christian hipsters wonder: Can't the music itself be a channel of transcendent truth? Warren's message reinforces a sinking suspicion that evangelicals have largely abandoned form for the sake of content. In a nutshell, Christians have forgotten the implications of the incarnation: truth comes in a package, and that package is just as important as the message it carries.

Christian hipsters have worked hard to strike down the notion of "Christian music" as representing only that which carries overt Christian content. They've aggressively made the case that *any* music—whether made by a Baptist or a Buddhist—can be sacred and truthful and beautiful, if it reflects excellent musical craft and/or honest, creation-revealing lyrics. Magazines like *Relevant* have strict policies about covering a higher percentage of secular music than Christian music. *Paste* magazine—though founded and run by Christians—avoids talking in language of "Christian" or "secular," but focuses only on what's good. A whole genre of Christian-written books discuss Bob Dylan, U2, and other secular musicians who nevertheless seem "Christian" in more ways than one.

Perhaps the poster boy for the Christian hipster approach to music is Sufjan Stevens, who makes music that is first and foremost *good*—pushing the boundaries of musical ingenuity through his unique brand of low-fi ensemble folk—and yet also deeply rooted in his soul. Sufjan's music is Christian to the core, albeit much more subtly Christian than your average contemporary Christian artist—something John Totten observes in an article on theotherjournal.com:

> While "CCM" artists only know how to speak about Jesus in their songs, Sufjan is good at addressing the Jesus in other people or other situations. . . . While contemporary Christian musicians try to inject

Essential Christian Hipster Albums

Can you tell a Christian hipster by their iTunes music library? Maybe. There are definitely some albums that every true Christian hipster is likely to own. Check this list and see if you fit the bill:

Sufjan Stevens, *Seven Swans*
Damien Jurado, *Rehearsals for Departure*
Pedro the Lion, *It's Hard to Find a Friend*
Danielson, *Ships*
Starflyer 59, *Fashion Focus*
Waterdeep, *Everyone's Beautiful*
Denison Witmer, *Philadelphia Songs*
Over the Rhine, *Ohio*
Innocence Mission, *Befriended*
Sunny Day Real Estate, *LP2*

as much of Jesus into mainstream culture as they can, religious hipster musicians spend time pointing out that he already was and is. Sufjan may not be talented at rocking our socks off but he can find the Gospel in the pettiest of stories and situations. He can point it out in the most mundane of characters or in the most evil of serial killers.[14]

This idea—that God is already present in the world through general revelation, and that anyone with a keen eye and a sharp pen can discover and artistically articulate truth—is the core of the Christian hipster perspective on art. Though vague and even problematic, the idea rings true to experience, and that is exactly the point.

Hipsters give special privilege to experience. As we've seen in the last few chapters, in their approaches to politics, religion, art, and culture, hipsters tend to accept that which fits their own experiential paradigm or standards of authenticity and reject that which is artificial, imposed, contrived, or manipulative. Because so much in their upbringing turned out to be phony, they are intensely skeptical of most anything that masquerades under labels like "objective," "definite" and "capital-T Truth." To be hip is to champion the evasive and ambiguous, the ill-defined and subjective; to be hip means favoring process and relationship and questions over purpose and utility and answers.

These universal characteristics of hipsterdom have hopefully been manifested in this chapter, and indeed, in all the chapters thus far in this book. Everything up till now has, to some extent, been an attempt to summarize the details of hip, hipsters, and Christian hip. My intention was to render a fairly comprehensive portrait of what hip means, who Christian hipsters are, and what they think about everything from theology to missions to—in the case of this chapter—art.

Though our discussion has largely been expository and descriptive up to this point, the rest of the book is a bit more evaluative. Now that we have a solid grasp of this phenomenon of Christian cool, we can begin to think more critically and biblically about it. What does it all mean in light of our faith? How does cool correspond to our calling as Christians? What are the problems and paradoxes the question of cool Christianity presents us with? How do hip's requisite commitments to things like subjectivity, individualism, and ambiguity correspond to the commitments of the Christian life?

Let's get to the task of answering some of these questions.

part three

problems and solutions

ten

wannabe hip churches

*O*f all my church visits during the research for this book, the churches that frustrated me the most—the ones that, to be honest, I had a hard time sitting through—were those that I call "wannabe hip churches." These churches had million-dollar stage lighting and bands that played David Cook songs as worship. They had skate parks and bowling alleys inside their "Xtreme!" youth group buildings. They preached endlessly about how judgmental and hypocritical Christians usually are. These churches were the worst at disguising their desperate hope to be hip. They clearly endeavored to be palatable to the cool kids. But mostly they just looked sad and desperate, uncomfortable in their skin and too hip for their own good.

Up until now, this study of hipster Christianity has focused on the beliefs, convictions, and alignments of the Christian hipster movement—their emergent and missional beliefs, their political and artistic convictions, and so on. The picture I've painted, however, has been one of relatively organic Christian hip: a trend that has bubbled up in recent years, mostly without the aid of any top-down institutional guidance.

To be sure, those at the top—even the stodgiest of institutional stalwarts—do recognize that they have to make some efforts to be cool and relevant so that young people won't run for the secular hills. But hip in its truest form can never sustain itself as a top-down phenomenon. And it rarely works when it is a means to an end (i.e., a secret weapon to keep the kids from fleeing).

Thus, this chapter (and much of the remainder of this book) is something of an admonishment against those who would push for an aggressive strategy of Christian hip in their ecclesiological efforts. It's a cautionary reflection on the presiding impulse these days for churches to be culturally savvy (up on all trends and technologies and entertainment), stylish (designed and packaged to fit the "young, edgy, hip" mold), and shocking ("not your mother's church!"). We see more and more evangelical churches focusing on these things in efforts to stop the hemorrhaging of young people (especially twentysomethings).

But I question whether or not these top-down hip initiatives have truly hit their intended mark; and even if they do in the short term, I wonder if in the long term they are damaging the church's legitimacy.

We can discuss that question later. For now, let's take a closer look at the distinguishing marks of wannabe hip congregations.

Leveraging Pop Culture

To be anticulture, prudish, or behind the times is anathema in the mind of any pastor who wants to have a "cooler" church. On the contrary, they want to project an image of cultural awareness, open-mindedness, and a general up-and-up on the ever-fluid zeitgeist of the day. For them, the church should not shy away from leveraging the culture to reach people for Christ. Their position is that the church has lagged behind the cultural curve for far too long, and it's high time Christians take a more proactive approach to being culturally savvy.

This takes many forms. For some pastors, it means they incorporate references to Paris Hilton and *The Hills* in their sermons. For others, it means they play Coldplay or Sigur Rós music before or after the service, or use clips from *Lord of the Rings* or *Lost* to hammer home a point. It means that worship bands can (gasp!) play secular songs on occasion and secular-ish bands can play special concerts at the church. In some cases it has meant fashioning an entire Eucharist liturgy around U2 songs, as in the Episcopal Church's U2charist innovation.[1]

Whatever it takes.

A lot of these pastors are motivated by the desire to "meet the culture where it's at." Tim Stevens, pastor of Granger Community Church (GCCwired.com), emphasizes this in his book *Pop Goes the Church*.

Reasons Why Eighteen- to Twenty-Two-Year-Olds Drop Out of Church

According to a study from Lifeway Research, 70 percent of young adults ages twenty-three to thirty stopped attending church regularly for at least a year between ages eighteen and twenty-two. What were their reasons? Curiously, "The church wasn't cool enough" did not make the list.

"I simply wanted a break from church" (27 percent).

"Church members seemed judgmental or hypocritical" (26 percent).

"I moved to college and stopped attending church" (25 percent).

"Work responsibilities prevented me from attending" (23 percent).

"I moved too far away from the church to continue attending" (22 percent).

"I didn't feel connected to the people in my church" (20 percent).

"I disagreed with the church's stance on political or social issues" (18 percent).

"I was only going to church to please others" (17 percent).

[Jesus] wore the clothes, used the language, and illustrated his stories with the signs and symbols of the day to communicate the Gospel of an upside-down kingdom here on earth. He didn't wear God-clothes, speak God-words, and expect the culture to connect. He didn't spend years learning big words so he could impress but not communicate. He didn't look for music that was unfamiliar to the culture and expect people to learn to like it.[2]

This sort of thinking is pervasive among the wannabe hip church crowd. They are committed to bending over backward to meet the culture where it's at, even if it means sponsoring church film clubs that show gritty movies like *Fight Club* and *Sweeney Todd*, playing music with an f-word or two, or making reference to TV shows like *Mad Men* and *Entourage*. (None of this is so terrible in and of itself, but we probably all agree it's just a little strange when coming in a steady stream from the pulpit.)

At the church I attended in Los Angeles, Bel Air Presbyterian, pop culture was inescapable (in part because pop culture icons like Britney Spears, Jessica Simpson, and John Tesh—yes, *that* John Tesh—occasionally attended). The drama and video ministry at the church cleverly infused current pop culture references into skits and parodies of such things as *The Twilight Zone, The Office, The O.C., Fear Factor,* and VH1's *Behind the Music.* A ministry called "The Beacon" sponsored screenings of films such as *Lars and the Real Girl* and *The Secret Life of Bees.* Kanye West's "Jesus Walks" video was once played during a morning service. Pop culture was in the DNA of the church, but for Bel Air Presbyterian, this was organic. The church sits atop the Hollywood Hills in the center of the entertainment industry. Actors, writers, singers, and entertainment industry professionals make up a large percentage of the congregation. For other churches, pop culture doesn't come as easily as it does for a church like Bel Air. But other churches often see it as no less important.

Bil Cornelius, pastor of Bay Area Fellowship in Corpus Christi, Texas (bayareafellowship.com), argues that to ignore pop culture is to ignore an important opportunity for outreach. We must not be afraid of harnessing secular culture—even controversial aspects of it—to gain the interest and affinity of the audience that can relate to it. Says Cornelius:

> Either we can quote dead preachers like Spurgeon (who is awesome, but only preachers even know who he was) or we can quote Oprah, Dr. Phil, Bono, and Kanye West. I'm not comparing their wisdom to Spurgeon, but they are listened to, and we can harness their insights, even when they are wrong, which is often the case.[3]

Things can get a little out of hand when pastors no longer care about the rightness or wrongness of something in pop culture, only that it can be used as an attention-getter or gateway to a theologically apropos discussion. Hipsters don't really appreciate these far-reaching attempts. They like Kanye West, but why force him to say "Christian" things in church? They love *The Office,* but I doubt they go to church with hopes of seeing a clip from that show. Pastors who think they'll win over the cool kids by forming the church in the cool kids' pop-culture image are liable to find themselves even less relevant than when they started.

Looking Cool

For the church or Christian trying hard to be cool, image is of the utmost importance. This very self-conscious endeavor requires wearing the trendy clothes, sporting the right haircut, and having the coolest design.

The wannabe hip pastors can be spotted a mile away. They are firmly entrenched in their midthirties or forties, and yet wear clothes from Hot Topic, Hollister, Element, or Ed Hardy. They have the requisite ever-changing arrangement of scruffy facial hair, and they frequently sport earrings or (if they are really committed) tattoos. They wear tight-fitting clothes, a lot of black, and often don thick-rimmed glasses. The ones who are not bald spend a lot of time on their hair, frequently sculpting it into a spiky variation on the faux-hawk. The more daring wannabe hip pastors might even wear jewelry or wallet chains. All of them care very much about shoes.

But image goes beyond dress. It also involves the way people carry themselves, and for wannabe hip pastors, it's all about being laid-back and chill. They do everything necessary to avoid appearing out-of-touch, legalistic, or obsessed with structure and control. They aim to not take themselves so seriously, and yet take Christ very seriously. Their image is about being real and (the favored buzzword) "authentic." It's also about presenting an image of cultural savvy that is aware of the current pop culture zeitgeist and whatever YouTube video was the viral sensation that week. Key characteristics of their image include relevance, compassion, empathy, adaptability, and approachability.

Wannabe hip pastors strive to embody this image not just in their own lives, but also throughout the whole church—in its design, branding, font choices, and so on. The websites, bulletins, videos, and all other visual communications of these churches have in recent years become critically important. Having an awesome, trendy design is priority number one. As Phil Cooke writes in *Branding Faith*, "We live in a design-driven generation, and if the Church is going to make an impact, design is the language we must learn."[4]

But I'm not sure that pastors' learning the ins and outs of design and fashion will help them be hip. On the contrary, the successfully hip churches are those that solicit the talents of their stylish, artistic young congregations for their design-related services. As I've visited hip churches such as Mosaic in L.A. and Mars Hill in Seattle—churches with impressive and cohesively cool design aesthetics—and spoken with the pastors there, I have consistently heard some variation of, "We don't pay top dollar to outsource our design to professionals; we let the designers who attend our church offer their services as a tithe. So however stylish or cool our design or brand is, it's only because those are the types of people who are in our congregation." These pastors live in the worlds of design and fashion.

> ## *James Harleman, Pastor, Mars Hill Church*
> ## *(Lake City Campus)*
>
> We don't want to mimic what the cool kids are doing. We want the cool kids to be a part of the congregation. We want to let them serve with us. . . . Instead of trying to be cool, we should seek out and support the places in culture that we believe are hitting the nail on the head. We need to retrain our minds in how we engage culture. Why do we listen to the music that we do? Why do we like the films that we like? Rather than force ourselves to like what is cool, we should seek to understand better why we like what we like. Be authentic to what you like. You can't become a prizefighter if you've never trained your whole life.

Being on the Technological Forefront

Though it would seem like hipsters would like high-tech gadgetry and flashy technological doodads, they resolutely do not, at least when it comes to church. This is perhaps the biggest mistake wannabe hip churches make: bending over backward to be on the technological forefront and believing that this is where the hip young people want to be.

Many churches are now pouring gobs of money into the kind of high-tech hoo-ha more befitting of a U2 concert than a Sunday service. But Christian hipsters decidedly tend toward the opposite direction. They may be severely over-connected in their everyday lives (iPods, TVs, cell phones, computers, etc.), but for things sacred such as church and worship and community, they are seeking something simpler than fog machines and strobe lights. They've also become more critical and questioning of the impact of technology on their humanity and relationships.

Authors such as Quentin Schultze and Shane Hipps have recently written books exploring the impact of technology on church. In *The Hidden Power of Electronic Culture: How Media Shapes Faith, the Gospel, and Church*, Hipps emphasizes that "within the *forms* of media and technology, regardless of their *content*, are extremely powerful forces that cause changes in our faith, theology, culture, and ultimately the church."[5] Ken Myers pointed this out in his classic 1989 book, *All God's Children and Blue Suede Shoes*, writing, "A generation after Marshall McLuhan, the Church still behaves as if the forms of culture, especially the forms of mass media and the role they play in our lives, are value-neutral."[6] More and more Christians feel uneasy about the unintended consequences of technologies on religion—realizing that not all that is divine can be digitized.

Some people also express an increased skepticism about why we even need some of the new technologies the church is using. Does displaying the words to a hymn on a centralized jumbo screen make the process of singing corporately that much easier or more convenient than reaching down to the pew and flipping to the correct page in the book? Sure, there are some benefits involved with trading hymnbooks for PowerPoint (for one, it's cheaper), but do they outweigh the costs (for example, the loss of a collected canon of sacred church music)? We are very quick to justify the change because of the pros, with scarcely little pause to consider the cons. Because its newness appeals to us, and because we live in a fast-paced, ever-changing world, we embrace the new technology with open arms, even when the old technology (hymnbooks) seemed to work fine for hundreds of years. We show words up on the screen because we can, not because the former alternatives were ineffective.[7]

This same logic leads many wannabe hip congregations to adopt such things as in-service texting or online campuses. I've visited numerous churches that now encourage their congregations to text in questions to the pastor during the service from their mobile phones or PDAs. But is this ability—for congregations to be able to anonymously put forth a query as it comes to them during the service—really an improvement on anything? Does it offer anything groundbreaking or gamechanging to the church? Or is this just a case of "well, we all have phones and we all like texting, so how can we make this a cool churchy thing?"

The same goes for online church campuses. I've visited a few churches that proudly advertise the availability of an "online campus," where on Sunday (or any day or time of the week) interested churchgoers from anywhere in the world can simply "attend" church on their personal computer. At Central Christian Church in Las Vegas, for example, the bulletin and website advertise four campuses and services: Henderson, Summerlin, Southwest, and Online. At Liquid Church in New Jersey, the options are New Brunswick, Morristown, and Internet Campus. At Liquid Church's so-called iCampus, "churchgoers" are encouraged to join "online life groups" where, via technologies like Skype and TokBox, groups of four to nine people from around the world can meet online for a small group Bible study.

Now I am not saying that these sorts of things have no merit or do not contribute to the spiritual enrichment of Christians. Certainly the church should be engaging with the creative use of technology. To abandon technology altogether would be just as foolish as leveraging it in an extreme or reckless way. Technology itself doesn't make anything cooler, and increasingly the younger generations are looking for a tech-free space wherein they can quiet themselves and focus on the transcendent truths of the gospel, apart from the media and digital overload of the rest of their lives.

They wonder whether, when we express Christianity so thoroughly through the avenues of pop culture, we lose an element of sacredness in the message. Phil Cooke speaks to this issue in *Branding Faith*. "It's difficult to portray the transcendent through the same medium that broadcasts the World Wrestling Federation or *American Idol*," writes Cooke, who questions the push to make the gospel so available on multimedia channels. "In our well-intentioned efforts to reach the largest audience possible, we've forgotten that the Christian faith isn't always easy, and this generation is starting to recognize the disconnect."[8]

Wannabe hip pastors would do well to realize this crucial point: technology and all its accompanying methods of making things easier and more efficient (e.g., "go to church on your laptop at home!") are often contrary to the true nature of cool. Cool is difficult, elite, for the few and the brave. Narrow is the path.

Amping Up the Shock Value

Wannabe hip churches love to use this popular tactic. What better way to appeal to younger generations of Christians than to push the envelope and go where no fundamentalist has gone before? What better way to prove the hip credibility of Christianity than to do the sorts of things that would make church ladies cringe and Baptists blush? Amping up the shock value will surely attract rebellious, subversive-friendly young folks, right?

This is the assumption. And it motivates a lot of churches to take some pretty drastic measures to brand themselves as daring, dangerous, and cool. Some churches hold their services in bars and nightclubs—Mosaic in L.A. meets in The Mayan nightclub, and North Brooklyn Vineyard in New York meets at a place called The Trash Bar. Some churches host wine tastings or schedule outings to microbreweries (like Grace Chicago). I even attended an Anglican church a few years ago that sponsored a cookout with fine wines, beer, and a selection of cigars from the priest's own humidor.

But this element of shock value goes beyond the imbibing of certain potentially harmful substances. Some churches focus more on the shock value of sermons, delving into touchy subjects such as homosexuality, child abuse, sex trafficking, AIDS, and so on, sometimes with an f-bomb or two thrown in for good measure.

One of the trendiest ways for many wannabe hip churches to be shocking is to talk frankly about sex. If you're a pastor and you haven't done a sex series or at least a mildly scandalous sermon on Song of Solomon, you're behind the times. Sex is so hot right now for Christians. Hip Christian authors are writing books about it (see Rob Bell's *Sex God*, for example, or Lauren Winner's *Real Sex*), pastors are issuing forty-days-of-sex challenges to the married folks in their churches, and a growing cottage industry of books urge married Christians to vigorously rip off those chastity belts and get busy having wild and experimental sex as often as possible.

Sex sells. It always has, but Christians have only recently begun using it to sell their own messages. Christian-run websites like XXX Church.com, for example, help people who struggle with porn and sex addiction. Churches are finding creative ways to use sex-themed marketing gimmicks to shock people into coming to church. Oak Leaf Church in Cartersville, Georgia, created a website called yourgreat sexlife.com to pique the interest of young seekers. Flamingo Road Church in Miami created an online, anonymous confessional (Ive ScrewedUp.com), then had a web series called MyNakedPastor.com, which featured a 24/7 webcam televising five weeks in the life of the pastor, Troy Gramling.

Mars Hill Church in Seattle is infamous for these sorts of shock-value gimmicks. The senior pastor, Mark Driscoll, is the king of controversy and someone the *New York Times* described as having "the coolest style and foulest mouth of any preacher you've ever seen."[9] Driscoll delivers sermons with titles like "Biblical Oral Sex" and "Pleasuring Your Spouse," and has been known to scream obscenities from the pulpit and instruct the married women in his flock to "be visually generous" with their husbands. When I spoke with James Harleman (who is on staff at Mars Hill with Mark Driscoll) about the shock value and rebellious reputation of Mars Hill, he said it's a means to an end. "The edginess of the church is more of an icebreaker," he said. "The tattoos, body piercings, and salty language are just an entry point. It's meant to show non-Christians that Christianity might not be in the box they thought it was."[10]

Shock value ultimately comes down to this: making the case that Christianity isn't the boring, whitewashed, clean-cut, safe religion people assume it to be. Whether or not pastors believe it, they're increasingly trying to brand Christianity as one of the most rebellious, subversive things you can possibly get involved with.

Saying Jesus Was a Rebel

It is not a stretch to say that Jesus was a rebel. He was. He bucked the system, turned over tables, and said all sorts of subversive things in the days when he was walking the earth. It is perfectly appropriate, then, for churches to call Jesus a rebel or a subversive. And it certainly fits neatly into any sort of a "Christianity is hip" PR ambition a church might be undertaking. Hipsters love rebels, and even if they loathe church or Christians, most of them still think Jesus is pretty dang cool.

But one person's rebel is another person's square. The phrase "Jesus was a rebel" means different things to different people. Some tend to play up the judgment side of things, imagining a warrior Jesus in the vein of Mark Driscoll's infamous "Jesus is a prizefighter with a tattoo down his leg" portrait. Others, like the Shane Claibornes of the world, emphasize the "turn the other cheek" Jesus of peace, love, and harmony. Both types are subversive; both are rebellious. Jesus is a dynamic enough figure to be an icon of rebellion, activism, and subversion for pretty much any type of person or cause—whether for a hippie, a CEO, or an immigrant farmworker.

But there are dangers in getting too much mileage out of this rebel talk. Sure, Jesus was a rebel. Yes, Christianity is subversive. But that should not be the end goal of our faith. We shouldn't enlist young hipsters to join the cause because they think Jesus is a Che Guevara–type revolutionary. They should join the cause because they need God's grace, not because they want to take down some system or join some romantic revolutionary movement. A faith built upon rebellion is, at the end of the day, not going to be very sustainable. We can't be a church primarily organized around fighting *against* things.

Eric Bryant, Pastor, Mosaic

It's funny using the word *cool* to describe Jesus, but in many ways, Jesus is still hip. There's something about Jesus that people haven't been able to put their finger on. They're intrigued by him, they look to him. But what makes Jesus cool is that he is real, authentic, relevant. He spoke with honesty. He was a man on a mission. He was a radical, a revolutionary, yet tender and kind and loving. If that is what it means to be cool, then aspiring towards that is certainly worthwhile.

Donald Miller expressed this idea—that we have to be devoted followers of Christ first, and rebels second—in an article for the *New York Times*:

> If you're a Christian, you need to obey God. And if you obey God, you're going to be seen as a rebel, both within American church culture and popular culture. But that's not the point. The point is to obey God.[11]

Indeed, of all the marketing tactics wannabe hip churches might be engaged in, "Jesus was a rebel" is one of the more legitimate. But it also has the potential to backfire in the worst ways. Portraying Jesus as the world's most badass rebel is not likely the best way to advance the cause of Christ. Will it really benefit the church to have an army of anarchists and anti-institutional young revolutionaries running around tipping over the tables of the world? Perhaps. But I'm certain that we will not benefit Christianity by making it primarily an exercise in rebellion. Especially considering that Christ came to right the rebellion of man. All else but the gospel is rebellion. The cause of Christ is the one obedient cause.

Last Words to Wannabe Hip Churches

Lest all of the above sound overly critical or unfairly dismissive of what I'm calling "wannabe hip" churches, let me just say a few things in closing. First of all, I want to reiterate that my purpose in this book is to build the church up, not to tear it down. I hope that if pastors read this chapter and feel implicated, they won't take it personally. I hope this discussion serves instead as a helpful corrective or gut check; or even better, as a source of freedom for those who felt enslaved by the chains of cool.

The never-ending quest for cool is arduous and draining. I'm not sure you can ever *learn* cool, so my advice would be to stop trying so hard. What churches should be doing is engaging their communities and cultures and seeking to equip their congregations to express themselves in whatever way is truthful and authentic (in the nonclichéd sense of the word). No recipe or how-to formula will provide instructions on how to be a cool church that is appealing to fashionable young people, and I suspect that the harder you try, the harder it becomes to sustain such a community. No one stays hip for very long, after all—especially when the "hip" is never completely comfortable in its own skin in the first place.

It seems a risky proposition for a church to focus so much energy and resources on this quest to be cool and culturally relevant. Indeed, I suspect that David Wells is right when he says, in *The Courage to Be Protestant*, "the miscalculation here is enormous."

> The born-again, marketing church has calculated that unless it makes deep, serious cultural adaptations, it will go out of business, especially with the younger generations. What it has not considered carefully enough is that it may well be putting itself out of business with God. And the further irony is that the younger generations who are less impressed by whiz-bang technology, who often see through what is slick and glitzy, and who have been on the receiving end of enough marketing to nauseate them, are as likely to walk away from these oh-so-relevant churches as to walk into them.[12]

This chapter has examined why hip doesn't work as a means to an end, especially for churches. I've tried to suggest that the goal of becoming a cool church almost always costs more than it is worth and frequently results in an inadvertently uncool Christianity. But what about hip Christianity in general? Can it *ever* work? In the next two chapters I tackle this question head-on—a question that is in many ways the core of this whole exploration: can cool and Christianity ever truly exist in harmony?

eleven

what's so wrong with cool?

I'm not sure when it first dawned on me—this notion that *Christian* and *cool* are words that may not actually go together all that neatly; that in fact pairing them in tandem might be troublesome. Perhaps I began to sense it in high school, where the most popular and attractive kids participated in Young Life and Fellowship of Christian Athletes, but also wore Abercrombie & Fitch, drove BMWs, and drank beer at parties. Or perhaps I became aware of this awkward alliance when I attended an evangelical college and discovered a prevalent subculture of Christian hipsters who smoked pot to the music of Pink Floyd by night and took Old Testament survey classes by day. But the predicament really came to a head when I started writing for *Relevant* magazine and experienced cool Christianity firsthand as a deliberate, packaged, legitimized media enterprise. Looking at myself and my peers, I realized we were the market for this magazine. And it made me slightly uncomfortable.

The question at hand is this: Are the pursuits of Christianity and cool irreconcilable? In this chapter, I will argue that the answer is yes. But I'm not going to write off the possibility that the answer could be maybe or even no. Chapter 12 will explore this possibility further and ponder the existence of authentic and truly Christlike hipster communities, but for now I want to dig deeper into the qualities of cool

191

that I think are resoundingly inconsistent with a Christlike life. What are the aspects of cool (as defined in previous chapters) that become problematic in light of the gospel of Jesus Christ? There are probably more than this, but here are seven "cool" traits to start with.

1. Individualism

Way back in chapter 1 of this book, when I put forth my very rudimentary definition of cool, you probably noticed the language was heavy on characteristics like freedom, liberty, independence, and the Frostian "road less traveled." That's because at its core, hip is an individual pursuit. It highlights *me* and seeks to determine how I can set *myself* apart, how I can advance *my* standing in the world, turn heads toward *me*, be noticed, be envied, and so on. Hip thrives wherever individualism is promoted as a cultural virtue. It tends to be tamer in collectivist cultures where group identity reigns supreme. In Europe and America, hip has prospered, and in Westernized countries all around the world, it is increasingly a dominant mode of expression. Hip enables a person to announce oneself to the world; to assert one's agency against the behemoth of abstracted culture; to advertise one's privileged knowledge about how to look and act in a fashionable way. And all of this is thoroughly an individualistic affair, meant to distance, or at least distinguish, one's self from the pack.

In terms of Christianity, this self-centeredness is a problem. Evangelicalism already suffers under the effects of individualism, which permeates so much of the Western context of the post-Reformation Christian tradition. We've drifted away from the corporate tradition of Christianity and adopted a more malleable spirituality that traffics in phrases like *do-it-yourself*, *self-help*, and *your best life now!* We have moved from a collective Christianity to one of personal preference. As a result, individualism no longer seems to Christians like the cancer it is. We've gotten so used to the idea of individualism that something so wholeheartedly individualistic and self-serving as hip has become commonplace and even virtuous. But I'm convinced that it is actually a hindrance.

Being a Christian should mean being others-focused, not self-obsessed. "We" and "us" should be exalted above "me" and "I." We must resist our culture, our technologies, even our instincts that all seemingly push us toward individualism. As God's church, we should not neglect to meet together, "as is the habit of some" (Heb. 10:25). Christ said he would be in our midst whenever two or three gathered in his name (Matt. 18:20). He did not say, "The Christian life is a solitary, go-it-alone affair."

We are the body of Christ—one body, unified in harmonious purpose. We are never to forsake meeting together, praying together, and breaking bread together, as the early church did (Acts 2:42). The Bible clearly establishes the importance of community—of holding each other up, being vulnerable and accountable, in love and spirit and truth.

Hip pulls us in exactly the opposite direction. The necessarily individualist, egocentric nature of hip makes it a poor companion for a faith that calls us into community and collective purpose. Hip says we can and should rely on our own devices in terms of how we define ourselves. It calls us to be different and unique and not bound by the norms and standardizations of group culture. People rarely talk about how "that group or institution or belief system is so cool!" Cool by nature happens in small doses and in the expressions of people fighting for recognition and affirmation in a crowded marketplace of attention-seeking individuals.

2. Alienation

One of the most ironic things about hip is that while the desire for it comes out of a deep-seated and very universal longing for acceptance, its outworking in our lives typically breeds alienation rather than affirmation, and bitterness rather than acceptance. We all want and need to be accepted—God made us this way. But for good reason, we will always fail in this quest for acceptance when we focus on becoming cool and fashionable. God is the only one who truly accepts us. And he doesn't care what clothes we wear. All the energy we spend on looking cool for the approval of fickle people is ultimately wasted. No one loves anyone primarily because they look or act cool. It's a stupid reason to love. But it's a good (or at least common) reason to hate.

Being fashionable alienates us from others. Some will argue that it is attractive, to which I say yes, but it is attractive mostly in an invidious way. Being fashionable is attractive in the way that someone driving a Porsche is attractive: mostly because we really wish we could be that person. Being fashionable might gain you friends, but more often than not these "friends" are attracted to the fashionable image of association with you more than they are attracted to your personhood or spirit. Chances are, they actually can't stand you. Like the Gatsby syndrome, if you are cool, wealthy, fashionable, and throw awesome parties, you'll always have people around you. People will talk about you. The paparazzi will stalk you. But in the awful event of your death, most of these people will not attend your funeral. What use are you to them at that point?

This is cynical, yes, but unfortunately it's true. Cool is ultimately a lonely world because it makes people fear you. It signifies elitism, which makes uncool people really uncomfortable. Cool people and not-so-cool people struggle to mix and enjoy each other's company.

In my social history, I've been something of a chameleon who can fit in with many different types of people. In grade school I was friends with both the nerds and the cool kids. In college I had a lot of hipster friends, some totally nonhipster friends, and a few friends who became hipsters after college. Mixing the groups was always a bit awkward. My nonhipster friends rarely wanted to hang around with my hipster friends, and vice versa. These sorts of divisions are pretty natural (whether along class or ethnicity lines or according to interests), but they are only compounded by a disparity in fashion or the question of cool.

In most of the hipster churches I've visited, the demographics have been pretty homogeneous: mostly white, mostly twentysomething. This is probably the case for several reasons: (1) most every church these days is homogeneous, (2) hipsters flock together, and (3) when lots of hipsters get together, most other people (especially older people and soccer moms) move as far away as they can. The reasons are clear: we simply feel uncomfortable to be around people who confidently flaunt their fashion-forwardness or transgressive antiestablishmentarianism.

When I talked with Chris Hildebrand, who serves as associate pastor at Brooklyn's Resurrection Presbyterian, I wasn't at all surprised when he told me that he felt a bit uncomfortable when he started as a pastor there. He's not a hipster, but a redheaded young father in his thirties. The church's main pastor—Vito Aiuto—and the majority of its congregation *are* hipsters, so "it took a period of adjustment" for Chris. Feeling like a fish out of water is hard in any circumstance, but when you're in the nonhipster minority among throngs of hipsters, I can imagine that it's especially tough. So you can see why these churches rarely draw a diversity of ages or perspective. When hipsters dominate, most everyone else feels too afraid to even come in the door.

3. Competition

The hip mentality builds on a larger Western value of in-the-know, forward-looking, dog-eat-dog autonomy. Everyone wants to have that "one step ahead" uniqueness that sets them apart and produces advantage in the cultural rat race. As a result, the world of hip is highly competitive and frequently cutthroat. How does this jibe with the compassionate, cooperative notion of Christ's church? I'm not sure.

Hip breeds competition and antagonism, because the only way to be hip is to be one better than the next guy. At any given moment, only a handful of people can be true mavens or trendsetters in the world. Hipsters constantly battle for this prized position—to be in on a trend or fashion before any other hipsters (i.e., the masses) get on board. In such a high-stakes race, cooperation and collective purpose fall victim to the powerful instincts of Darwinian self-preservation. In the pursuit of hip, everyone ultimately thinks only of his or her own survival.

People committed to being cool do not trust each other. They're cynical, skeptical, and suspicious of one another. Cool people tend to look at each other with derision and worry that someone else might soon assume the crown of cool. Thus, a definite sense of withdrawal and removal goes along with hipster relationships: they only let so many people in, and those who do get in are allowed only limited access. Cool people tightly guard the inner sanctum of their hip cachet. All of this bodes ill for Christians, who are called to put away all malice, deceit, and envy, and rather "be harmonious, sympathetic, brotherly, kindhearted, and humble in spirit" (1 Peter 2:1; 3:8).

As Tullian Tchividjian writes in his book *Unfashionable*, "In a culture where people don't trust each other, everyone looks out for himself, not for others. People who don't trust those around them live lives of self-protection *from* others rather than of self-sacrifice *for* others. And this posture ruins the possibility of real community."[1]

Having grown up in a world so thoroughly infused with the desire for hip, I can attest to the exhausting, dog-eat-dog nature of the whole rigmarole. Time and time again I have found that the pursuit of hip doesn't bring people together as much as it pushes them apart.

"Cool is a form of callus," writes Paul Grant in *Blessed Are the Uncool.* "But the way of Jesus is not to get tougher or stouter of heart but to grow in love and hope and faith."[2]

Indeed, Christians need to consider how hip affects their unity and their mandate toward selflessness and love. We are instructed to put off our old ways and our unkindness, and instead to love one another, regardless of how nerdy or cool any one of us might be.

4. Pride and Vanity

Being cool does not help diminish our egos. Quite the opposite. The whole notion of cool says we are better than the majority—we are a minority with privileged knowledge and narrow access to whatever is "in" at the moment. Cool advertises the idea that we have everything together and can execute a style or fashion better than just about anyone. It expresses self-aggrandizement and provides coals for the fires of our pride and arrogance. To be hip is to be haughty and elit-ist, scorning those less-thans and have-nots who can't compete with our fashionable aesthetic.

Hip also fosters vanity. To be overly concerned about one's appear-ance—even the "I just rolled out of bed!" look (a popular one among hipsters)—necessitates a huge amount of time in front of the mirror. Cool people lose sleep over shoes and whether or not a pair of jeans fits. They have to be very strategic about every piece of clothing they put on their body, even if it only cost four dollars at a thrift store. You don't have to read far in the New Testament to recognize that this self-obsession is pretty un-Christian. In the Gospels, Christ tells us that we should not be anxious about clothing (Matt. 6:25, 28; Luke 12:23). In his letter to the Philippians, Paul instructs Christians to "do nothing out of selfish ambition or vain conceit, but in humility consider others better than yourselves" (Phil. 2:3 NIV). In Romans there is the directive to not think of ourselves more highly than we ought (Rom. 12:3). And what about the Sermon on the Mount? How do we reconcile such Beatitudes as "blessed are the poor in spirit" (Matt. 5:3) and "blessed are the meek" (Matt. 5:5 NIV) with hip's call to lavish vanity and pride? And what do we make of the mandate for every follower of Christ to "deny himself, and take up his cross and follow [Christ]" (Matt. 16:24)?

It's hard to deny yourself or take up any cross daily when you're chained by the shackles of hip. You cannot be humble when you are obsessed with your image. You cannot be poor in spirit when you spend five minutes trying to decide which pair of sunglasses to wear or how high to roll up your skinny jeans before leaving the house in the morning. And you cannot put others before yourself if you are sold out to the pursuit of your own cool persona.

5. A Focus on the Now

By definition, hip is temporary and transitory. To be cool is to be cool *now*, not forever. Nothing cool lasts very long, let alone forever. Hip is a fast-moving train. The minute something cool becomes recognized as such, it is likely on its way out of fashion. Thus, *cool* almost always and exclusively functions as a present-tense word. Cool lives for the moment and has no use for the past, apart from appropriating it in an ironic way (e.g., sixties sunglasses and vintage furniture). In this sense, we might call cool a chronological snob, as it values the past only insofar as it can serve some quirky aesthetic purpose in the present. Otherwise, it's all about the current—what's hot *now*. Cool bucks convention and past standards, and doesn't even think about the future, particularly in terms of consequences. It thinks only of living in the moment and seizing the day.

But being a Christian means being a part of something that transcends. Though we have finite bodies, we recognize that we are part of an eternal kingdom. Our purpose as Christians is to embody that "now and not yet" kingdom space, between present and future, reflecting God's future, renewed world in the present one. We have to view the current world as just a foretaste or pale reflection of a more glorious, more perfect future world. We have to be both present-minded and future-minded, recognizing that our actions right now do matter and that living for the moment is ultimately not a responsible Christian mind-set.

Being a Christian also means having knowledge of and respect for the past—especially our Christian past. Hip churches these days fashionably disregard Christian history and tradition because of some "emerging" desire to reinvent the wheel. In some cases, hipsters romanticize the past (Candles! Ancient prayers! Latin!), but rarely revisit, and almost never understand, the whole of history. Hip needs only the present, the now, the instant. It is fast-moving, disposable, and intensely cannibalizing—and nothing ever lingers for very long.

For followers of Christ and a gospel that has lasted two millennia and promises to extend indefinitely into the future, the hip perspective on time seems counterproductive and irresponsible. We still have to live in the present—day by day—but our minds must be driven by eternal things, not just the fads and fashions of the moment.

As Tchividjian writes, "Daily Christian living means daily Christian dying—dying to our fascination with the sizzle of this world and living for something bigger, something thicker, something eternal."[3]

6. Rebellion

The central logic of hip is rebellion. In striving to be cool, we assert our own personal agency against the forces that be and all institutions of control that might otherwise dare to suppress our voice. Every incarnation of hip rebels against something. Trendy fashion rebels against convention. Jazz rebels against strict meter. Riding a fixed-gear bike rebels against gasoline. The point is, to be a hipster is to be a rebel. If you want to keep the rules and abide by established conventions, you can only be so cool.

I should say, however, that rebellion itself is not a bad thing. Rebellion is sometimes necessary and frequently productive. And remember, Jesus was a rebel. He was God incarnate; how could he not be a rebel? But his purpose was higher than just subverting the norms and standards for rebellion's sake. Hip culture today elevates rebellion as an end unto itself, and this is problematic. A lot of rules exist for a reason, and authority has its purpose. But being cool requires that we bend or break the rules, because rules are oppressive and systems of control are highly dubious.

As a result, the hipster existence is frequently rife with vices. If hipsters can't completely overthrow the structures that bind them, they can at least destabilize and unnerve them by engaging in hedonistic, naughty behavior. This means smoking (everything from cloves to hookah to marijuana), drinking (everything from Wild Turkey whiskey to hard apple cider to absinthe), drugs, cursing, sexual experimentation, and so on and so forth. Hipsters care only about freedom, partying, and transgression. And if you aren't willing to engage in at least some of these vices, it will be hard for you to maintain any sort of hipster credibility.

This requisite behavior is one of the most important and common sources of tension for the Christian hipster. The inherent dissonance in cool Christianity creates the most ruptures in this area. I've known many young Christians (myself included) who have engaged in these "vices" to an unhealthy extent—in the name of fun and cool, but chiefly for rebellion's sake. The evangelical Christian college I attended forbade these activities. But as soon as summer hit, it was open season on drinking, smoking, and so on.

I recently went to a party with a lot of Christian hipsters in Los Angeles. It was a really fun party, and everyone seemed to be having a great time. But I wondered that night, and especially in the days that followed: would a non-Christian who came to that party have *any* clue that these revelers were people devoted to following Christ? After all, the party was full of alcohol, drunkenness, people doing shots,

Cool vs. Christianity

Cool and Christianity clash on a myriad of points. In fact, they share very few attributes in common. No wonder "cool Christianity" frequently becomes so awkward and ugly! It's like mixing oil and water.

Cool	Christianity
Self-obsessed	Selfless
Vain/narcissistic	Giving/Altruistic
Self-sovereignty	Submitting to God
Exclusive club	Inclusive/open to all
Elitist/arrogant	Humble
Alienating	Inviting
Transient	Transcendent
Focused on the now	Eternal
Style is king	Substance is king
Cutthroat	Trustworthy
Ironic	Earnest
Hedonism championed	Asceticism/sacrifice championed
Jaded	Hopeful
Better than the masses	First shall be last

dancing to filthy music, smoking, cursing, and who knows what else. This behavior is hedonistic and "cool," yes. But is it Christian?

Numerous times in the Bible, Christians are described as new creatures, freed from the shackles of sin and old ways. Paul gives the instruction "to put off your old self, which belongs to your former manner of life and is corrupt through deceitful desires, and to be renewed in the spirit of your minds, and to put on the new self, created after the likeness of God in true righteousness and holiness" (Eph. 4:22–24).

In the Christian life, we put to death our earthly desires (Col. 3:5). We meditate on things that are true, honorable, just, pure, lovely, and commendable (Phil. 4:8), rather than flirt with darkness and the corrupt. So then, how can we justify giving into the patterns of hipster hedonism and rebellion, which esteem vice and shun the alternative as prudish legalism?

I think the Christian hipster lifestyle has become far too accommodating and accepting of sin, something that should actually shock and disturb us. If it's uncool to draw lines about what behavior is permissible and prudent for the Christian, then Christians should start getting used to the idea of being uncool.

7. A Reduction of Our Identities to the Visual

As I've plunged myself into the study of hipster culture over the last few years, I've learned that it is almost impossible to agree on a stable, uniform meaning of *hipster*. As a result (and perhaps it was always this way), I've come to understand the meaning primarily in superficial, visual terms—in hipsters' dress, look, style, and immediate visceral appearance. Hipsters today can only exist as such by way of the visual: their identity as a member of the group "cool" is for all intents and purposes derived from their outward appearance, for a number of reasons.

For one thing—and I thank my friend Joanna for talking me through this train of thought when I met her in Brooklyn last year—we have to understand the idea of "hipster" in terms of its sociological and geographical location; that is, primarily big cities or urban areas. In this context, people are public creatures by default—riding on public subways, walking along busy streets, wandering through crowded markets, and so on. Unlike their suburban or rural counterparts who can live largely anonymous lives enclosed in SUVs and cul-de-sacs and office cubicles, most urbanites of a certain age live very public lives. People *see* them. People bump, shove, glimpse, and frequently ignore them in the crowded urban labyrinths through which they daily move. As such, hipsters feel a greater pressure to distinguish themselves visually—to stand out in the crowd and (at least for themselves) to assert some sort of originality. I suspect this is an important reason why hipster culture thrives in cities and why it is first and foremost a visual mode of identity expression.

Another reason concerns the fact that in our postmodern context, the visual has indeed become the primary channel of communicating meaning. Ours is a visual culture, no longer concerned with what we say but rather what we do, how we live, and how we appear to outsiders. Somewhere along the line in our technologically advanced, media-driven culture, meaning has moved from being static and objective to being dynamic and defined in the interchange—between viewer and performer, artwork and observer, satellite and receiver. In this way, what we mean becomes less crucial than what we are *taken to mean* by others. Thus, whether or not a person means anything political or ideological by wearing skinny jeans or a Bad Religion T-shirt, the immediate impression on others is the same: "That person is a hipster." A rich, conservative Republican teenager who wears a Che Guevara T-shirt communicates the same thing as a poor, liberal Democrat who wears the same shirt. Unless you get to know them, in which case the meaning might change.

These examples mean to hammer home one crucial point: the clothes we wear and the way we appear matters, and they always have. Clothes connote meaning. Our appearance is part of our identity, whether we like it or not. But appearance has never mattered as much as it does in the hipster world, where it is pretty much everything. Yet, while appearance holds the lion's share of meaning, hipsters treat it in a fairly reckless, haphazard manner. Most hipsters could care less whether or not they have a cohesive wardrobe or a consistent aesthetic that reflects a consistent ideology. On the contrary, most aim for chaos and unpredictability by unlikely mixing and matching. By and large, they give little thought to what anything they wear might mean or how it might affect who they are to the world.

And herein lies the problem for Christian hipsters. For whatever they might mean by the clothes they wear or hairstyle they sport, the only thing that really matters in our visual culture is in how others perceive them. Does their appearance connote "hipster" in the minds of observers? And if so, what are the ramifications of that?

Throughout the New Testament, it seems clear that Christians should think seriously about how they look and what their clothing or appearance conveys. Should Christians look just like every other person? Or should our appearance (like our actions) set us apart? In his commentary on Matthew, theologian Craig Keener suggests that Jesus's directives on what his disciples should carry were meant to distinguish them from other travelers:

> Jesus here forbids the normal basic apparatus for travel. By prohibiting a bag (Matt. 10:10; Mark 6:8) Jesus forbids begging, the survival method of the otherwise almost equally simple cynics. Mark allows at least a staff (for self-protection) and sandals, but Matthew's demand for simplicity is still more radical, prohibiting even these. This is not a matter of asceticism but of priorities, as in 6:19–34. These prohibitions would distinguish the disciples from other kinds of wandering preachers.[4]

Elsewhere, as in the 1 Peter 3 passage where Peter lays out instructions on women's dress, there is a similar sense that we are to take seriously both our own intention in dress and also the interpretation of others—that both are important and should align with our identification as followers of Christ. "Do not let your adorning be external—the braiding of hair and the putting on of gold jewelry, or the clothing you wear," writes Peter, "but let your adorning be the hidden person of the heart with the imperishable beauty of a gentle and quiet spirit, which in God's sight is very precious" (vv. 3–4).

Paul seconds this notion in his directives to the women at Ephesus, when he tells them to "adorn themselves in respectable apparel, with modesty and self-control, not with braided hair and gold or pearls or costly attire, but with what is proper for women who profess godliness—with good works" (1 Tim. 2:9–10). Both of these passages should not be read as a literal, transcendent instruction to not wear braids or gold, but rather as a reminder that our adornments should honor God and reflect our Christian commitments.

A recurring theme in these Scriptures about clothing is that Christians should keep it nondescript and avoid opulence or overly ostentatious appearances. This creates definite friction between a Christian and a hipster visual style—the latter of which is typically quite ostentatious and intentionally attention-grabbing. On the contrary, when the Bible mentions the clothing of Christians in a positive light, the attire is typically pretty shabby, spare, and humble. The heroes of the faith mentioned in Hebrews 11:37–38, for example, are described as going around "in sheepskins and goatskins, destitute, persecuted and mistreated" (NIV), and John the Baptist is described as wearing camel hair and a leather belt (Matt. 3:4; Mark 1:6), which was customary garb for the biblical prophets. James gives specific instructions for Christians to not show favoritism to the man who wears "a gold ring and fine clothing" over the "poor man in shabby clothing" (2:1–3).

In each of these cases, the Christian aesthetic is counter to that which is elaborate, rich, and showy. Clothes matter, yes, but they should not distract people from what *really* counts: our inner person.

I ended this chapter with a lengthy discussion of visual appearance, possibly the most important piece in this discussion. Coupled with the bit about rebellion and behavior (which is also largely about our appearance), this notion of how we, as Christians, are perceived by the outside world is of the utmost importance.

Theologians and biblical scholars who speak about mission and translation often talk in terms of form and function. Function never changes, they'll say, but the form can. But I firmly believe (à la Marshall McLuhan and Neil Postman) form and function cannot be so easily separated. The way something is presented necessarily affects the message being conveyed. Indeed, the medium is often the message itself.

That's why the discussion (and this chapter's critique) of hipster Christianity is so utterly important. The form and style of cool cannot help but affect the content of Christianity when the two are fused together (whether intimately or loosely). To the churches and pastors who are rushing to brand themselves as cool and hip, and to fashion themselves in the accompanying image, I would say this: tread carefully. The message cannot be divorced from its presentation, and for all the reasons mentioned in this chapter, a hip presentation carries with it quite a bit of baggage that I'm not sure can be reconciled with the core assertions of the gospel.

twelve

authentic christian cool

*O*ne of the last churches that I visited as research for this book was in one of my favorite cities in the world: Paris. I visited a few churches in London and then took the Chunnel train over to Paris to unwind for a few days and, if it worked out, to visit Hillsong Paris, a bilingual church that I'd heard was one of the youngest and liveliest evangelical congregations in the city. While in Paris I stayed at a hostel in the area of town where *Amélie* was filmed. It was fine—a lively, party-type hostel for twentysomething backpackers from all over the world—but on the night before my planned visit to Hillsong Church, things got a little nasty in my communal room (which I shared with about eight other people).

The night before, I had made friends with some of my room-mates: Aussie university students from Melbourne, a Texan soldier on leave from Iraq, a guy from Berlin, and a girl from Rome (origi-nally Ethiopia). We played cards late into the night and had a good time. But on this particular night, everything became thoroughly debauched. I was asleep (or trying to sleep, in that "please just let me sleep through this" sort of way) when the partiers (i.e., pretty much everyone in the hostel but me) started filtering in around 4:00 a.m., drunk and with random hookups in tow. These kids began scurrying around and bed swapping, and before long the bunk apparatus on which I was sleeping began to shake in a decidedly risqué, thrusting, rhythmic cadence. You guessed it: the bunk below me was doubling as an hourly rate cheap motel. And then minutes later, I heard more shaking and muffled moans from the bunk to my immediate right! It was happening all around me. I felt so very violated.

The next morning I got up before anyone else awoke and made a hasty getaway, kicking aside empty wine bottles and beer cans at the foot of my bed. I don't think I've ever been more relieved to be going to church. I made my way on the labyrinth of Parisian subways to the location of the slightly difficult-to-find church. I arrived early but was happily greeted by a number of friendly young people who managed to converse with me in English and make me feel welcome. The vibe there was so welcome, so therapeutic. It was a smaller congregation of impressive age and ethnic diversity, and everywhere I looked, people were hugging and kiss-kissing each other (on the cheeks, French style). The worship and preaching were in French and English, and the crowd was energetic. As the band played familiar worship songs with alternating verses in French and English, and as I shook hands and exchanged blessings with strangers, I knew I was home.

The appeal of this church was not primarily in its hip factor or cultural relevance but rather in the fact that it was such a welcome change from the harried, depressing, unsatisfying depravity of the fallen world around it. The church wasn't trying to mimic the culture; it was set apart. Coming from the den of iniquity that was my hostel room the night before, I felt the contrast acutely and appreciated it. This church wasn't perfect, but it was striving to be an authentic, loving, holy community of Christ followers. It was a place where people loved each other genuinely, not cheaply as in the one-night-stand-in-a-hostel sense. It was a supercool church, but only because it didn't try too hard to be anything but the body of Christ and a light in a dark place.

If cool Christianity exists, it will not be because that is how we have packaged it and sold it. It will rather be an organic phenomenon that happens because of the nature of the community that the gospel has entered and transformed. Or it will be an outgrowth of the nature of the gospel itself—which is certainly counter to the prevailing mainstream values of the world.

The bottom line is this: To the extent that hipster Christianity can exist in a legitimate, biblical sense, it must not come from a top-down, "join Jesus because it's punk rock!" sales pitch. If Christianity is perceived as cool, it is because Christianity *is* cool. The lifestyles of Christ followers do, at the end of the day, end up looking cool because that's what the gospel is. That's what kingdom living looks like.

Though I spent the previous chapter arguing that cool and Christianity can never really coexist in a biblical way, I suppose that, with a shift in how we understand "cool" and a rehabilitation of the term *hipster*, we might be able to envision a respectable, Christlike embodiment of Christian hipster living.

But what might these sorts of "authentic Christian hipster communities" look like? Under what circumstances are such communities an appropriate embodiment of Christ? In this chapter I will lay out some criteria for when I think hipster Christianity can actually work in an organic, authentic way.

When It's a Sincere Celebration of Art and Culture and Good Things

I recently had this epiphany sitting in a café in the Shoreditch neighborhood of London, in the heart of one of the trendiest boroughs of the British capital: Hipsters have good taste. They like good things. On first glimpse, they appear to shun quality (what with their affinity for thrift-store, secondhand clothes), and certainly many of them can't afford the highest quality of anything, but by and large they are passionately appreciative of the finer things in life. I'm talking about material things here (clothes, jewelry, sunglasses, cameras, antiques, food, wine, etc.), but also the experience of life in general. With childlike awe and wonder that betrays their otherwise cynical demeanor, hipsters glory in the little pleasures of life like riding bikes along rivers, eating homemade macaroons on a blanket in a friend's front yard, or playing Frisbee in the park.

This realization is not necessarily something I didn't recognize before, but that evening in Shoreditch reminded me: Of all the dumb reasons to be annoyed by hipsters, perhaps the dumbest one is to be annoyed by the fact that hipsters have really good taste, that they know how to let loose and have a good time, and that they seem adept at smelling the roses of life. As I sat there at Macando Café on the edge of Hoxton Square Park, sipping an amaretto sour, eating a piece of lime cake, and listening to Bob Dylan's "Mr. Tambourine Man" playing in the background, I wondered, *Isn't this actually a good thing?*

Isn't it a good thing to take joy in good food, drink, music, and an outdoor café on a beautiful Sunday night?

A lot of hipsters certainly engage in things (music, fashion, even food) because it ups their fashion quotient or makes them look like an arbiter of all things chic. But some hipsters, as my friend Olivia maintains, "embrace indie rock because they love the sound of musical innovation, not just the image and the idea of indie rock; who love the raw food movement because they find the lifestyle sensible; who love Sauconys and Chucks and big glasses and skinny jeans because they honestly love the aesthetic."

We must allow that this type of hipster exists—the type that actually values the fashion and aesthetic and quirky accoutrements apart from whatever trendy cachet they might carry. And in terms of Christian hipsters, perhaps this attitude is something the rest of Christendom might do well to model. These Christian hipsters take joy in God's material creation, in the colors and sounds and textures and tastes of all the good things he has created. They glory in the little pleasures of life in a way that is worshipful and thankful and full of the sort of passion that stirs within us a longing for God and his more perfect kingdom, of which these little pleasures are just a glimpse.

Of course, there is a fine line between taking Christian joy in the material pleasures of this world and indulging too much in them to the point of hedonism. The pleasure of culture is in itself a good thing, wrote C. S. Lewis in "Christianity and Culture," but pleasure can become sinful when something good is "offered, and accepted, under conditions which involve a breach of the moral law."[1] There is also a fine line between liking trendy things because they are truly worthwhile and edifying and liking them because they are trendy status symbols. I'm not sure the former can ever be completely free of the latter, but I'm willing to concede that some hipster communities do have a sincere appreciation for these things.

And so, to the extent that this is the case with Christians—that the things of earth that elicit joy and worship of God also happen to be trendy and fashionable—I think it's perfectly legitimate that there might be Christian hipsters whose tastes align with the fashionable tastemakers of the world. I would still caution, however, that some apparent difference should set the Christian hipster's appreciation for art and culture and good material things apart. If we as Christians truly do see God and his pleasure in these things, we should make it known. If we see God in the films of Terrence Malick (as I do), we should communicate this whenever and wherever we can. Chances are, secular hipsters will resonate with the language of spirituality and transcendence in discussions of why a certain art piece or film or song moves us. To put a name to that transcendence is our job as Christians (or Christian hipsters, as it were).

For example, in an interview for her article in *The Believer*, Judy Berman—a secular columnist for Salon.com—asked me to explain why it is that Christians sometimes claim to experience God in non-Christian art or culture. I talked about general revelation and all the experiences of God that I've had through secular film and music, and then she admitted to me that she had recently felt a pang of some sort of unknown spirituality or transcendence while listening to the Animal Collective album *Merriweather Post Pavilion*. I had felt the same thing, of course (because that album is a stunning artistic achievement), and so it afforded us the chance to talk about God and music and why albums like that *really* affect us the way that they do.

When we enjoy things like Animal Collective because they genuinely move us toward God, or when we appreciate a Pimm's & Lemonade on a summer afternoon in England because it feels like a little bit of heaven, I think it's okay to be part of something that might be called "cool."

When It's Centered on Christ, Not on Consumption and Image

If we are making the case that cool Christianity can be a good thing, we have to be clear that the "cool" part of Christianity must exude out of the "Christ" aspect of it, not from the stylish packaging or trendiness it might otherwise be associated with. In other words, an authentic Christian hipster community looks attractive and hip and cool, not because it tries to fashion itself in the world's image, but because it does exactly the opposite—it fashions itself after Christ's strange kingdom and his transforming gospel for a world that desperately needs it.

People should look at this type of Christian hipster and see Christ, not cool. And this goes for any type of Christian, regardless of the question of hip. People should look at us and want what we have. Beyond style, beyond fashion, we've got to be appealing and sought after for what we have that the world doesn't: Christ's love and kingdom values. We should be a taste of the kingdom for the world, a fragrance of goodness and peace and love and mercy that makes us far more fulfilling than the fickle fashions of the day. The gospel has to be apparent in the way we live our lives—the way we minister to the poor, the way we treat each other, the way we treat our families and friends and strangers, the way we have victory over sin and death—and this will be immediately cool to onlookers if we live it out in a full-bodied manner.

Churches throughout the world spend a ton of money, time, and resources every Sunday on making the church "attractive" to seekers and consumers and otherwise unchurched "prospects." Whether this means having Starbucks coffee or a dynamite rock band or hundreds of candles and IKEA decorations, the rationale is the same: The church must look good on the surface so people will come and enjoy it and not be alienated. But we forget that the church is not a building, and it is not in the stuff. No, the church is *us*. The buildings and design are important, but the church is ultimately people. It is lives transformed. Whatever designs on being attractive we might have as a church, they must first and foremost start with our own lives.

If Christian cool exists, it exists as a sort of happy accident—not as an intended consequence of careful planning and high-level marketing meetings, but as an unintended by-product of a faithfulness to the gospel and an authentic community's outworking of that in everyday life. It's not about managing one's image or carefully selecting a color scheme based on months of market research, but about living lives that are loving, giving, sacrificial, righteous, and resurrection-minded. It's about not being conformed to the world, but being transformed, Romans 12 style, by the renewal of our minds.

Christian cool is also about what we can offer the world. Hip, as we saw earlier, tends to be self-focused and all about me, but Chris-

David Fitch, Pastor, Life on the Vine

We can't go out and make ourselves more attractive. We'll be fake. We've got to be real. There's something inherently attractive and compelling about the Gospel lived out. God is beautiful, and that beauty should be manifested in our lives. I don't think you can manufacture cool and I don't think you can manufacture attractiveness. It has to be natural. When you try to manufacture it, when you try to coordinate or structure an environment to be cool so people will want to come there, weird, sad things happen. It's not the gospel anymore; it's like a sales job.

tian hip must be outward-focused—about giving rather than taking, producing rather than consuming. Hipsterdom today is largely defined in terms of consumption—in terms of the bands and brands that signify acceptance in the elite circles of fashion and good taste. On their Facebook profile pages and blogs and biographies, hipsters today tend to define themselves in terms of the media they consume rather than the causes they champion. If they position themselves in terms of politics or ideology, they usually do so in a negative sense (being opposed to this or in rebellion against that).

The motivating forces of Christian hip, on the other hand, are positive. They are *for* the world, offering God's answers and hope to anyone—of any race or disposition or proclivity or vice—who opens himself or herself up enough to receive the gift of grace. Christianity cares not about self-congratulation as much as loving the prostitutes, widows, and vagrants of the world. It is not concerned with maintaining a stylish demeanor as much as coming to the rescue of white-collar criminals, stressed-out soccer moms, and anyone in the world who feels overcome by a gaping lack. And when you think about it like that, Christianity seems infinitely more hip than even hip itself.

And so given that hipsterdom at large is now devoid of significant countercultural meaning beyond the superficial level, and that hipsters are typically aimless, irresponsible, and apathetic about all but the vainest and most immediate pursuits, perhaps the positive, proactive Christian version might actually serve to rehabilitate the notion of cool—to recover its forgotten activist roots and move cool in a direction away from shallow elitism and vanity, to a place of passionate engagement and kingdom activism. It would require a shift in how we think about and use the word *cool*, however. We would have to abandon the notion of "cool" as meaning "elite, trendy, fashionable" and start thinking of it more in the "admirable, inspiring, moving" sense, like when you tell a friend who works with the homeless that what they're doing is "way cool." Or something like that.

When It's Different from the World (and Different from the Hipster World)

One of the chief values of hip has always been difference: setting oneself apart from the masses and being unique and one-of-a-kind. But this sort of difference is typically only surface-deep, because at the end of the day, the hipsters of the world live in many of the same patterns as anyone else—they just do it with perhaps a little more subversive attitude and stylistic panache. But Christian hip has the potential to be truly different. Our identity in Christ requires a difference and set-apartness that goes way beyond how we express ourselves through fashion or music tastes.

Being a Christian means being transformed. Christianity changes who we are and radically shifts our position from sinners trying to get by on our own devices, to citizens of God's eternal kingdom, saved by grace and enlisted to work on earth for God's purposes. Scripture reinforces the radical transformation that happens when we join Christ, assuring us that our old self was crucified with Christ and that we are no longer enslaved to sin (Rom. 6:6). We are to put on the new self, created after the likeness of God in true righteousness and holiness (Eph. 4:24). We are new creations, and the old has passed away (2 Cor. 5:17). How can we go on living like we did before once we have become Christians? And how can we possibly live like everyone else in the world when something so radical and transformative has happened in our lives?

Tullian Tchividjian argues in *Unfashionable* that if we as Christians don't have a clear sense about what makes us different, we are going to be less able to actually make a difference in the world. "Christians make a difference in this world by being different from this world," he writes. "They don't make a difference by being the same."[2] We must not conform to the world. Our transformation, writes Dick Staub, requires a deliberate decision to stop conforming to our culture's zeitgeist.[3]

If anyone is a new creation, the old is gone and the new has come (2 Cor. 5:17). We have to be mindful that we are not *of* the world, just as Christ is not of it. We are citizens of a higher realm—an eternal kingdom—and as such, we should not get too comfortable fitting into the fallen patterns of this world. We are resident aliens, in the world but not of it. We are a *new* creation, and we have to live that way—not as individualistic hipsters, but as a joyous cohort of kingdom believers. We are God's agents of renewal for the world.

But what does this sort of "difference" look like? What does it look like to be citizens of God's kingdom? For starters, it means we don't take our cues from the trends of the day or the demands of cultural relevance. In *Jesus for President*, Shane Claiborne and Chris Haw suggest that Christians in the postmodern world must be "people who spend their energy creating a culture of contrast rather than a culture of relevancy. If we are to be relevant to the world we live in, we must be relevant nonconformists."[4]

Later in that book, Claiborne and Haw go into great detail about what a real countercultural Christianity should look like, and I think they come as close as anyone to envisioning an authentic Christian hipster lifestyle. They describe Christian hipsters as political misfits, cultural refugees, ordinary radicals, resident aliens, exiles in their own land, living a life of countercultural habits and norms largely inspired by the Sermon on the Mount. These "ordinary radicals" practice such things as: holy nonconformity, resurrection ("making ugly things beautiful"), diverse community, making and growing things (clothes, food, etc.), loving people, forgiveness and "revolutionary patience" (as opposed to preemptive attacks to rid the world of evil), alternative economics (pooling money, sharing everything, being a "village of interdependence"), and the art of "bustin' out a can of grace" whenever necessary.

Of course, this description is of a particularly "Shane Claiborne" sort (i.e., hippie-ish), but I think it gets the point across. We are to be the salt of the earth as Christians. And if the salt loses its saltiness, what is it worth? As Christians we are truly meant to be a society of contrast, argues Claiborne, not just a hip counterculture:

> What marks us as different must be more than something external or superficial: it must be a peculiar way of living. The New Testament speaks of the circumcision of the heart, cutting away the things of culture, keeping ourselves from being "polluted by the world." Preserving this distinctiveness of the kingdom of God has always been the most important and most difficult task of the church.[5]

But we must be careful that this commitment to "preserving the distinctiveness" doesn't become just another hipster movement to be different and strange for the sake of difference. And on this account, perhaps we should be very careful the next time we brand Christianity as "rebellious" or "subversive" or "countercultural" for the sake of winning over young dissident hipsters. We don't want to win converts who are attracted by the romance of a countercultural movement; we want to win converts who are attracted by Christ and his gospel of grace. Only after we become a part of this community and learn what it actually means to live life as a "little Christ" (denying ourselves, loving our enemies, believing in the resurrection, etc.) can the appearance of radicalism or subversion (and yes, hip) become a by-product. But as I've noted several times in this chapter so far, hip should not be the end goal. If we are true to the nature of gospel living and loving, it is very possible that we might be seen as a hipster community in spite of ourselves. And in that case, I think it's okay.

When It's Willing to Say No to Sin

This may seem like an unlikely quality for anything hip, and indeed, most hipster cultures throughout time have been resolutely *against* legalism and prohibitions on behavior. But if Christians want to be authentically cool and different from the world, they must be brave enough to live righteously and say no to sin. And I don't mean in a private, "what I do is my own business but I would never judge you" way. We can easily retreat into our own relativistic bubble of morality; it's harder to speak the truth about sin in any sort of universal way and call a spade a spade. It might not gain us friends or make us popular, but ultimately it will fortify our Christian distinctiveness and give us a consistent moral witness.

For a lot of Christian hipster communities and hip churches these days, talking about sin in any sort of potentially offensive way is completely off-limits. The last thing young people want is to be told they can't do something, right? Actually, I'm not so sure. My suspicion is that younger generations are actually longing for the opposite: for authority and structure and limits and laws. They've grown up as spoiled, coddled children in an "anything goes," "you can be anything you want to be" world, where parents are so busy with their own divorces and jobs and problems that they don't want to deal with the stresses of discipline. Kids grow up having hardly ever been told no, and yet when they become young adults they encounter a world run amok on such wishy-washy amorality. As adults they are confronted with the wages of sin and an undeniable, ever-present fallenness. To them, sin is obvious and everywhere. It makes no sense to simply avoid talking about it.

I also suspect that Calvinism appeals to the younger generations for this reason—they are drawn to its frank approach to sin and the depravity of man. Throughout their lives they've been met with yesses at every turn, but they are longing for noes. They recognize that they

> ### James Harleman, Pastor, Mars Hill Church (Lake City Campus)
>
> Where are we going to be markedly different? We have to naturally and demonstratively disconnect at certain points. We might redraw the lines of where we can go, but we still have to have lines. We can't say yes to *all* films or *all* art. Relevance is becoming secondary to the truth. Market research is not going to solve the problem of relevance.

are far from the angelic harbingers of goodness that their parents, teachers, and advertisers have deemed them. Calvinism tells it like it is and refuses to sugarcoat anything or avoid calling people out for sinful behavior.

Paradoxically, Christianity's hip potential is tied to the extent to which it is willing to be disliked and unpopular for the sake of fidelity to its principles and moral mandates. A morally tepid, politically correct Christianity will not look cool in anyone's eyes, if for no other reason than because it looks no different than anything else. A Christianity that doesn't have a problem with homosexuality or premarital sex? Big deal. Join the rest of the secular world. But a Christianity that stands up and speaks out against sin, even when it's hard and might offend someone? That has some subversive hipster appeal. We can't be afraid of offending others. "There comes a time when we must show that we disagree," said C. S. Lewis in an interview shortly before his death. "We must show our Christian colours, if we are to be true to Jesus Christ. We cannot remain silent or concede everything away."[6]

However, we must not be crazy zealots who dole out judgment and black-and-white moral assessments at every turn. Certainly that would not be hip or cool by anyone's standards. Rather, we should have a nuanced position that is both charitable and understanding but also firm and resolute with regard to sin and discipline. I like the idea that Dick Staub presents in *Too Christian, Too Pagan*—that Christians should live in a way that is too irreligious for our religious friends and too religious for our irreligious friends. As a result, we frequently anger everyone, but the legitimacy and moral authority we gain by being steadfast and nuanced makes it totally worth it.

The truth is, Christians should be horrified by sin wherever we find it. We must never grow accustomed to it or permissive of it to the point that it doesn't cause us pain in the way that it would Christ. We must never call ourselves Christians and then live exactly like the foulest-mouthed, wildest-living party pagans we brush shoulders with every day. No, we must be different. Like everyone, Christians are sinners and have fallen short. We believe that we've been washed and sanctified by the blood of Christ and have a new, fresh outlook and freedom from our own depravity. But sin is still a struggle that we deal with every day. For Christians, the topic of sin has got to be on the table and open for discussion. We can't be shy about it for fear of scaring anyone away. Sin is a harsh reality, and like it or not, it has everything to do with our Christian faith.

To say that there is such a thing as "authentic Christian cool" is largely an exercise in rehabilitating the term. It requires an understanding that *cool* is actually a marker of distinction that connotes something profoundly unique, respectable, and against the grain (and not just in a perfunctory way). Do I think it possible that authentic Christian hipster communities exist? Yes, I think that true Christianity can't help but be perceived as countercultural and daringly subversive. When we live like aliens and exiles, in and not of the world, resonating with truth and beauty but feeling the dissonance of sin, we are not going to fit comfortably into the prevailing patterns of the world. We are going to be oddballs, outsiders, humble prophets speaking truth to a world that isn't sure what it needs. We will alienate people, and some of them will run for the hills. But if we do our job right and live our lives in this strange, out-of-sync, Christ-centric kingdom way that is outward- and upward-focused (rather than inward), we should not be surprised when some people find the whole thing pretty dang cool. But whether they do or not shouldn't matter. And we should never wear such a distinction as any sort of badge of honor. We must just be who we are, authentic and faithful to the final breath. Blessings and fruit will follow suit.

thirteen

reversing the ripple effect

I am a C. I am a C-H. I am a C-H-R-I-S-T-I-A-N. And I have C-H-R-I-S-T in my H-E-A-R-T and I will L-I-V-E-E-T-E-R-N-A-L-L-Y . . ."

When I was a kid in Sunday school, that was my favorite song. Mostly because it was fun to sing over and over again, faster and faster, until everyone was just saying gibberish and laughing. Among other things, "I Am a C" taught kids how to spell *Christian*. But it was also a sort of creedal, confident, straight-to-the-point declaration of identity. Who am I? I am a C! I am a C as in C-H-R-I-S-T-I-A-N. Simple as that. It was a cool song to sing because "Christian" was a cool thing to be. It meant Jesus Christ was in my heart. It meant I was going to live eternally in his kingdom. What an amazing thing! Who would be ashamed to be a Christian?

But then I grew older and started to notice that a lot of Christians were really annoying, hypocritical, and, well, disappointingly human. A lot of them were hardly distinguishable from non-Christians. I knew of Christians who cheated on their wives, Christians who cursed and drank like sailors, teenage Christians who drove BMWs. I started to wonder: What was it that made us different again? I wondered what it really meant to be a Christian, beyond just "being saved," and why it might be something to be proud of and excited about. No one seemed to have a very good answer. Most Christians I knew kept pretty quiet about their faith and kept their "church life" comfortably segregated from their "worldly life." Their identity, however they might conceive it, was certainly not as assured as the "I Am a C" song.

When it comes down to it, this book—this whole discussion about cool and Christianity—concerns Christian identity. It explores who we are as Christians, how we conceive of our role as the church and our identity in Christ, and how the world perceives us. Whether talking about wannabe or authentic Christian hipster communities, we ask these important questions: Do we know who we really are? From what source do we define ourselves? Is it the culture, the fashion magazines, the billboards or runways? Or is it God, Scripture, and theological tradition?

The contemporary church finds itself in the midst of an identity crisis unrivaled in the history of the faith. Barna statistics are more gloom-and-doom than ever, underscoring the frightening extent to which people both inside and outside the Christian tradition are uncertain about just what Christianity means and why it's important.

One of the main reasons for this crisis, I think, is that the church has increasingly let itself be defined by the outside and by its own reactions to the culture at large. A by-product of so many developments in recent centuries (capitalism, consumerism, technology, postmodernism, democracy, advertising, etc.), this unfortunate situation has led the church to a place of looking to the outside for its internal direction. It is on the periphery rather than the center, on the outer rings of the ripple chain rather than the inner, adjusting according to the movements and motions of the cultural center to which the church is now only tangential (or so we think, in our worried, defeatist mind-set). Whereas previous generations of Christians confidently asserted their identity in terms of *sola scriptura*, *sola fide*, *sola gratia*, *sola Christus*, and *soli Deo gloria* (by Scripture, faith, grace, Christ, and to God's glory alone), today's Christians are more apt, in their wayfaring, postmodern panic, to live by the *sola cultura* philosophy: by culture alone.

But why do we think it a good idea to take our cues from culture? Is there anything more screwed up, incongruous, fractured, and inconsistent than the culture in which we live today? If, when we are talking about what is cool, we are referring to the fickle, fast-moving, over-before-it-started status symbols to which everyone (hipster or not) is captive, why would we ever spend so much time and energy fashioning our identity around it?

As a pendulum-swing reaction against its anticultural, hermit past, the contemporary church has become utterly obsessed with culture. How will we brand Christianity to appeal to the culture? What are the "in" things that the church must adopt in order to stay relevant in the culture? What kinds of music, colors, and coffee brands do seekers like? What are the latest statistics about teenagers and Twitter? Should we have Twitter in our worship services? These are the sorts of questions we are asking—questions that are turning Christianity into a shape-shifting chameleon with ever-diminishing ecclesiological confidence and cultural legitimacy.

It's high time we take back our Christian identity from the clutches of marketing, consumerism, and the accompanying soulless bric-a-brac of mass-market capitalism. It's time we rediscover who we really are (and always have been) as the body of Christ.

In this chapter I will outline three problems I see as contributing to our eroding sense of identity, and one solution. The problems are basically faulty approaches that Christians are taking with respect to culture, in efforts to position, brand, and sell Christianity in the twenty-first-century world. The solution is basically that we need to look above and beyond our current context and get a grip on the transcendent meaning of being a Christian.

Problem #1: Reacting to Ripples

My little nephew Gabriel loves throwing rocks into rivers, ponds, and pretty much any body of water. I remember loving that as well when I was his age. It must be the excitement of seeing the impact one little object can have when hurled in just the right way and against just the right substance (in this case, water). The rock makes a fun plop noise, creates a splash, and in previously still waters creates ripples that push out from the center and get larger and larger the farther out they go. Everyone loves to make an impact and see its ramifications—to see that one little rock can ripple out to impact an area hundreds of times larger than its original size.

The ripple image can be aptly applied to Christianity in terms of how it started and what it's become. Candlelight services in churches on Christmas Eve convey the same idea. The world was dark, still, needy, and expectant. But then a little baby was born in a humble corner of nowhere, to nobody parents and in a nondescript setting (a manger!). Slowly but surely this little baby grew into a man who proceeded to shake things up in the Middle East. Then he died, rose again, and his message began to really take off. Soon Christianity had spread to multiple continents and eventually nearly everywhere. It became the most important ripple effect event in history, and we're still feeling it.

But these days, most "big ripple" events don't have much to do with Christianity. When was the last time you saw a world-shaking, viral phenomenon that stemmed from the church or began with a Christian? Our inside-out impact is increasingly negligible. More often than not, we are *reacting* to the impacts and ripples of the secular world. We are living according to the trends, ideas, technologies, and innovations trickling out from some distant, crucial center. And frequently we are among the last to receive the ripple message; we are on the outer rings.

Christians have, over the years, lazily relinquished their culture-making, innovative reputation. Instead, we've become really good at imitation. When something popular, whether important or unimportant, happens in culture, we respond by copying it in a "Christian" way, typically eighteen to thirty-six months after the original version hit its peak. After slap bracelets captured the imagination of preteens in the early nineties, Christians eventually created Jesus-fish slap bracelets. After YouTube took the Internet by storm, along came "GodTube." That sort of thing. And invariably, the Christian versions turn out to be subpar counterparts, lacking any of the depth, insight, or innovation that made the original worthy to be imitated in the first place.

Whenever Christians play copycat like this, whenever we define ourselves in this mimetic way, we do ourselves harm. We become just another subculture trying to appropriate pop culture for our own purposes. This imitative role reduces Christianity to a featherweight faith with so little internal combustion energy that it might very well topple over if the ripples and waves coming at it get too fast and furious. Dick Staub calls it "Christianity-Lite"—a faith that "has abandoned the mandate to build a richer intellectual and aesthetic culture on earth, choosing to settle for a mindless, insipid, imitative artistic subculture instead."[1]

Why is the church like this today? Have we so little confidence against the threat of postmodernity and other twenty-first-century challenges that we are relegated to this sorry state of reactionary irrelevance? Are we so uncertain about the future of Christianity and its appeal to the next generation that we don't know where else to turn but to the external cultural whims and waves that are churning all around us? Whatever happened to being confident that "he who began a good work in you will bring it to completion at the day of Jesus Christ" (Phil. 1:6), or believing that "all things work together for good, for those who are called according to his purpose" (Rom. 8:28)? Why are we frantically, desperately trying to monitor, copy, appropriate, and adjust to the culture in such a frightened and defensive manner, when we are repeatedly instructed in the Bible to have confidence that God is going to do what God is going to do, and it's going to be awesome?

Of course, we cannot just sit back and relax. We are the hands and feet and conduits of God's work in the world, and we have to be proactive. Though we shouldn't let the culture determine our course of action, we also shouldn't completely write it off. We *should* pay attention to the things in culture that are popular—the trends and ideas that are capturing the hearts and minds of the masses. But it has to be more than just a cursory glance at the billboard charts or Nielsen ratings to see "what the kids are into." No, we must pay attention and look at these things in terms of *why* they are popular, not just *that* they are.

In other words, our reaction to cultural ripples should not be that we feel immediately (or eventually) obliged to take part in the trend or jump on the bandwagon, but that we seek to understand the source of the ripple and why it caught on in the first place.

But even better than that, we should seek to reverse the ripple effect entirely—to see if we might regain that position of stone thrower and ripple creator, rather than always being just a ripple-absorber and cultural reactionary. We should throw off our copycat, lily-livered caginess and assert ourselves with confidence in Christ, remembering that we are part of a world-altering faith tradition that, from one candle to billions, has never been extinguished and never will be.

Problem #2: Scratching Where They Itch

One of the most troubling things I see when I look at contemporary Christianity is the mentality that the church should fashion itself according to the needs and wants of the "audience." This idea grew out of the evangelical church growth and seeker movements and is practically an epidemic today. Almost every evangelical church thinks, to some extent, in terms of what the audience wants and how churches can provide them with a desirable product. This unseemly pressure to bow to the masses is just a symptom of the consumerist culture we live in. Presumably, it is simply how things must be done. Whatever else you might say about a product you're trying to sell, the one thing you know for sure is this: the audience is sovereign.

But of course, the question the church must reckon with is this: Is Christianity a product we must sell? Looking at the language many pastors and Christian leaders use today, this certainly seems to be the case. In *Pop Goes the Church*, Tim Stevens argues that effective churches are those that identify the needs of their audience, speak their language, and "scratch where they itch."[2] In *Branding Faith*, Phil Cooke says the church needs to "start thinking in reverse," by focusing on the audience rather than the message and realizing that "it's not the message you send, it's the message that's received that counts." Cooke also says this:

> Pastors, Christian leaders and broadcasters always thought they had the answers to what their audience wanted and, more important, the audience would listen. Today the audience is in charge. In a virtually unlimited channel universe, the audience has more choices than ever before, and for us to justify their attention, we need to get on their wavelength.[3]

Indeed, it may be true that people have more choices than ever before and that Christianity is competing for increasingly depleted pockets of attention, but I hardly think the answer to this dilemma is to start with the conceit that "the audience is in charge." Especially for Christians, it should be clear that the audience is *not* and should not be sovereign! The audience consists of broken, depraved, ne'er-do-well sinners. *God* is sovereign. He comes first, not the audience's idea of what they want God to be or what they want from religion.

In the problematic "audience is sovereign" approach, audiences rarely want what is really in their best interest. A company might make money by giving the audience what they want, but this rarely satisfies the audience in the long run. And it hardly ever edifies their soul. Furthermore, in terms of Christianity, what the audience wants has very little bearing on what Christianity actually *is*. In a market economy, consumer needs are those that *consumers* identify for themselves. But as David Wells points out, "The needs sinners have are needs *God* identifies for us, and the way we see our needs is rather different from the way he sees them. . . . The product we will seek naturally will not be the gospel."[4]

To "scratch where they itch," then, seems like a futile pursuit for a church trying to win converts to the gospel. People are itching for a lot of things, and some of them might actually add up to what the gospel of Christ offers, but at the end of the day, the gospel is defined

Decisions Churches Waste Too Much Time On

The marketing mind-set within Christianity leads churches to become obsessed with all the tangential particulars of being seeker-sensitive, at the expense—perhaps—of more important things like simply being the body of Christ and preaching the gospel. Here are some examples of questions consuming inordinate amounts of time on the agendas of worship-planning meetings everywhere:

How much standing vs. sitting time will the congregation have in the service?

Should name tags be used in the college group?

Shade-grown or fair-trade coffee? What brand?

Bagels or donuts?

Should the announcements be in a serif or sans serif font? Which announcements get the coveted space in the printed programs?

Should the pastor speak with a pulpit or music stand? Standing or sitting on a stool?

Encourage or discourage texting during service?

What is the most strategic pop-culture reference for our target demographic?

Can the pastor pull off a V-neck sweater and/or skinny jeans?

Should Satan be batlike in the Passion Play, or more like Mel Gibson's Devil?

What color and kind of fabric to drape from the cross? And how should it be draped?

Port, sherry, or Welch's for the communion cup?

Should the pastor go with mousse, gel, or hairspray? Or bald?

Which swear word is the line that can't be crossed during church?

outside of and with little regard to whatever people think Christianity is or should be.

Consumerism asserts that people want what they want and get what they want, for a price. It's all about *me*—the brands I buy, the products I consume, the "gimme more" mind-set of never having to wait long to have any desire fulfilled.

I'm not sure there are any circumstances under which Christianity fits comfortably into this paradigm.

To position the gospel within this consumerist framework is to open the door to all sorts of distortions, mutations, and "to each his own" cockamamy variations. If Christianity aims to sell a message that scratches a pluralism of itches, how in the world will a cohesive, orthodox, unified gospel survive?

In his article "Jesus Is Not a Brand" in *Christianity Today*, Tyler Wigg-Stevenson warns that by adopting a marketing mind-set, the church "will subtly contort the gospel into mere personal fulfillment," focusing only on the benefits of becoming a Christian and presenting a message "not fundamentally different from commercial advertising about the existential benefits of this car or that soap."[5] And this sort of "what can the church do for me?" mind-set is completely contrary to living a God-centered, neighbor-focused life.

To conceive of Christian identity in terms of consumer satisfaction is the wrong way for the church. We cannot let ourselves—or our message—be form-fit to the fickle demands and fluctuating interests of the market. As Wells puts it:

> Relevance is not about incorporating something else as definitive in the life of the church, be it the hottest marketing trend, the latest demographic, the newest study on depression, what a younger generation thinks, Starbucks, or contemporary music. None of these is definitive. None should be allowed a defining role in how the church is strengthened and nourished.[6]

A lot of things "scratch" where the average person itches—like aspirin, coffee, reality TV, cookies, cigarettes, sleep, sex, and orange juice. To place Christianity as one in that category of many desires is to do it a monumental injustice. Christianity transcends all that. It is much bigger and above all earthly whims, fads, desires, and emotional cravings. If we think we can sell it best on the terms of the consumer, we are gravely mistaken.

Problem #3: Marketing a Noncommercial Message

The church today has a weakness for numbers. We are infatuated with measurements and quantified data: statistics, opinion polls, market research, attendance figures, bestseller lists, budgets, and so on. We want specific numbers so we can keep tabs on things like market saturation, return on investment, and consumer satisfaction. We want to monitor what the masses are buying, where the people are flocking, and what is hot right now, so that perhaps our warehouse churches will overflow with seeker-consumers. In other words, the church today operates like a corporation, with a product to sell and a market to conquer.

But what happens to our faith when we turn it into a product to sell? What does it mean to package Christianity in a methodical manner so as to make it salient to as wide an audience as possible? What does Christianity lose when it becomes just one piece of a consumer transaction? These are questions that the brand managers of cool Christianity would do well to consider.

In *Branding Faith*, Phil Cooke talks about how Christianity's brand appeal is strengthened due to its mystery, in the same way that Kentucky Fried Chicken's brand is enhanced by the mystery of its secret spices, and McDonald's by its special sauce. He also compares the sensory appeal of liturgical churches' "smells and bells" (incense, etc.) to that of stores like Victoria's Secret and Bath and Body Works, which enhance customers' experiences with smells.[7] Christians constantly make comparisons like this, using the language of mass-market capitalism to talk about how to polish and position the "brand" of Christ. But it strikes me as incredibly unseemly and wrongheaded to speak of Christianity in this way—as if it were just like any other organization or business to be marketed. We market products, sports teams, movies, and . . . Jesus? We trivialize and demean Jesus when we place him in the company of yellow pages products like hairspray and hot wings.

Let's think for a minute about what Christianity is and why it doesn't make a good "product." For one thing, products must be subject to markets, yet God is not subject to the consumer needs or wants of any market. God only and ever deals on his own terms. His grace comes from within him, and he bestows it on us as he pleases. It doesn't come when we are ready for it or when we long for it. We struggle to fathom something that can't be purchased "on demand" in this day and age, but Christianity is one such thing. God saves at his discretion and on his watch.

Another reason why Christianity doesn't make a good product is that it doesn't lend itself to an easy commercial sale. Sure, there are appealing things about it, but there are also not-so-appealing things about it (um . . . taking up one's cross, avoiding sin and worldliness, etc.). And although the gospel is wonderfully simple in the sense that even a child can recognize its truth, it is also mind-blowingly complex in a way that doesn't lend itself to thirty-second jingles. Marketing requires simplifying, cutting out all friction and obstacles to a sale, and focusing solely on the beneficial, feel-good aspects of a product. To market something is to empty it of all potentially controversial or difficult elements, which is maybe not the best method of communicating the gospel, notes Wells:

> [Marketing] flattens, simplifies, and converts everything into what is appealing. That is what it has done in the evangelical church. The gospel, understood as a product, loses its depth and cost. This happens so that its appeal and salability can be elevated, but along the way Christianity becomes flat, empty, and banal.[8]

Not only that, but Christianity also becomes indistinguishable from any other marketed commodity. When people are "sold" Christianity in the same way that they are sold a pair of shoes or a cell phone upgrade, they will naturally think of Christianity in the same way they do any other consumer product; that is, as a lifestyle choice and brand with which they currently identify but might easily abandon if a better offer comes down the pike. If I primarily choose Christianity because it is slickly marketed, like I might choose an iPhone, the risk is high that I won't stay loyal to that "brand" forever. I never was attracted to the "thing" itself, after all—just the attractive marketing, which can easily be one-upped in the future by competitors. Attempting to sell the gospel as cool, then, is a dangerous proposition, because it bases the attractiveness of the gospel on an external definition of marketability and cool that will appeal to people but has very little to do with the actual content of the message. Converts to this gospel will likely be like the seeds on rocky soil in Matthew 13—rootless. As Tyler Wigg-Stevenson notes:

Any salvation that needs a sophisticated sales pitch is a salvation that won't really do anything. It will make you holy the same way a new pair of Nikes makes you athletic—which is to say, not at all. It only changes your religious brand. . . . Spiritual shoppers have no reason to think that Christianity is anything but one option among many.

Just as cool has become little more than a cheap happy-meal product to satiate the desires of young people to "purchase empty authenticity and rebellion,"[9] pop Christianity is on the verge of becoming little more than just another vacuous moniker and feel-better-about-myself, over-the-counter drug. It's always easier to consume cool or buy a satisfactory status (whether emotional, spiritual, or physical) than it is to legitimately work for it, earn it, and become it. The church must make sure we aren't selling an empty, easy, superficial product devoid of anything truthful or real. It's easy to sell Christianity-Lite when you mention only the positive, "this will make your life so much better" selling points; it's significantly harder to convince people to adopt a full Christian life that makes no promises about instant gratification and almost guarantees hardship. Such a thing isn't as easily "sold," but it's worth more than anything you might ever buy.

Solution: Finding Our Core

These three problems I've outlined stem from and underscore contemporary Christianity's identity crisis and fear-induced overcompensations for its increasingly marginalized place in culture. As it becomes clearer in this post-Christian world that Christians don't run the show like they once did, many in the church have reacted in one of two extreme ways. On one hand, people have thrown in the towel completely and conceded that Christianity should occupy a quiet, apolitical, inoffensive spot on the sidelines of culture where it can't do anyone any harm. On the other hand, aggressive and excitable Christians have become obsessed with rehabilitating Christianity's image and stop at nothing to reestablish a relevant Christianity in its proper (and prominent) place within culture.

Both extremes belie a lack of confidence, faith, and understanding of just what the church is to be in the world. Both are reactive and worried more about Christianity's image than its substance, and its reputation in culture more than its evangelical impact. And both do more to confuse our twenty-first-century situation than they do to clarify it.

The church's only way out of this quagmire, I believe, is to commit to rediscover and rearticulate its core, biblical purpose in the world, and to devote itself to being the divine and eternal body of Christ, not the flimsy and ephemeral thing the world wants it to be.

I'm convinced that most secular seekers today care very little about how cool church is, but very much about how authentic it is. They are interested in the church being the church. They want the church to know what it is and be honest with itself and the world, and to quit putting on airs of glossy marketability and perfection. People see through that. They know that Christianity—like anything else in life—is not perfect. They sense that Christianity is maybe inherently uncool and difficult to live out. But they also sense that it might actually be true, and they're waiting for the church to just speak that truth clearly to them, without all the distracting bells and whistles.

"There are a lot of ways the church isn't doing its churchhood well," wrote a Christian hipster in an email to me, "and slathering on a layer of cool is a total distraction from the real work that needs to be done."

An aggressively "cool" Christianity is not what younger generations want from our faith. They aren't looking for something trendy and fashionable and transient; they want something deep and lasting and transcendent. They don't want a copycat church that looks just like their own cool culture (only a few steps behind); they want something alternative, unique, profound, lasting, and transformative. Our world is in flux, and lives are crumbling on shaky foundations every day. Uncertainty, skepticism, and fear are ubiquitous. People desperately desire something certain, true, and solid—something the church can certainly be if it only gets its head on straight and mounts an epic reversal of the ripple effect.

As Tchividjian writes, "The world desperately needs the church to be the church, reflecting the kingdom of God so that those who are lost will know where to turn when their own kingdoms begin to collapse."[10]

Paul Grant makes this point in *Blessed Are the Uncool*:

A lot of the world's hostility to the church is actually a plea for the church to be the church. It's capricious, to be sure: the world will also ridicule believers no matter how cool we try to be. At the same time, the world desperately wants the church to be authentic and spiritually powerful. The world doesn't want the church to be cool.[11]

Nothing is more see-through for younger people today than an institution of power or control that feigns countercultural credibility. Young people are already inclined to doubt and rebel against all authority and institutions, and those institutions don't help matters by being dishonest and inauthentic about their identity, function, and purpose. Churches would get a lot more respect these days if they focused less on infiltrating cool culture and more on doing the things that they are supposed to do.

But what are those things? What is this "authentic church," and what exactly is its purpose in the world?

I'm not entirely equipped to answer this big question. But I don't think the answer will come by looking around at the world, assessing its needs and deriving or adjusting our identity based on those needs.

In 2006, *Christianity Today* ran a series entitled "What's Next?" in which various evangelical leaders weighed in on the challenges that the church faced and would face going forward. One of the voices surveyed was Simon Chan, a professor of systematic theology at Trinity Theological College in Singapore, who honed in on ecclesiology—the "ontology of the church."

Chan asserted that while most evangelicals have tended to view Christian identity through the lens of the larger world—that the church is God's plan to make things right in a broken creation—the proper ecclesiological perspective is actually the opposite. In contrast to the views of people like N. T. Wright, Chan says this:

> The church does not exist in order to fix a broken creation; rather, creation exists to realize the church. To be sure, the church's coming into being does require the overcoming of sin, but that is quite different from saying that the problem of sin is the reason for the church's being. God made the world in order to make the church, not vice versa.[12]

According to this train of thought, we should view the church as something far bigger and more ancient and important than just "one voice at the pluralist table" or "something that can do good things for the suffering of the world." No, we are a body that was chosen before the foundation of the world (Eph. 1:4), suggests Chan, and we must remember that our names were written in the Book of Life before the first human ever took a breath (Rev. 13:8). The church is not our creation; it is *prior* to creation. We must have confidence that we are the body of Christ and not just some transitory means to an end. We *are* the end.

The church—the eternal, glorious centerpiece of the universe, infused with the power of God himself—is nothing less than the goal and point of all God's redemptive work in the world. In the first chapter of Ephesians, Paul describes the "immeasurable greatness" (v. 19) of Christ and his "rule and authority and power and dominion" (v. 21) over all creation, but then he adds that God gives Christ—and Christ's subsequent authority over all things—*to the church* (v. 22), which is Christ's body, "the fullness of him who fills all in all" (v. 23). At Christ's feet, the world cowers and all creation converges. And as the church—as the body of Christ—we share in this unique, cornerstone-of-creation destiny.

In light of this reality, how could any Christian lack the confidence to be the church in the world—a body constantly spreading itself outward and expanding the reach of the gospel? How could we ever worry that the fate of Christianity rests on *this* generation and *these* immediate challenges, when we know that we are part of something that will outlast time?

The Christian church is not just a Sunday-morning place with steeples and stained glass; a type of music or a brand of breath mints; an extracurricular club or recreational activity. The church is the action of God in the world through Christ, and the ultimate purpose for creation. Christians are invited to participate—indeed, *gifted* with this

---

C. S. Lewis on the Church Eternal

The structural position in the church which the humblest Christian occupies is eternal and even cosmic. The church will outlive the universe; in it the individual person will outlive the universe. Everything that is joined to the immortal Head will share his immortality. . . . As mere biological entities, each with its separate will to live and to expand, we are apparently of no account; we are cross-fodder. But as organs in the Body of Christ, as stones and pillars in the temple, we are assured of our eternal self-identity and shall live to remember the galaxies as an old tale.[13]

amazing opportunity—and we must view our role in the church with appropriate humility. But humility does not mean timidity. Far from being tenuous, we must be bold and confident that this thing—this church—is not ours to create or destroy or confuse or mess up. And it's not the culture's to shape and distort and contextualize as it sees fit. On the contrary, notes Chan, the church is something far sturdier and everlasting: "It is the body of Christ, a reality in existence before culture ever was."[14]

fourteen

relevance is not a fad

$\mathcal{B}$ack in 2005, I wrote a piece for *Relevant* magazine entitled "A New Kind of Hipster." In the article—the first thing I ever published about hipster Christianity—I charged my generation of Christians to remember that we were never called to be a cool subset of the larger culture.

> We are to be a counterculture—in and not of the world, accepting yet not acquiescent, flexible but not compromising, progressive though not by the world's standards. True relevance is not about making faith fit into a hipster sphere as opposed to a fundamentalist box. True relevance is seeking the true faith that transcends all boxes and labels.[1]

I wrote the article a few weeks after returning from England, where I had attended the Oxbridge 2005 conference in Oxford and Cambridge, followed by a few more weeks of traveling around the British Isles with my best friend, Ryan. My time in the UK that summer changed my life on a number of levels, but perhaps the biggest thing it offered me was a deeper, broader, richer sense of the longevity and culture-redefining magnitude of Christianity. That summer I attended worship services in cathedrals that were a thousand years old. In Northern Ireland I saw the birthplace of C. S. Lewis and the grave of St. Patrick. In Edinburgh I visited the church where John Knox did his part to spread the Protestant Reformation. All of it made real something I had previously only read about in history books: that Christ and his church are really the biggest things this world has ever seen.

Christianity wasn't born yesterday, and it won't die tomorrow. It's been around for quite a while, and it will live on for eternity. Unlike leg warmers, pogs, shoulder pads, aviator sunglasses, Cabbage Patch kids, and socks with sandals, Christianity is not just some flavor-of-the-week fad. The church is bigger than cool and transcends trendiness. It is vital and relevant not because it is well coifed or dolled up in hot-off-the-runway fashion, but because its truth has always existed and always will exist. God loves, and he created the church out of that love. All creation points to this end, the church. Christianity doesn't have to dig around for relevance on the sales racks at H&M. True relevance is not a fad.

The logic of today's hipster Christianity, however, operates under a somewhat less confident assumption—the assumption that to be truly relevant, Christianity must rethink everything and throw all its chips into the contextualization pot. This mind-set assumes no one will listen to us if we aren't loud and edgy; no one will take us seriously if we aren't conversant with culture; and no one will find Jesus interesting unless he is made to fit the particularities of the zeitgeist.

But this sort of "relevance" is defined chiefly and inextricably by the one thing Christianity resolutely defeats: impermanence. Things that are permanent are not faddish or fickle or trendy. They are solid. The word *relevant*, however, seems to imply temporality. I think we need to fess up to the truth that nothing temporal is really all that relevant at all, in the long run. True relevance *lasts*.

~~Cool~~ Lasting Christianity

A far more compelling facet of Christianity than its ephemeral, contextual, hipster cool is its longevity. Christianity has already lasted two thousand years and is destined to last infinitely longer. *Eternally* longer. When we approach it through the lenses of trend and fashion, we tend to conceive of Christianity in a very narrow, anachronistic manner that reeks of ahistorical chronological snobbery.

Because cool so thoroughly relies on a privileging of newness and "the next," as well as a commitment to shedding the past and reinventing the wheel, our generation—so wholly devoted to the pursuit of hip—naturally finds little reason to learn where we came from or what the past teaches us. Sure, we view history and "the old" as hip in a commoditized, "look how vintage!" sort of way, but in terms of its being vital, instructive, and centering to our present situation, we increasingly overlook the past in favor of *what's happening now* and—perhaps more importantly—*what's coming next.*

We saw this in the discussion of the emerging church in chapter 7—this sort of overdetermined analysis of change and reinvention for the sake of change and reinvention. And we saw it in chapter 10's discussion of wannabe hip churches that are pouring untold resources and energies into the pursuit of the new and changing face of contemporary culture.

Christianity's haphazard embrace of the present and future tenses (while also dabbling in largely à la carte past-tense explorations) is entirely symptomatic of the broader postmodern culture, which, having loosed itself of the chains of connected thinking and holistic, well-rounded rationalism, increasingly finds itself recklessly adrift. Wells describes it in this way:

> Today, we are neither rooted nor do we have much sense of belonging. We are in fact the uprooted generations, the disconnected, the drifters, the alone. . . . Our roots in families, place, and work have all withered or been cut off. . . . We float free of the past. We are cut loose.[2]

It may be cool to be "cut loose" in a free-spirited, independent-thinking sort of way, but how on earth could such a position be appropriate for Christianity? Christianity is necessarily a past, present, and future phenomenon. When we sever our faith's ties to the past (or even downplay them), we immediately do it harm. Think of the church as an ancient rock formation. Naturally, it will change and morph because of the erosion of passing generations—the winds, rain, and weather of history. It will always be changing because of the nature of history. Change is natural; adaptation is a good thing. But when we intentionally ignore or gloss over history and put so much favor on the present, we are unnaturally expediting the process—taking a chisel and chipping off a healthy bit of rock, so to speak.

Many church leaders today too quickly assume the role of change agent. They brush our sometimes controversial past under the rug and put our "better" (i.e., present and future) face forward. But do

Hipster Fads That Will Have Passed by the Time You Read This Book

John Lennon small round spectacles	Anthemic indie songs about virgin sacrifice
Huge Dan Deacon big-frame glasses, even for people with perfect eyesight	Bands who use the f-word in their name
Tribal Pocahontas headbands on girls	Band names that only use cnsnnts
Sparkly iridescent face paint	Autotune
Tennis star chic (headbands, short Ocean Pacific shorts)	Victorian era suspenders, arm garters, and vests
Ironic appreciation of Lady Gaga and *Twilight*	Vintage straw fedoras
	Bacon-and-chocolate desserts

people really want this? Even non-Christians are asking the question: Why are Christians today so quick to hide their heritage?

In his article for the *New York Times*, "Ideas & Trends: Alt-Worship; Christian Cool and the New Generation Gap," John Leland describes the push among many young churches to create "alternative" environments in coffee bars and warehouses that "come on as anything but church," and notes that the younger generations of Christians are rapidly reinventing church to be something far from what their parents' and grandparents' generations experienced. Leland ends his article by posing this question: "If religion is our link to the timeless, what does it mean that young Christians replace their parents' practices?"[3]

Indeed, what *does* it mean that contemporary Christianity so aggressively and consistently supplants its precedents and cannibalizes its incumbency? What does it mean that we feel like our relevance has more to do with how we dress and what buzzwords we use than it does with our ancient creeds and orthodox practices? We need to wake up to the fact that, as Phil Cooke says, "relevance isn't about chasing trends; it's about standing the test of time."[4]

We must work to remember—and educate our children—that church is not just a twenty-first-century cultural activity we participate in once a week. It is not a passing fad. Christians today participate in God's mission just as Christians did in the ninth century, the 1860s,

> ### Things about Christianity That Will Not Have Changed by the Time You Read This Book
>
> | | |
> |---|---|
> | God the Father | The Holy Spirit's presence in our lives |
> | God the Son | The universal church |
> | God the Holy Spirit | Justification |
> | Jesus's death on the cross and atonement for our sins | Sanctification |
> | | Prayer |
> | Jesus's resurrection and defeat of sin and death | The sacrament of Eucharist |
> | | The Apostles' Creed |
> | The ascension of Christ | Mayo-based casseroles at church potlucks |
> | The transforming power of the gospel | |

or the 1990s. The Holy Spirit is working through us now but has been working for centuries prior as well, bringing God's work through the church to fruition in the fullness of time.

In order to be truly relevant, we have to look beyond our own framework and fleeting cultural context. We have to look at the things that last—things like, first and foremost, Scripture. I like what Kevin DeYoung, pastor and author of *Why We're Not Emergent*, wrote on his blog on the occasion of Calvin's 500th anniversary in July 2009:

> Strive for relevance in your day, and you'll may [sic] make a difference for a few years. Anchor yourself in what is eternal and you may influence the world for another five centuries. . . . The only way our lives will ever touch that which is eternal is to admit that our lives are hopelessly temporal. . . . The truly significant people in this world know that God is everything and they're nothing. Fads and fashions will rise and fall, but the word will keep on accomplishing its purposes. It will outlast us all.[5]

Amen and amen. If we must rediscover anything about the true nature of relevance, it is that relevance comes from humility and the acknowledgment that Christians make the biggest impact when they don't overestimate their individual impact or agency—when they don't think of themselves or their generational significance more highly than they ought.

~~Cool~~ Selfless Christianity

Christianity's true relevance also lies in its fundamentally self-effacing and others-focused nature. It isn't primarily about our individual happiness, but about the power of the collective—the sum of its parts. Where cool emphasizes the self—the elevated, elitist, hipper-than-thou self—Christianity emphasizes community. Christianity frees the self from the burden of narcissism and mercifully focuses us on something much bigger and better than we could ever be.

Christianity humbles us—something that the pursuit of cool never does. To live a life of fashion and trendsetting desirability is to obstinately refuse to cower to the reality of one's smallness. But in the dark recesses and unpolished anxieties of every hipster's life is an abiding, deeply troubling recognition that the coolest we could ever be—we're talking David Bowie, Miles Davis, Bob Dylan cool—still doesn't make up for lingering existential dilemmas such as, say, mortality. At the end of the day, every hipster knows in his heart this one unfortunate truism: that he who dies with the most hip still dies.

Christianity not only embraces humanity's smallness and infinitude, but it manages to turn it into a galvanizing call to action. I like what Paul Grant writes in *Blessed Are the Uncool*:

> Cool contains enough contradictions and illusions to make one's head spin. But those afterparty moments of honesty, when we know—*really know*—that we're lost and going nowhere, are moments of opportunity. Weakness, not success, is our way out. When we feel lonely and vulnerable—when we feel uncool—God is inviting us to a whole life.[6]

And as it turns out, a "whole life" has less to do with inflating our egos than it does with dying to ourselves. It has less to do with image and artifice than it does with sacrifice (Rom. 12:1; Luke 14:33; Phil. 3:7). And rather than obsessively seeking the love and approval of the world, Christianity recognizes and accepts what Jesus said on his last night with his disciples—that in all likelihood, the world will hate you if you are a Christian (John 15:19).

We should not, however, take countercultural pride in being a massively hated and oppressed minority. Other things about Christianity are more worthy of being designated countercultural—like our emphasis on community above self and mission above personal gain.

Whereas cool puts individual gain and self-sovereignty at the center point, Christianity puts it on the edges. We are still individuals and our happiness is important to God, but the focal point is God's pleasure and his purposes for Christ's church. Our happiness and satisfaction should trickle down from God's happiness. As John Piper often says, "God is most glorified in us when we are most satisfied in him."[7] And this truly is a revolutionary concept: that happiness is not something *we* establish for ourselves or strive for in all of our ambitions of status and renown; rather, it comes when we get over ourselves and rest in God's grace, accepting his love at a deep level and spreading it outward to anyone and everyone, even if they have nothing to offer us in return.

This outward, selfless love is a hallmark of Christianity and one of the things that should make us stand out as the picture of true relevance. They will know we are Christians by our love, as the song goes. People will know it by seeing *who* we love: not just our lovers and our families and those desirable people we like to surround ourselves with for our own elevated status, but also those who are unlovable and different from us in ways that sometimes make it hard to even talk to them.

But because Christianity—unlike cool—isn't afraid of awkwardness or discomfort in the name of selflessness and love, community becomes much more natural (if not necessarily easier) and absorbed as a foundational principle of who we are as the body of Christ. We become a community of disparate believers who nevertheless fuse together under the auspices of that most binding and barrier-breaking of all sealants: Christ's all-surpassing love. Naturally, this will look countercultural to a world that more often than not divides itself along whatever lines (ethnic, class, gender, nationality) it can come up with. Ideally, the Christian church distinguishes itself by putting aside these dividing lines. As D. A. Carson famously described, we are a band of natural enemies who love one another for Jesus's sake:

> The church itself is not made up of natural "friends." It is made up of natural enemies. What binds us together is not common education, common race, common income levels, common politics, common nationality, common accents, common jobs, or anything else of that sort. Christians come together, not because they form a natural collocation, but because they have all been saved by Jesus Christ and owe him a common allegiance.[8]

239

As cool as this aspect of Christianity is, we should never get a big head about it. But neither should we be ashamed of it. Christianity should be humble, yes, but not timid or insecure. And this leads us to another characteristic of Christianity's true relevance.

~~Cool~~ Confident Christianity

Something "cool" will typically have an air of confidence to it. The hipster guy who struts around in feminine skinny jeans and a bright pink T-shirt? Yeah, that takes confidence. But is this true confidence, or simply a daring performance of visual overcompensation? Are hipsters who wear ridiculous outfits really confident or are they just trying ridiculously hard to be noticed? I suspect the latter.

Hipster Christianity tends to dress itself up in noticeable, gaudy, memorable ways, in efforts to turn heads and hopefully lure in the masses. But, like the hipster in skinny jeans and a pink shirt, this performative spectacle frequently comes across as an annoying act of desperation by someone who was probably picked on in gym class as a kid.

Do we really want the world to perceive Christianity as having an inferiority complex? If we are constantly trying to fashion ourselves in the trends of the day, that's what it will look like. But, if we ignore the call to be cool and simply exist as we are—even if it looks lame or nerdy on the surface—my sense is that people will then be curious and respect us more. They will recognize, as Paul Grant does, that authentic faith is unashamed and actually has a lot of meat to offer without the dressing of cool. "Christians are far richer than the empty bravado behind cool," writes Grant, "because our story is a great story: a God dies to give us life in abundance."[9]

We easily forget that our Christian beliefs are actually pretty radical, unheard of, life-changing, world-shaking, and elegant. We forget that Christianity offers the world hope that is a gazillion times greater than any hope (ahem, Obama) that might otherwise excite us—a hope that raises the dead, which should excite people even without a stylish "hope" logo of an O rising above a patriotic field.[10] But we worry that the hip kids (who often declare everything hopeless and adopt a misanthropic world weariness as a cool posture) won't buy the shocking optimism that is Christianity. We fret about making the wrong moves or saying the wrong things or dressing in a way that repels the next generation of seekers. We worry that Christianity might contain so much baggage and negative cultural connotations that it might not be salvageable without major overhaul.

We in the contemporary evangelical community worry about a lot of things. But as David Wells writes in *The Courage to Be Protestant*, we are mostly worrying about the wrong things.

> [Evangelicals] are deeply apprehensive about becoming obsolete, of being left behind, so to speak, of being passed by, and of not being relevant. Never mind that they should first and foremost be relevant to God and his truth. That seems like a small consideration as long as they are relevant to the latest ways of being and behaving in this (post)modern culture.[11]

Wells suggests that relevance (or the lack thereof) is a red herring distraction in the proper ordering of concerns, and I think he's right. The type of relevance that drives so many evangelical churches today is not the type of relevance that Christianity has or ultimately will have to offer the world. If we want to be a relevant religion in the sense of fitting into the contours of current spiritual trends, cultural expression, and the ebb and flow of ideas, we can certainly do that. *The Secret* sold a lot of copies and made Oprah really happy. Christianity could also aspire to that. But it would mean a lot of compromise. And it would likely mean that we'd pass out of popularity much sooner than later, dying the death of a thousand faddish religions.

That type of relevance is easy and fulfilling to pursue, at least in the short run. It offers more immediate return on investment and makes people feel good and like us. But the true type of relevance— the relevance that is at the core of Christianity and that has kept it chugging along all these years, in spite of our best efforts to derail it—is a bit harder. It's harder for us to exhibit and harder for the world to swallow. But Christians must confidently assert this true type of relevance.

True relevance, for example, does not fear unpopularity. Because it clings to eternal truths, relevant Christianity doesn't feel hurt when people don't smile and nod affirmingly at everything it says. It doesn't flinch when accused of being "out of the loop" or "behind the times." Accusing something eternal of being behind the times is, of course, laughable.

We shouldn't fear the ire of cultural mavens or tremble at the prospect of being offensively unfashionable. But neither should we revel in dissonance or wear our distinction like a badge of separatist honor (for how is this different than the countercultural hipster?).

As Os Guinness writes in *Prophetic Untimeliness*, an awareness of the unfashionable rather than the fashionable ultimately keeps Christianity relevant: "Nothing sharpens us better for resistance thinking and guards us from slipping into lazy, cowardly thinking than wrestling with truths that are unpopular."[12]

On my hipster church visits during the course of writing this book, I was somewhat encouraged by the fact that many of the churches I visited had no qualms about tackling tough, controversial issues. In this way they bore striking contrast to the seeker-sensitive megachurches I've visited. But were the "controversial" subjects tackled at these hipster churches really all that controversial? And were the churches actually taking a biblical stand on these things?

In my interviews with pastors, most of them assured me that yes, their churches were confidently taking positions on things that rubbed the culture the wrong way.

"We talk about things that are uncool," said Eric Bryant of Mosaic. "We believe that God's design for sexuality is in the context of heterosexual marriage, and that is uncool. We believe Jesus is the only way, and that is uncool, but it's a belief that we are not going to change."

That's the sort of attitude I hope more hipster pastors assume: an unswerving, confident attitude that doesn't sacrifice Scripture to the idol of relevance and doesn't worry too much about stepping on secular toes. It's one thing to step on toes when you're off the beaten path, preaching heresies and hate (like the abortion clinic bombers or "God hates fags" folks). But when you're walking with God and letting him lead you, what's to worry about?

~~Cool~~ God-Centered Christianity

One of the biggest problems of hipster Christianity is actually part of a larger problem that consistently plagues humanity: the problem of the aggrandized self. Hipsterdom at large focuses on the self as the center of all things. "The man," the masses, the machinations of everyday life and its mundane impositions . . . it's all to be usurped and transgressed by the self, which can and should do whatever it wants. And we see this mentality in Christianity today as well, as the individual self becomes elevated over things like tradition, authority, doctrine, discipline, and even God. Wells situates the current understanding of the self in this way:

> [The self] has become loosed from every external constraint, be it in God, the past, or religious authority. We *demand* to be free. We today, postmodern though we may be, are more unconstrained, more emancipated from everything except our own selves than were the proponents of the Enlightenment.[13]

But when we unfasten ourselves from all external solidities, where does that leave us? We find ourselves in a freewheeling, indulgent joyride that will evade predictability and homogeneity but will likely never arrive anywhere worth staying for very long. This endless flux avoids constants and authorities in favor of movement, change, transformation, reinvention, and remixability. Absolutes and eternal things like God—as something that stands outside of and above the self—are deemed retrograde. We may want to believe in a god, but we'd rather believe in one that won't demand anything from us, cramp our style, or tell us we can't be whoever we want to be.

Hipster Christianity, which traffics in change and reinvention and self-styled innovation, is in a dangerous dalliance with the cultural obsession with self. Its insistence on reenvisioning Christianity for the next generation and doing it in new and "organic" ways (whether this means haphazardly organized house churches or epistemologically tenuous emergent theology) belies an unseemly narcissism that bodes ill for the church's future.

Quite simply, the church needs to remember that this whole thing is not about us, but God. We should not go to church to get something, because church is not about us. There is admittedly much to dislike about church: placating church ladies, gossipy youth groups, Kenny G worship bands, and hellfire-and-brimstone sermons about sin. We have so many reasons to *not* go to church. I have Christian friends who don't attend church because "it has nothing to offer me anymore" or "I don't relate to the church anymore." Others have created their own house churches or ministries where nothing ever annoys them because nothing is ever outside of their control. But this misses the point entirely! *Church is not about us.* Church is about God. He is the one who calls us into church and pulls us unto himself.

When people go to church, they should feel welcomed and loved. They shouldn't feel like they aren't cool enough, or that they are too cool to be there. They shouldn't feel like they are a prospective customer, waiting to be sold a product, but neither should they feel like an ambivalent passerby who can come and go with zero impact on the life of the church. But mostly, they shouldn't feel like *their* feelings matter all that much. Rather, the experience should be about God. If people go to church and get the sense that church is all about them—their preferences and cultural patterns and desires—then churches are entirely missing the point. Not only does this not do Christ justice, but it leaves people with nothing to cling to or take joy in other than their own unsteady whims and passions. Do we not see? When we make our churches all about the people who come and not about God, we're cheating everyone.

Whenever we make Christianity primarily about us, it always leaves us cold. It won't last. But when we make it about God, it will be far better and more fulfilling than we ever imagined it could be. We need to realize our own limits and stop aiming so low (i.e., at our own pleasure). In the words of C. S. Lewis, we need to stop being "half-hearted creatures . . . making mud pies in a slum because we cannot imagine what is meant by the offer of a holiday at the sea. We are far too easily pleased."[14]

I do not mean to say that the Christian life should be some horrible, pleasureless chore. On the contrary, God wants us to be happy. He wants his joy to be our joy (John 15:11). He wants us to rejoice in him forever (Phil. 4:4). He wants our pleasure, and he knows (though we often don't) that true pleasure comes from glorifying God and enjoying him forever. Being satisfied and pleasure-filled but also completely devoted and reverential to God are not mutually exclusive, John Piper argues in *Desiring God*. And so rather than living as Christian hipsters—always looking within and to the world for envious stares—we should be "Christian hedonists," looking to God and the Christian life not as a renunciation of our own happiness but as a consummation of our joy.[15]

Cool Christianity

As I've written and researched this book, it has been fascinating to see the defensiveness of many churches and pastors and Christians who absolutely run from any accusation of being cool or hipster. As I noted early in this book, hipsters never like to talk about "being hip." You don't pronounce yourself cool; you just are. So on one level it makes sense that people are so effacing when it comes to their association with the term.

But why are we so aggressive in publicly brushing off the label "hip"? Why do Christians squirm and get so uneasy and sometimes angry (as in the vicious comments I've gotten on my Christian hipster posts on my blog) when they are implicated in the empire of cool? It is probably because, deep down, we all know that we *are* concerned with being cool and that this is not necessarily a good thing. We know that the pursuit of cool is problematic and distracts us from our higher calling and purposes as Christians. We feel uncomfortable when we are confronted with this dissonance.

Indeed, part of my goal in writing this book is to make people uncomfortable. I want Christians to feel the dissonance, ask questions, and think deeply about their identity and place in contemporary culture.

How is technology impacting Christianity? How should we speak into the culture? How involved in politics should we be as Christians? I don't know the answers to these questions, but I know that we have to think about them. We have to rediscover the practice of critical thinking.

Christians, we have to think harder. We have minds, and we have to use them—not because it will appeal to the academic hipsters out there, but because in thinking about and considering God's world, we worship him. And so even with something that might seem trivial, like ideas of "hip" and "cool," Christians need to think long and hard about what it all means for our objective on this planet. What does it mean that there is enough material to write a book about hipster Christianity? The discussion can start with that question.

It's not that I don't think Christianity is cool. On the contrary, I think it is the coolest thing ever. It is eternal and life-changing in a world of waste and quick fixes. It's the answer to everything and everyone. For wanderers, laborers, lovers, poets, slaves, villains, heroes, hipsters, movers, doers, and dancers (and everyone else under the sun), Jesus Christ is the answer. In a world of power grabbing and war and insurgency, of institutions and rebellion and protest movements, of blood and bombs and endless battles, where all hands are clamoring for control of some contested bit of land or love or liberty,

Jesus Christ is the H-bomb force that levels it all and allows for the rebuilding of an eternal kingdom.

So yes, Christianity can be cool. It *is* cool. There's nothing wrong with pointing this out, or at least pointing out that we are not as stupid or uncool as previously thought. We can stand for some image maintenance. But we shouldn't obsess about fitting our image into the culturally acceptable or desirable ideal. Christianity's appeal comes not from culture but from *within*—and the minute we start looking outside our own identity for affirmation about our relative relevance, we immediately begin to lose our cool.

A Parting Thought

As I've stated at various points along the way, this book has largely been about identity. Who are we? How do we get noticed? What can we do to stand out in this crushing mass of anonymous hubbub we call life? Hipsterdom thrives on this scrambling and competing. Any cultural phenomenon begins with an aim to stand out, to be different. It's about distinguishing ourselves through expression and figuring out our place and our purpose in a world that is unlivable if we have nothing to strive for and no legacy to leave.

To be hip is to be empowered. Hip exercises agency in a world that is otherwise completely uncontrollable. It positions our self as superior to others, in an activity of the part of the soul Plato called *thymos*—the aspect of our self that produces the insatiable desire for recognition. We want esteem, prestige, and affirmation of our worth. Hegel posited that this is ultimately the desire that drives history forward. Not food, not survival, but *recognition*.[16]

No one is immune from this. I'm certainly not. So much of my life has been about wanting to make myself acceptable and desirable, to fit in and stand out and look good. Most of my shortcomings have been by-products of this never-ending pursuit. Most of the world's human turmoil and man-made calamity can be attributed to this pride, this *thymos*. Since Eve first thought of herself more highly than she ought, we have all been doing it daily—fighting each other for the spotlight and the throne, the power and the glory. To quote a line from my favorite film of all time, *The Thin Red Line*, "We were a family. How'd it break up and come apart, so that now we're turned against each other? . . . What's keepin' us from reaching out, touching the glory?"[17]

The thing keeping us from touching the glory is this idea of *thymos*—of desperately desiring notoriety or "better than" status. And we seek it in so many places and in so many sordid ways. We seek it in our dating lives and sports teams, our bookshelves and wine cellars and skinny-jeans-and-V-neck fashion. We seek it in our Facebook pages and porn addictions, our credit card debt and oedipal psychoses, our indie music know-how and on and on and on.

But recognition will never satisfy. We will never truly be at peace with ourselves, comfortable in our skin, and happy with who we are, outside of the one who created us and calls us into his presence and eternal fulfillment. Our demand for recognition and individuality will not be met on our own terms, because as long as we are on this planet, who we are will always be an open question.

"For now we see in a mirror dimly," wrote Paul to the church at Corinth, "but then face to face. Now I know in part; then I shall know fully, even as I have been fully known" (1 Cor. 13:12).

The desire to be cool, hip, fashionable, and recognized . . . it's all a vain pursuit and a waste of time. It comes from a very human place, but it's a distraction and a self-destructing futility. Our instinct toward cool will only be satisfied in Christ. As new creations, saved by grace and guided by the Holy Spirit, we are called to lives of selflessness and love and renewal. Here—in service of Christ and with God as the center and core of our being—our identities become more fully realized than we've ever known.

If that's not cool, I don't know what is.

notes

Introduction

1. C. S. Lewis, "Cross-Examination," in *God in the Dock: Essays on Theology and Ethics*, ed. Walter Hooper (Grand Rapids: Eerdmans, 1970), 265.

Chapter 1 Is Christianity Cool?

1. See Robert Lanham's *The Hipster Handbook* (New York: Anchor, 2003) or John Leland's *Hip: The History* (New York: Harper, 2005).

2. Joseph Heath and Andrew Potter's *Nation of Rebels: Why Counterculture Became Consumer Culture* (New York: Harper, 2004) is a self-conscious critique of hipsters.

3. Douglas Haddow, "Hipster: The Dead End of Western Civilization," *Adbusters*, July 29, 2008, http://www.adbusters.org/magazine/79/hipster.html.

4. Robert Frost, "The Road Not Taken," in *Mountain Interval* (New York: Henry Holt & Co., 1916).

5. Theodor Adorno, "The Schema of Mass Culture," in *The Culture Industry* (New York: Routledge, 1991), 91.

6. Dave Hickey, "Romancing the Looky-Loos," in *Air Guitar: Essays on Art and Democracy* (Los Angeles: Art Issues Press, 1997), 149.

7. John Stuart Mill, *On Liberty and the Subjection of Women* (Hertfordshire, UK: Wordsworth, 1996), 8.

8. Leland, *Hip: The History*, 7.

9. C. S. Lewis, *Mere Christianity* (New York: HarperCollins, 2001), 199.

Chapter 2 The History of Hip

1. This is the argument of Jesse Sheidlower, editor-at-large for the *Oxford English Dictionary*, in a 2004 article about Leland's book: "Crying Wolf," *Slate*, December 8, 2004, http://www.slate.com/id/211081.

2. Jean-Jacques Rousseau, *On the Social Contract* (Mineola, NY: Dover, 2003), 1.

3. Victor Hugo, *Les Misérables* (Hertfordshire, UK: Wordsworth, 1994), 127.

4. Leland, *Hip: The History*, 39.

5. Haddow, "Hipster."

6. Allen Ginsberg, *Howl and Other Poems* (San Francisco: City Lights, 1956), 22.

7. Jack Kerouac, *On the Road* (New York: Penguin Classics, 2002), 6.

8. Theodore Roszak, *The Making of a Counter Culture: Reflections on the Technocratic Society and Its Youthful Opposition* (Berkeley: University of California Press, 1995), 62.

9. Heath and Potter, *Nation of Rebels*, 129.

Chapter 3 Hipsters Today

1. This is how Gavin McInness, cofounder of *Vice* magazine, defines *hipster*. It's "just like the flappers," he says. "Just fashionable young people."

2. Paul Grant, *Blessed Are the Uncool: Living Authentically in a World of Show* (Downers Grove, IL: InterVarsity, 2006), 27.

3. Julie Grisolano, "The Hipster Manifesto," *Salvo,* July 30, 2008, http://salvomag .typepad.com/blog/2008/07/the-hipster-man.html.

4. Sarah Nicole Prickett, "American Apparel: Now Hiring," *Torontoist,* November 6, 2008, http://torontoist.com/2008/11/american_apparel_now_hiring.php.

5. Steven Kandell, "How Looking Poor Became the New Status Symbol," *Details,* May 2009, http://men.style.com/details/features/landing?id=content_9418.

6. Thorstein Veblen, *The Theory of the Leisure Class* (New York: Oxford University Press, 2007), 106–7.

7. Haddow, "Hipster."

8. Robert Lanham, "Look at This Fucking Hipster Basher," *Dallas Morning News,* June 29, 2009, http://www.themorningnews.org/archives/op-ed/look_at_ this_fucking_hipster_basher.php.

9. Erik Hinton, "The Seventh Seal of Smug," *PopMatters,* October 3, 2008, http:// www.popmatters.com/pm/feature/63142/the-seventh-seal-of-smug/.

10. Joshua Errett, "The End of the Hipster," *Now,* December 9–16, 2008, http:// www.nowtoronto.com/lifestyle/story.cfm?content=166405.

11. Robert Dobbs Jr., "Obama Victory Renders Hipster 'Movement' Obsolete," *Street Carnage,* November 12, 2008, http://streetbonersandtvcarnage.com/blog/obama-victory-renders-hipster-movement-obsolete/.

Chapter 4 The History of Hip Christianity

1. Mark Oestreicher, "Youth Ministry 3.0, Part 8," April 7, 2008, http://www .ysmarko.com/?p=2657.

2. Larry Eskridge (associate director of the Institute for the Study of American Evangelicals), in discussion with the author, January 17, 2009.

3. "The New Rebel Cry: Jesus Is Coming!" *Time,* June 21, 1971, http://www.time .com/time/magazine/article/0,9171,905202-1,00.html.

4. Wise quoted in the film *The Life and Death of a Hippie Preacher*, DVD, directed by David Di Sabatino (Sparks, NV: Jester Media, 2005).

5. Os Guinness, *Prophetic Untimeliness: A Challenge to the Idol of Relevance* (Grand Rapids: Baker, 2003), 59.

6. John Leland, "Ideas & Trends: Alt-Worship; Christian Cool and the New Generation Gap," *The New York Times*, May 16, 2004, http://www.nytimes.com/2004/05/16/weekinreview/16lela.html.

Chapter 5 Christian Hipsters Today

1. Jerry Falwell, interview by Wolf Blitzer, *Late Edition with Wolf Blitzer*, CNN, October 24, 2004.

2. For examples of the effusive praise heaped upon Sufjan Stevens's *Illinois*, see http://www.metacritic.com/music/artists/stevenssufjan/illinois.

3. Shane Claiborne, *The Irresistible Revolution: Living as an Ordinary Radical* (Grand Rapids: Zondervan, 2006), 121.

4. Ibid., 230–31.

5. Quoted in a profile of Donald Miller by Beth Anderson in *The Relevant Nation: 50 Activists, Artists, and Innovators Who Are Changing Their World through Faith* (Orlando: Relevant Books, 2006), 97.

6. Seattle's "Humpfest" required its amateur porn video entries in 2008 to feature either Mars Hill Church or Mark Driscoll.

7. "7 Big Questions," *Relevant*, January–February 2007, http://www.relevantmagazine.com/god_article.php?id=7418.

8. Quoted in Andy Crouch, "The Emergent Mystique," *Christianity Today*, November 2004, http://www.christianitytoday.com/ct/2004/november/12.36.html.

9. Ibid.

10. John Leland, "Center Stage for a Pastor Where It's Rock That Usually Rules," *The New York Times*, July 8, 2006, http://www.nytimes.com/2006/07/08/us/08minister.html.

11. Robert Lanham, *The Sinner's Guide to the Evangelical Right* (New York: New American Library, 2006), 183.

12. David Van Biema, "The Hipper-Than-Thou Pastor," *Time*, December 6, 2007, http://www.time.com/time/magazine/article/0,9171,1692051,00.html.

13. Ben Paynter, "In God We Dress," *The Pitch Kansas City*, December 22, 2005, http://www.pitch.com/2005-12-22/news/in-god-we-dress/1.

14. "The New Rebel Cry."

Chapter 6 Christian Hipster Churches

1. Jason Byassee, "Emerging Model: A Visit to Jacob's Well," *Christian Century*, September 19, 2008, available online at http://www.christiancentury.org/article.lasso?id=2363.

Chapter 7 The Emerging Church

1. Tony Jones, *The New Christians: Dispatches from the Emergent Frontier* (San Francisco: Jossey-Bass, 2008), 40.

2. Ibid., 37.

3. Dan Kimball, *The Emerging Church: Vintage Christianity for New Generations* (Grand Rapids: Zondervan, 2003), 49.

4. Spencer Burke, "Entering the Conversation," in Mike Yaconelli, ed., *Stories of Emergence: Moving from Absolute to Authentic* (Grand Rapids: Zondervan, 2003), 29–35.

5. D. A. Carson, *Becoming Conversant with the Emerging Church* (Grand Rapids: Zondervan, 2005), 125.

6. Jones, *The New Christians*, 4, 7.

7. Kimball, *The Emerging Church*, 82.

8. Brian McLaren, *A Generous Orthodoxy* (Grand Rapids: Zondervan, 2004), 97.

9. Kevin DeYoung coins this term in the introduction to his book, cowritten with Ted Kluck, *Why We Love the Church* (Chicago: Moody, 2009), 13.

10. Donald Miller, *Searching for God Knows What* (Nashville: Thomas Nelson, 2004), 55, 57.

11. Jones, *The New Christians*, 141.

12. Rob Bell, *Velvet Elvis: Repainting the Christian Faith* (Grand Rapids: Zondervan, 2005), 171.

13. Scot McKnight, "Five Streams of the Emerging Church," *Christianity Today*, February 2007, http://www.christianitytoday.com/ct/2007/february/11.35.html?start=5.

14. David Fitch, *The Great Giveaway: Reclaiming the Mission of the Church from Big Business, Parachurch Organizations, Psychotherapy, Consumer Capitalism, and Other Modern Maladies* (Grand Rapids: Baker, 2005), 141, 146.

15. Bell, *Velvet Elvis*, 167.

16. Kimball, *The Emerging Church*, 14.

17. McLaren, *A Generous Orthodoxy*, 74.

18. Guinness, *Prophetic Untimeliness*, 64.

19. Grant, *Blessed Are the Uncool*, 49.

20. Ibid., 54.

21. Guinness, *Prophetic Untimeliness*, 66.

Chapter 8 Social Justice, Missional, and the New Christian Left

1. Claiborne, *The Irresistible Revolution*, 24.

2. Kimball, *The Emerging Church*, 95.

3. N. T. Wright, quoted in an interview with Tim Stafford, "Mere Mission," *Christianity Today*, January 2007.

4. David Kinnaman and Gabe Lyons, *unChristian: What a New Generation Really Thinks about Christianity . . . and Why It Matters* (Grand Rapids: Baker, 2007), 69.

5. McKnight, "Five Streams of the Emerging Church."

6. "On the Care of Creation: An Evangelical Declaration on the Care of Creation," http://www.creationcare.org/resources/declaration.php.

7. "Climate Change: An Evangelical Call to Action," http://christiansandclimate.org/.

8. "A Southern Baptist Declaration on the Environment and Climate Change," http://www.baptistcreationcare.org/node/1.

9. Jonathan Merritt opens his book *Green Like God* with this assertion, which he says he is "as sure of . . . as I am that two plus two is four" ([New York: FaithWords, 2010], xiii).

10. Laurie Goodstein, "Obama Made Gains Among Younger Evangelical Voters, Data Show," *The New York Times*, November 6, 2008, http://www.nytimes.com/2008/11/07/us/politics/07religion.html?ref=politics.

11. "Black, Latino & Younger Christians Take Leadership Role in Deciding Election Outcome," *Sojourners* press release, November 5, 2008, http://www.sojo.net/index.cfm?action=media.display_article&mode=P&NewsID=7301.

12. "Q&A With Tony Campolo," *Relevant*, March 11, 2009, http://www.relevantmagazine.com/features-reviews/life/16256-lauren-thompson.

Chapter 9 Reframing Christian "Art"

1. Joe Carter, "Kinkade's Cottage Fantasy," *First Things*, June 23, 2009, http://www.firstthings.com/blogs/firstthoughts/2009/06/23/kinkade%E2%80%99s-cottage-fantasy/.

2. Dick Staub, *The Culturally Savvy Christian: A Manifesto for Deepening Faith and Enriching Popular Culture in an Age of Christianity-Lite* (San Francisco: Jossey-Bass, 2007), 155.

3. Paul Tillich, *On Art and Architecture* (New York: Crossroad, 1987), 94–95, 33.

4. C. S. Lewis, *An Experiment in Criticism* (Cambridge: Cambridge University Press, 1961), 85.

5. George Steiner, *Martin Heidegger* (New York: Viking, 1978), 134.

6. Rolf Joachim Erler and Reiner Marquard, eds., *A Karl Barth Reader* (Grand Rapids: Eerdmans, 1986), 91.

7. Dana Gioia, "Art and the Search for Meaning," lecture at the C. S. Lewis Summer Institute, August 1, 2008.

8. Dorothy Sayers, *The Mind of the Maker* (New York: Harcourt, Brace & Co., 1941), 22.

9. Tolkien's theory of sub-creation is most famously expressed in his essay "On Fairy Stories," in *Essays Presented to Charles Williams*, ed. C. S. Lewis (Grand Rapids: Eerdmans, 1970).

10. Andy Crouch, *Culture Making: Recovering Our Creative Calling* (Downers Grove, IL: InterVarsity, 2008), 171.

11. Quoted in Andrew Greer, "Figuring It Out," *Christianity Today*, April 21, 2009, http://www.christianitytoday.com/music/news/2009/figuringitout-apr09.html.

12. George Steiner, *Real Presences* (Chicago: University of Chicago Press, 1989).

13. Rick Warren, "The Good, the True, and the Beautiful: To What End?" address at Oxbridge, July 25, 2005.

14. John Totten, "Reconciling Sufjan Stevens: Religious Hipsters and the Inevitable Queerness of Christian Music," *The Other Journal*, April 2, 2006, http://www.theotherjournal.com/article.php?id=166.

Chapter 10 Wannabe Hip Churches

1. See "The U2charist," http://www.e4gr.org/u2charists/service.html.

2. Tim Stevens, *Pop Goes the Church: Should the Church Engage Pop Culture?* (Indianapolis: Power Publishing, 2008), 19.

3. Quoted in ibid., 186.

4. Phil Cooke, *Branding Faith: Why Some Churches and Nonprofits Impact Culture and Others Don't* (Ventura, CA: Regal, 2008), 153.

5. Shane Hipps, *The Hidden Power of Electronic Culture: How Media Shapes Faith, the Gospel, and Church* (Grand Rapids: Zondervan, 2006), 17.

6. Kenneth A. Myers, *All God's Children and Blue Suede Shoes: Christians and Popular Culture* (Wheaton: Crossway, 1989), 22.

7. This paragraph is excerpted from an article I wrote in 2007 for FaithVisuals .com, "The Whys and Ways to Use Media," http://www.faithvisuals.com/help/articles/thewhysandwaystousemedia.html.

8. Cooke, *Branding Faith,* 172.

9. Molly Worthen, "Who Would Jesus Smack Down?" *The New York Times,* January 6, 2009, http://www.nytimes.com/2009/01/11/magazine/11punk-t.html.

10. Personal interview with James Harleman.

11. Donald Miller quoted in John Leland, "Rebels with a Cross," *The New York Times,* March 2, 2006, http://www.nytimes.com/2006/03/02/fashion/thursday styles/02rebels.html.

12. David Wells, *The Courage to Be Protestant: Truth-lovers, Marketers, and Emergents in a Postmodern World* (Grand Rapids: Eerdmans, 2008), 49–50.

Chapter 11 What's So Wrong with Cool?

1. Tullian Tchividjian, *Unfashionable: Making a Difference in the World by Being Different* (Colorado Springs: Multnomah, 2009), 117.

2. Grant, *Blessed Are the Uncool,* 80.

3. Tchividjian, *Unfashionable,* 19.

4. Craig S. Keener, *Matthew,* IVP New Testament Commentary Series (Downers Grove, IL: InterVarsity, 1997), 204.

Chapter 12 Authentic Christian Cool

1. C. S. Lewis, "Christianity and Culture," in *Christian Reflections,* ed. Walter Hooper (Grand Rapids: Eerdmans, 1995), 21.

2. Tchividjian, *Unfashionable,* 9.

3. Staub, *The Culturally Savvy Christian,* 99.

4. Shane Claiborne and Chris Haw, *Jesus for President: Politics for Ordinary Radicals* (Grand Rapids: Zondervan, 2008), 240.

5. Ibid., 239–40.

6. C. S. Lewis, "Cross-Examination," 262.

Chapter 13 Reversing the Ripple Effect

1. Staub, *The Culturally Savvy Christian,* 72.

2. Stevens, *Pop Goes the Church,* 121.

3. Cooke, *Branding Faith,* 57, 34.

4. Wells, *The Courage to Be Protestant,* 53.

5. Tyler Wigg-Stevenson, "Jesus Is Not a Brand," *Christianity Today,* January 2009, http://www.christianitytoday.com/ct/2009/january/10.20.html.

6. Wells, *The Courage to Be Protestant,* 227.

7. Cooke, *Branding Faith,* 85.

Chicago Public Library
Edgewater
8/16/2014   12:32:22 PM
-Patron Receipt-

ITEMS BORROWED:

1:
Title: Confessions /
Item #: R0427903809
Due Date: 9/6/2014

2:
Title: Hipster Christianity : when church a
Item #: R0427469732
Due Date: 9/6/2014

-Please retain for your records-

RWISE

8. Wells, *The Courage to Be Protestant*, 213.
9. This is Haddow's description from "Hipster."
10. Tchividjian, *Unfashionable*, 79.
11. Grant, *Blessed Are the Uncool*, 107–8.
12. Mark Galli, "Stopping Cultural Drift," *Christianity Today*, November 2006, http://www.christianitytoday.com/ct/2006/november/33.66.html.
13. C. S. Lewis, "Membership," in *The Weight of Glory and Other Addresses* (New York: Macmillan, 1949), 128–29.
14. Galli, "Stopping Cultural Drift."

Chapter 14 Relevance Is Not a Fad

1. Brett McCracken, "A New Kind of Hipster," *Relevant*, September 2005, http://www.relevantmagazine.com/culture/music/features/3181-a-new-kind-of-hipster.
2. Wells, *The Courage to Be Protestant*, 66.
3. Leland, "Ideas & Trends: Alt-Worship."
4. Cooke, *Branding Faith*, 180.
5. Kevin DeYoung, "Withering and the Word: John Calvin at 500," July 10, 2009, http://www.revkevindeyoung.com/2009/07/withering-and-word-john-calvin-at-500.html.
6. Grant, *Blessed Are the Uncool*, 23.
7. John Piper has repeated this phrase in countless books, such as *The Dangerous Duty of Delight* (Colorado Springs: Multnomah, 2001), 20.
8. D. A. Carson, *Love in Hard Places* (Wheaton: Crossway, 2002), 61.
9. Grant, *Blessed Are the Uncool*, 16.
10. In case you missed it, that was a reference to the iconic Obama "Hope" poster by artist Shepard Fairey for the 2008 presidential campaign.
11. Wells, *The Courage to Be Protestant*, 48.
12. Guinness, *Prophetic Untimeliness*, 96.
13. Wells, *The Courage to Be Protestant*, 62.
14. Lewis, "The Weight of Glory," in *The Weight of Glory and Other Addresses*, 2.
15. John Piper, *Desiring God: Meditations of a Christian Hedonist* (Colorado Springs: Multnomah, 1986).
16. Francis Fukuyama discusses Plato's notion of *thymos* (or "spiritedness") as well as Hegel's interpretation of it in the introduction to *The End of History and the Last Man* (New York: Free Press, 2006), xvi–xvii.
17. *The Thin Red Line*, DVD (Los Angeles: 20th Century Fox, 2002).

Brett McCracken is a graduate of Wheaton College and UCLA. His day job is managing editor for Biola University's *Biola Magazine*. He regularly writes movie reviews and features for *Christianity Today*, as well as contributing frequently to *Relevant* magazine. He comments on movies, media, and popular culture issues at his blog, The Search, http://stillsearching.wordpress.com/. He lives in Los Angeles.